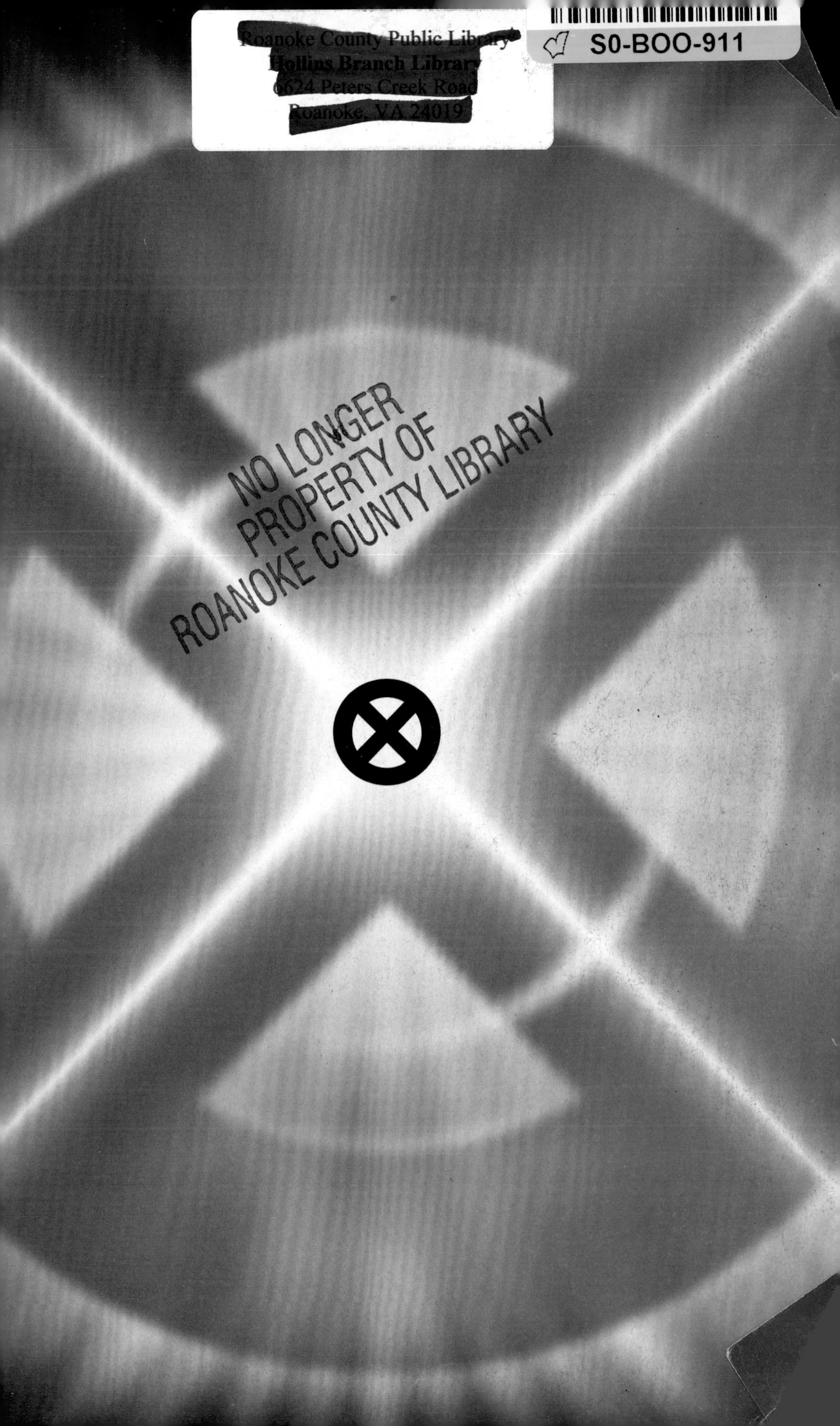

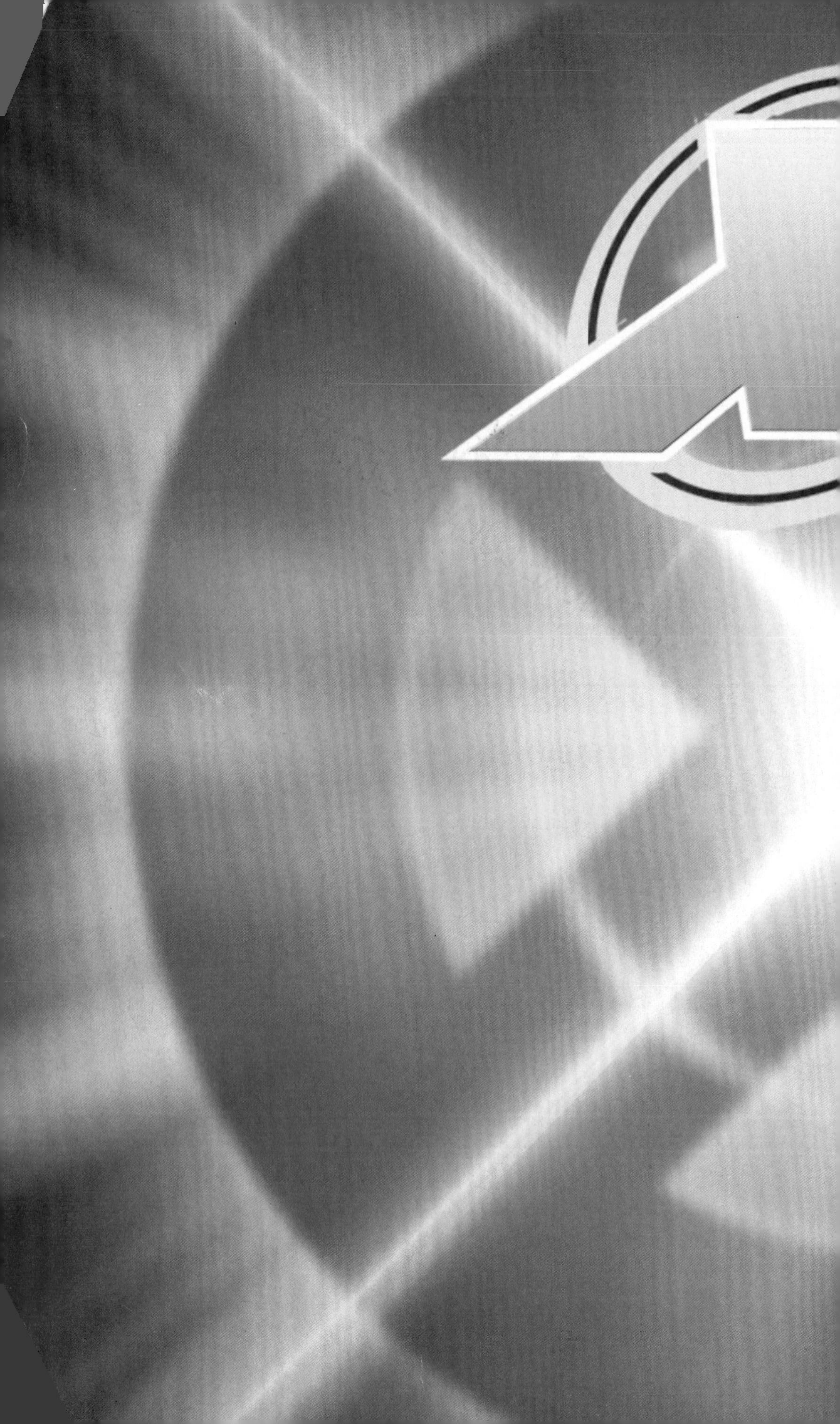

ASTONISHING X-MEN

TORN

writer_**JOSS WHEDON**

artist_**JOHN CASSADAY**

colorist_**LAURA MARTIN**
letterer_**CHRIS ELIOPOULOS**

assistant editor_**SEAN RYAN**
associate editor_**NICK LOWE**
editor_**MIKE MARTS**

collection editor_**JENNIFER GRÜNWALD**
assistant editor_**MICHAEL SHORT**
associate editor_**MARK D. BEAZLEY**
senior editor, special projects
_**JEFF YOUNGQUIST**

vice president of sales_**DAVID GABRIEL**
production_**JERRON QUALITY COLOR**
& **JERRY KALINOWSKI**
vice president of creative
_**TOM MARVELLI**

editor in chief_**JOE QUESADA**
publisher_**DAN BUCKLEY**

PREVIOUSLY:

The X-MEN's lives have been a roller coaster as of late. KITTY PRYDE discovered the long-thought-dead COLOSSUS to actually be alive! Colossus was Kitty's first love, and ever since his return, she has been a mess of emotions, not truly knowing how to handle the situation.

Meanwhile, at S.W.O.R.D. (Sentient Worlds Observation and Response Department), a creature from another world, named ORD, has come to Earth. He claims that his people have foreseen the destruction of their homeworld. This destruction shall be brought about by a mutant from Earth, an X-Man. Currently, Ord is in S.W.O.R.D. custody, and lead agent, AGENT BRAND, is still trying to find a peaceful solution to this problem.

Back at Xavier's, co-headmistress EMMA FROST has been communicating with a mysterious group, unbeknownst to the rest of the X-Men. They have no idea that Emma Frost has been meeting and communicating with the brand-new HELLFIRE CLUB!

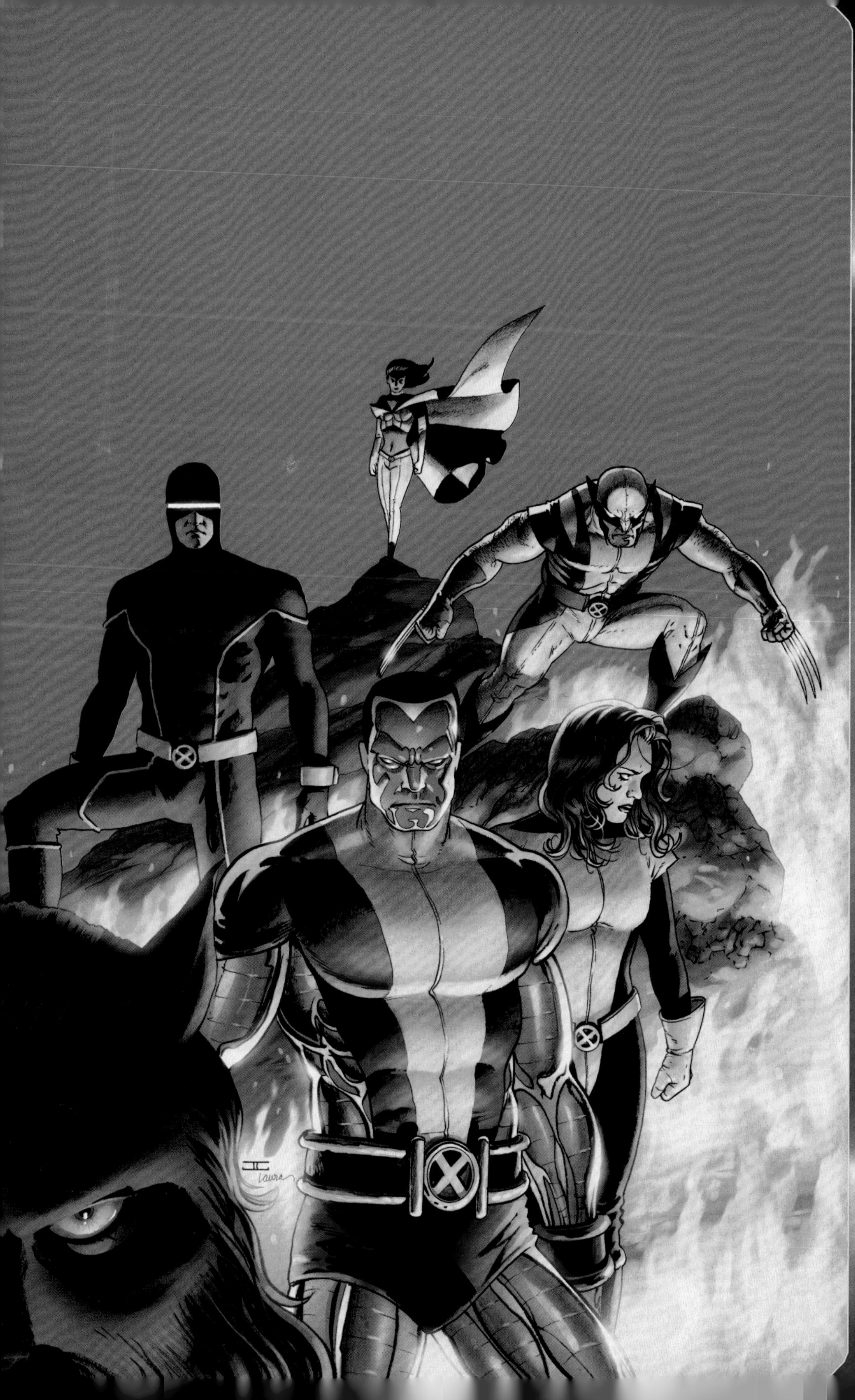

SOME TIME AGO

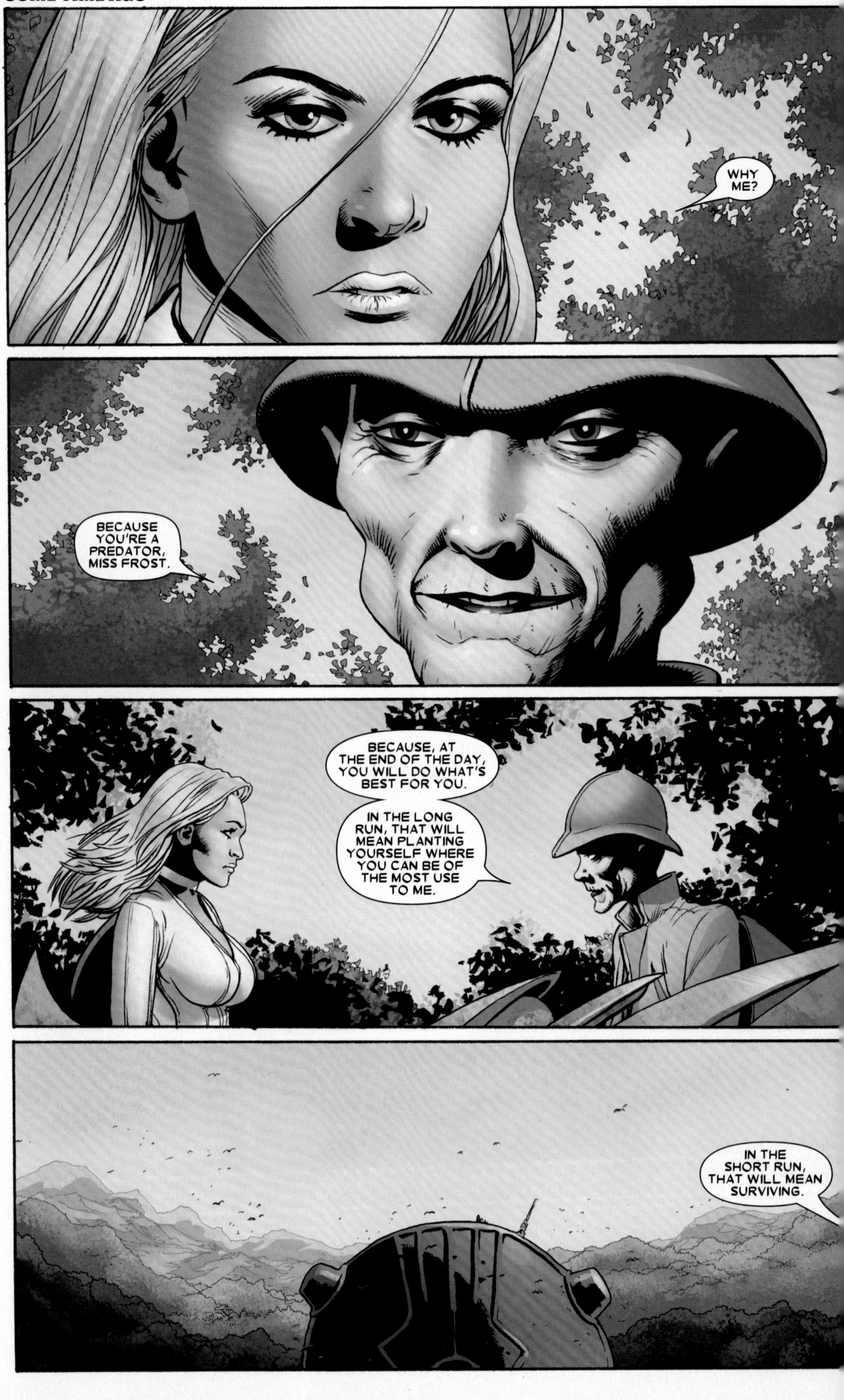
WHY ME?
BECAUSE YOU'RE A PREDATOR, MISS FROST.
BECAUSE, AT THE END OF THE DAY, YOU WILL DO WHAT'S BEST FOR YOU.
IN THE LONG RUN, THAT WILL MEAN PLANTING YOURSELF WHERE YOU CAN BE OF THE MOST USE TO ME.
IN THE SHORT RUN, THAT WILL MEAN SURVIVING.

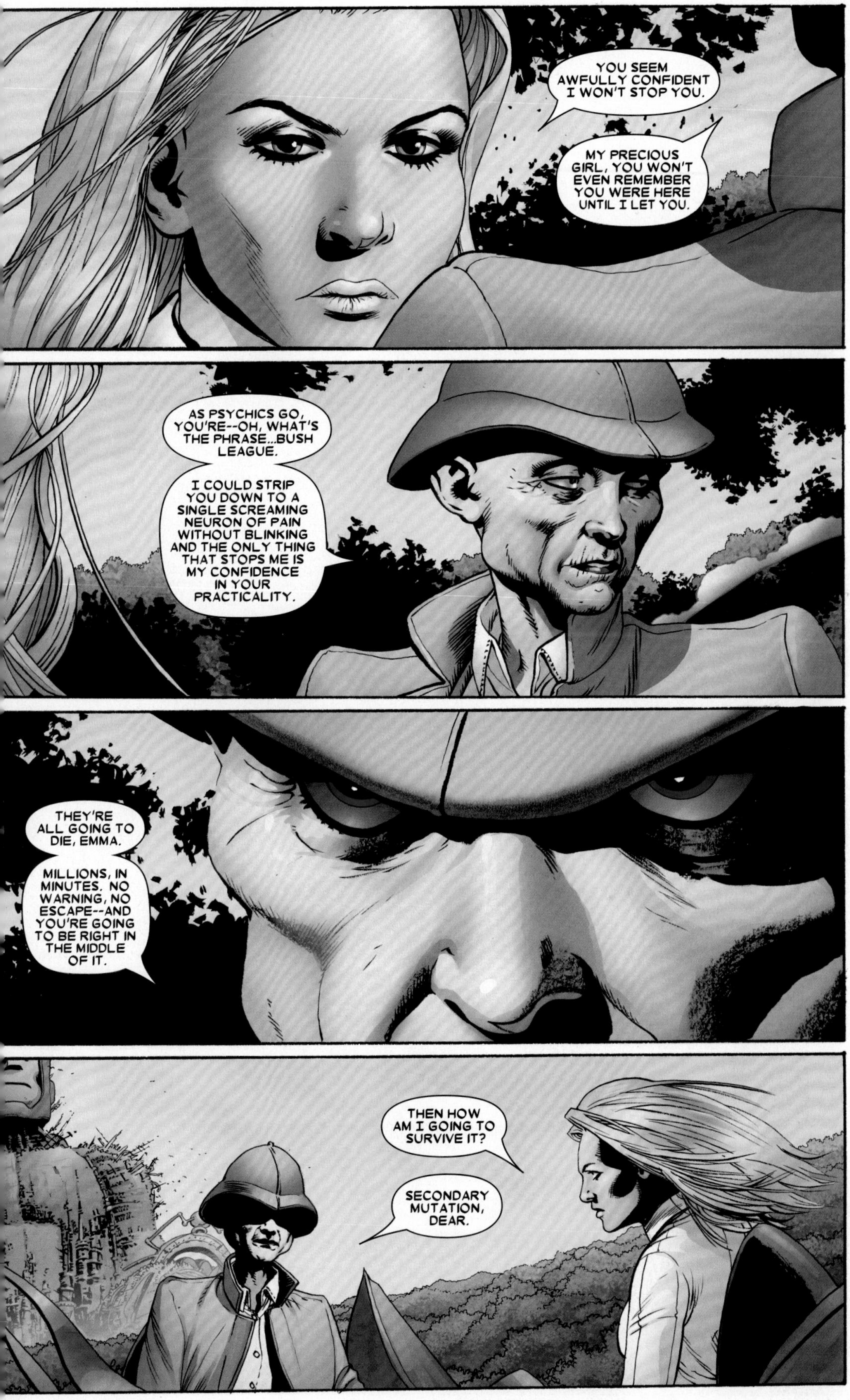
YOU SEEM AWFULLY CONFIDENT I WON'T STOP YOU.
MY PRECIOUS GIRL, YOU WON'T EVEN REMEMBER YOU WERE HERE UNTIL I LET YOU.
AS PSYCHICS GO, YOU'RE--OH, WHAT'S THE PHRASE...BUSH LEAGUE.
I COULD STRIP YOU DOWN TO A SINGLE SCREAMING NEURON OF PAIN WITHOUT BLINKING AND THE ONLY THING THAT STOPS ME IS MY CONFIDENCE IN YOUR PRACTICALITY.
THEY'RE ALL GOING TO DIE, EMMA.
MILLIONS, IN MINUTES. NO WARNING, NO ESCAPE--AND YOU'RE GOING TO BE RIGHT IN THE MIDDLE OF IT.
THEN HOW AM I GOING TO SURVIVE IT?
SECONDARY MUTATION, DEAR.

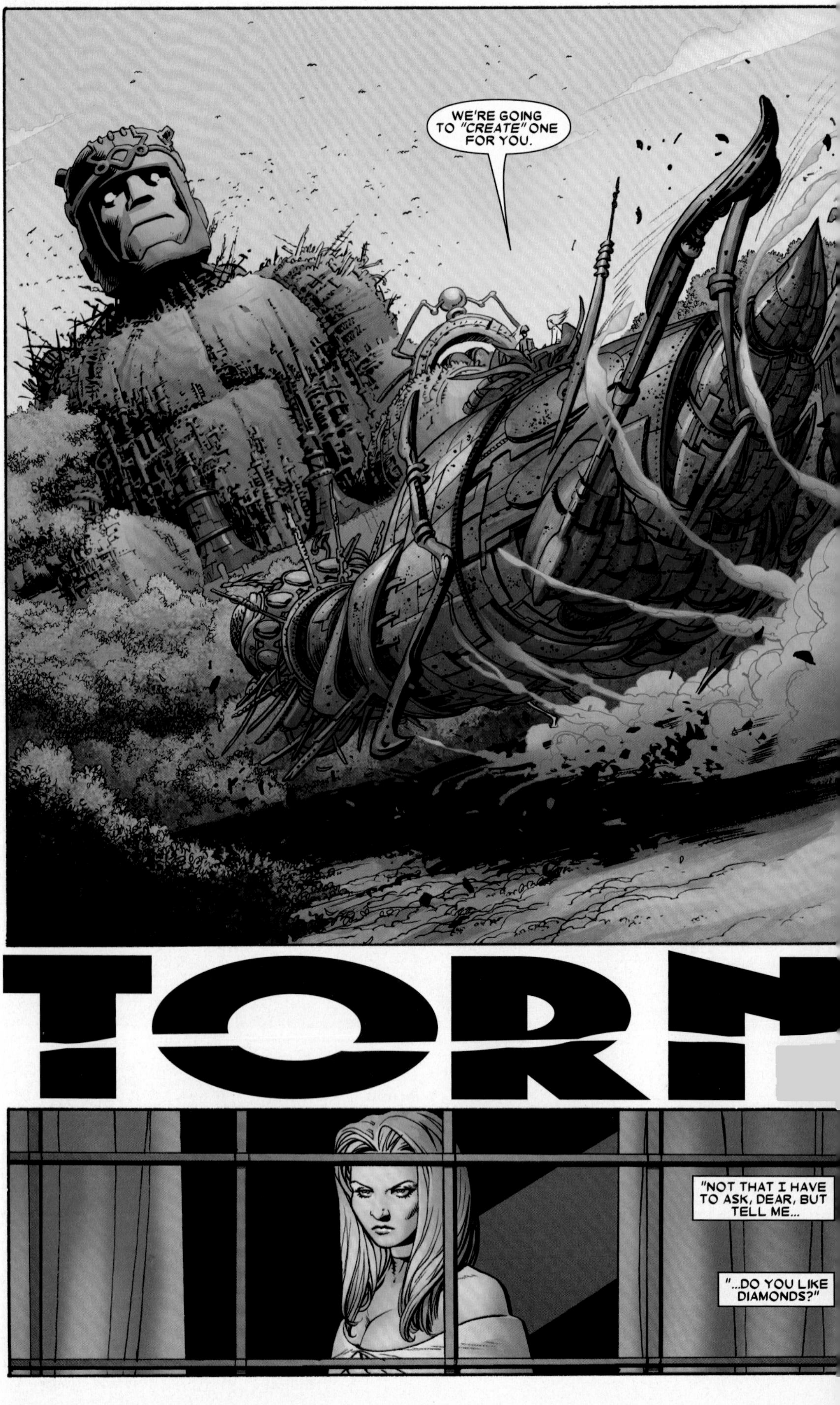
WE'RE GOING TO "CREATE" ONE FOR YOU.
TORN
"NOT THAT I HAVE TO ASK, DEAR, BUT TELL ME...
"...DO YOU LIKE DIAMONDS?"

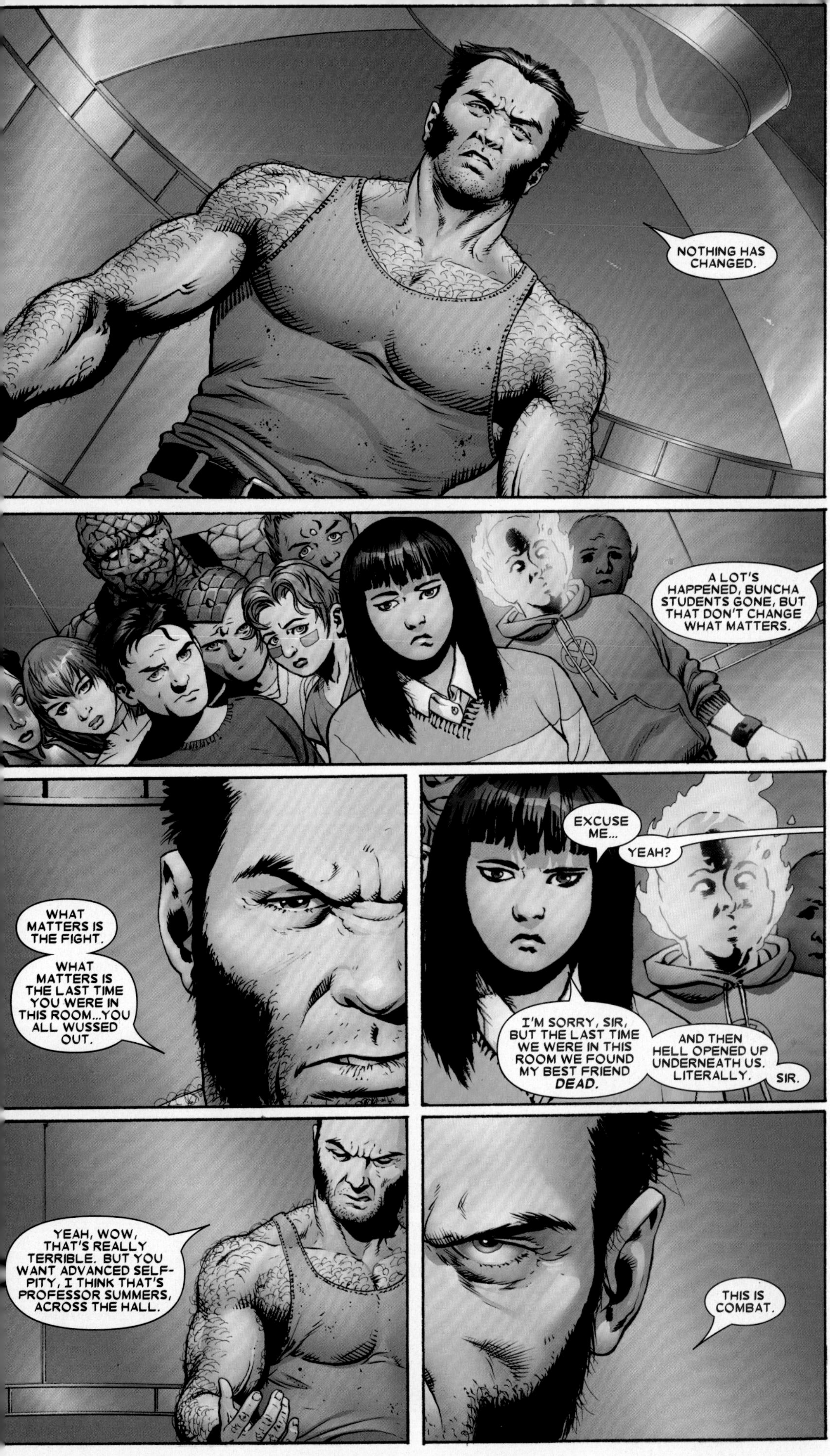
NOTHING HAS CHANGED.
A LOT'S HAPPENED, BUNCHA STUDENTS GONE, BUT THAT DON'T CHANGE WHAT MATTERS.
WHAT MATTERS IS THE FIGHT.
WHAT MATTERS IS THE LAST TIME YOU WERE IN THIS ROOM...YOU ALL WUSSED OUT.
EXCUSE ME...
YEAH?
I'M SORRY, SIR, BUT THE LAST TIME WE WERE IN THIS ROOM WE FOUND MY BEST FRIEND *DEAD.*
AND THEN HELL OPENED UP UNDERNEATH US. LITERALLY.
SIR.
YEAH, WOW, THAT'S REALLY TERRIBLE. BUT YOU WANT ADVANCED SELF-PITY, I THINK THAT'S PROFESSOR SUMMERS, ACROSS THE HALL.
THIS IS COMBAT.

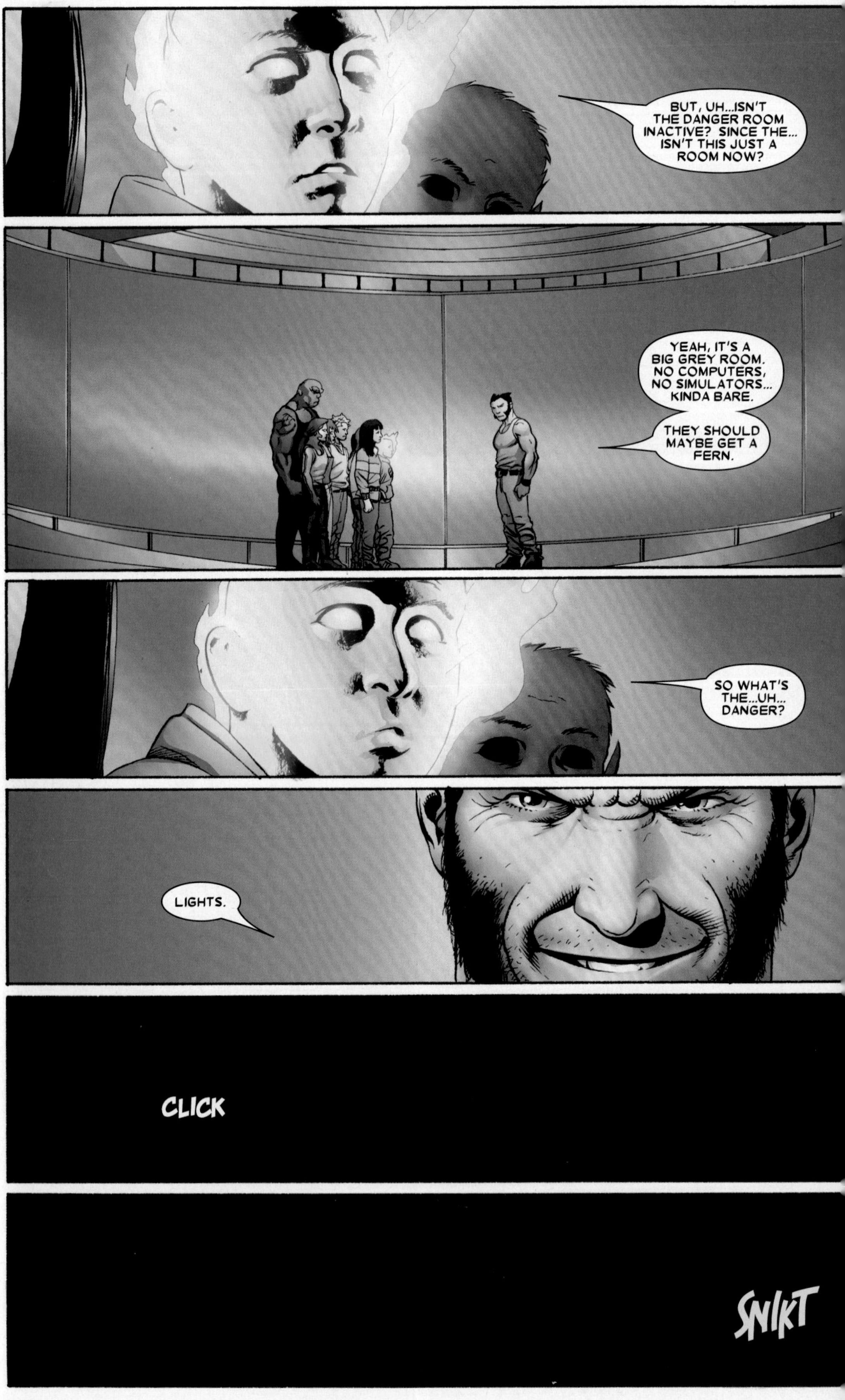
BUT, UH...ISN'T THE DANGER ROOM INACTIVE? SINCE THE... ISN'T THIS JUST A ROOM NOW?
YEAH, IT'S A BIG GREY ROOM. NO COMPUTERS, NO SIMULATORS... KINDA BARE.
THEY SHOULD MAYBE GET A FERN.
SO WHAT'S THE...UH... DANGER?
LIGHTS.
CLICK
SNIKT

AND WE ASSUME THE CHILDREN ARE GOING TO SURVIVE THIS EXPERIENCE BECAUSE...

LOGAN'LL GO EASY. WELL, FOR LOGAN.

IT'S WHAT THEY NEED.

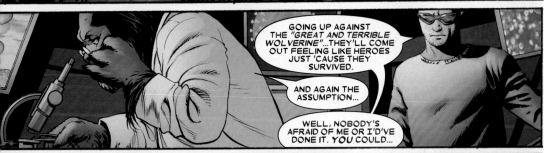

GOING UP AGAINST THE "GREAT AND TERRIBLE WOLVERINE"...THEY'LL COME OUT FEELING LIKE HEROES JUST 'CAUSE THEY SURVIVED.

AND AGAIN THE ASSUMPTION...

WELL, NOBODY'S AFRAID OF ME OR I'D'VE DONE IT. YOU COULD...

'COURSE, THAT WOULD MEAN LEAVING THE LAB FOR FIVE MINUTES. AND THAT'S NOT ON THE MENU, IS IT?

IF IT'S NOT A MISSION OR A CLASS YOU'RE HERE, NO EXCEPTIONS.

YOU WANT ME TO TELL YOU WHY YOU'RE DOWN HERE?

I'D LOVE IT. AFTER YOU TELL ME WHY YOU'RE HANGING AROUND HERE AND NOT UPSTAIRS WITH YOUR LADY LOVE.

YEAH.

HMM.

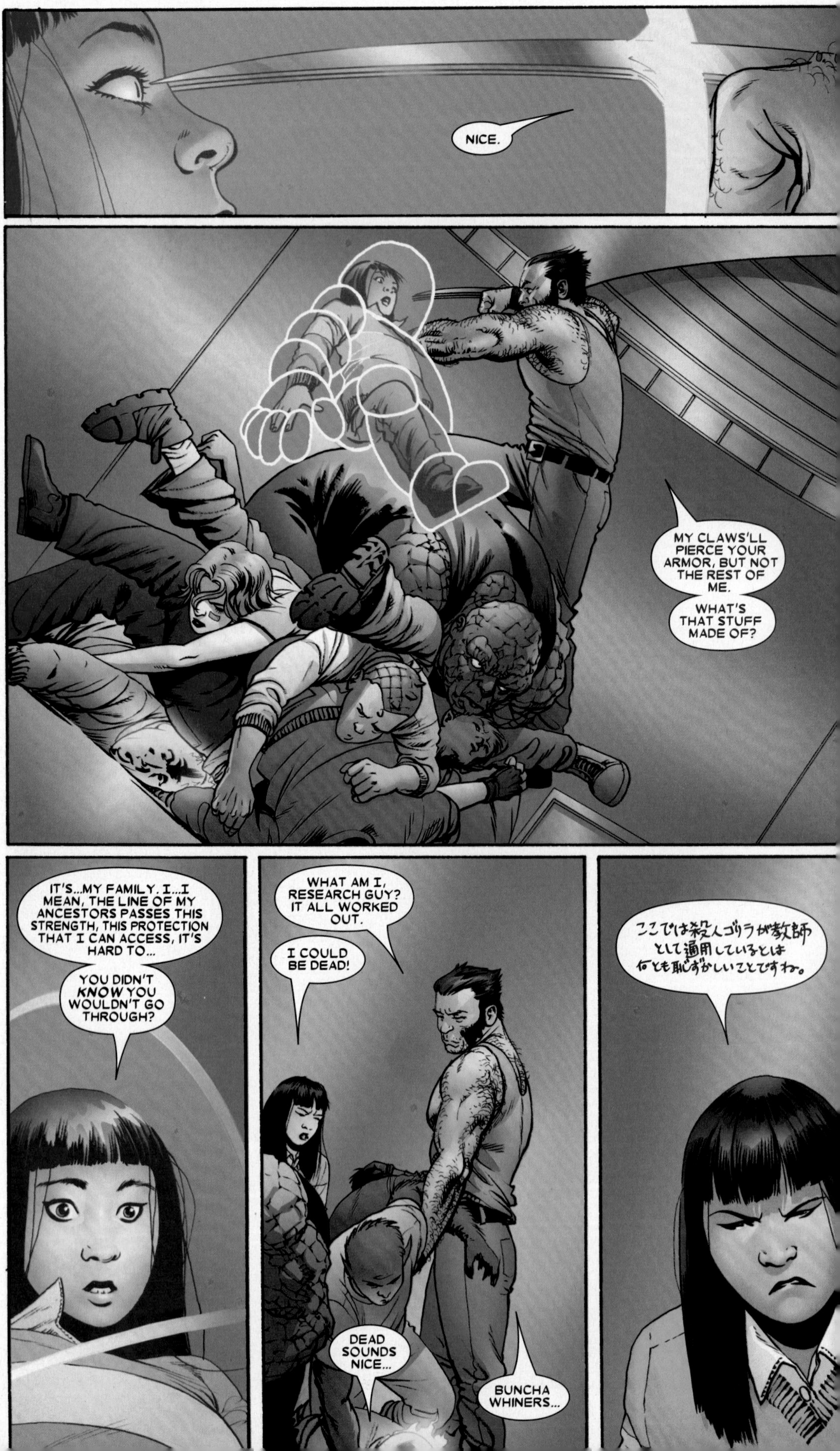
NICE.
MY CLAWS'LL PIERCE YOUR ARMOR, BUT NOT THE REST OF ME.
WHAT'S THAT STUFF MADE OF?
IT'S...MY FAMILY. I...I MEAN, THE LINE OF MY ANCESTORS PASSES THIS STRENGTH, THIS PROTECTION THAT I CAN ACCESS, IT'S HARD TO...
YOU DIDN'T KNOW YOU WOULDN'T GO THROUGH?
WHAT AM I, RESEARCH GUY? IT ALL WORKED OUT.
I COULD BE DEAD!
DEAD SOUNDS NICE...
BUNCHA WHINERS...
ここでは殺人ゴリラが教師として通用しているとは何とも恥ずかしいことですね。

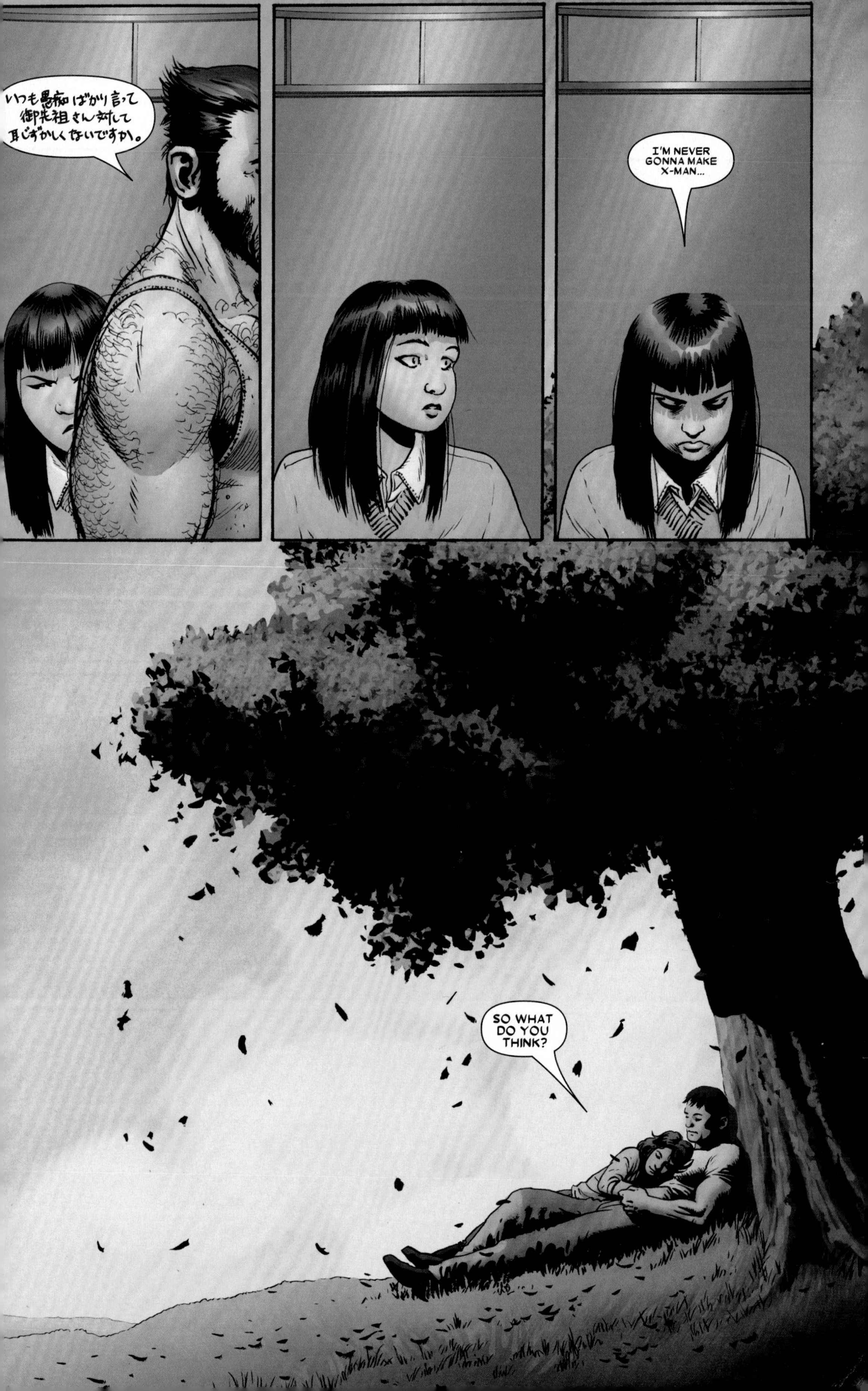

いつも愚痴ばかり言って
御先祖さん対して
耳じずかしくないですか。
I'M NEVER GONNA MAKE X-MAN...
SO WHAT DO YOU THINK?

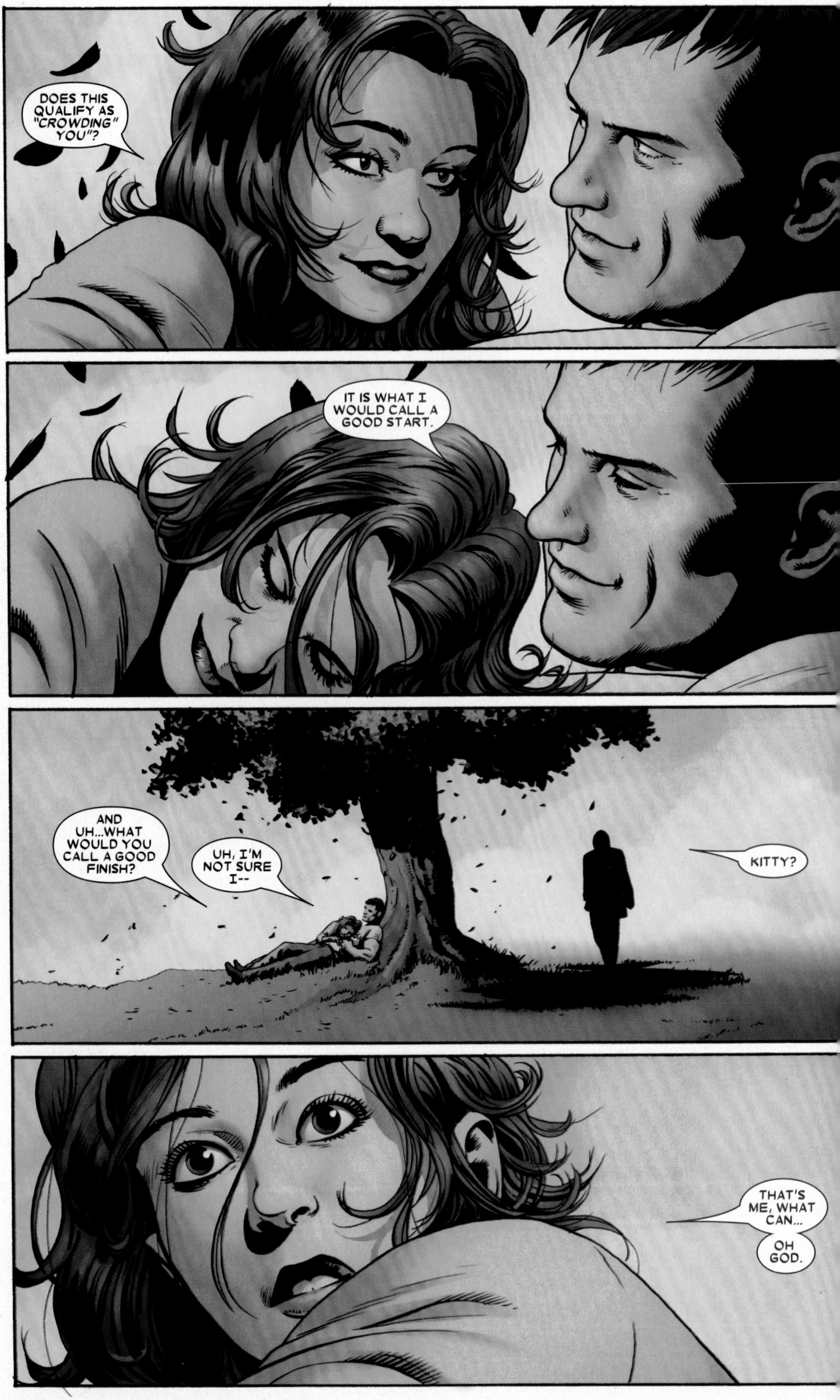
DOES THIS QUALIFY AS "CROWDING YOU"?
IT IS WHAT I WOULD CALL A GOOD START.
AND UH...WHAT WOULD YOU CALL A GOOD FINISH?
UH, I'M NOT SURE I--
KITTY?
THAT'S ME, WHAT CAN...
OH GOD.

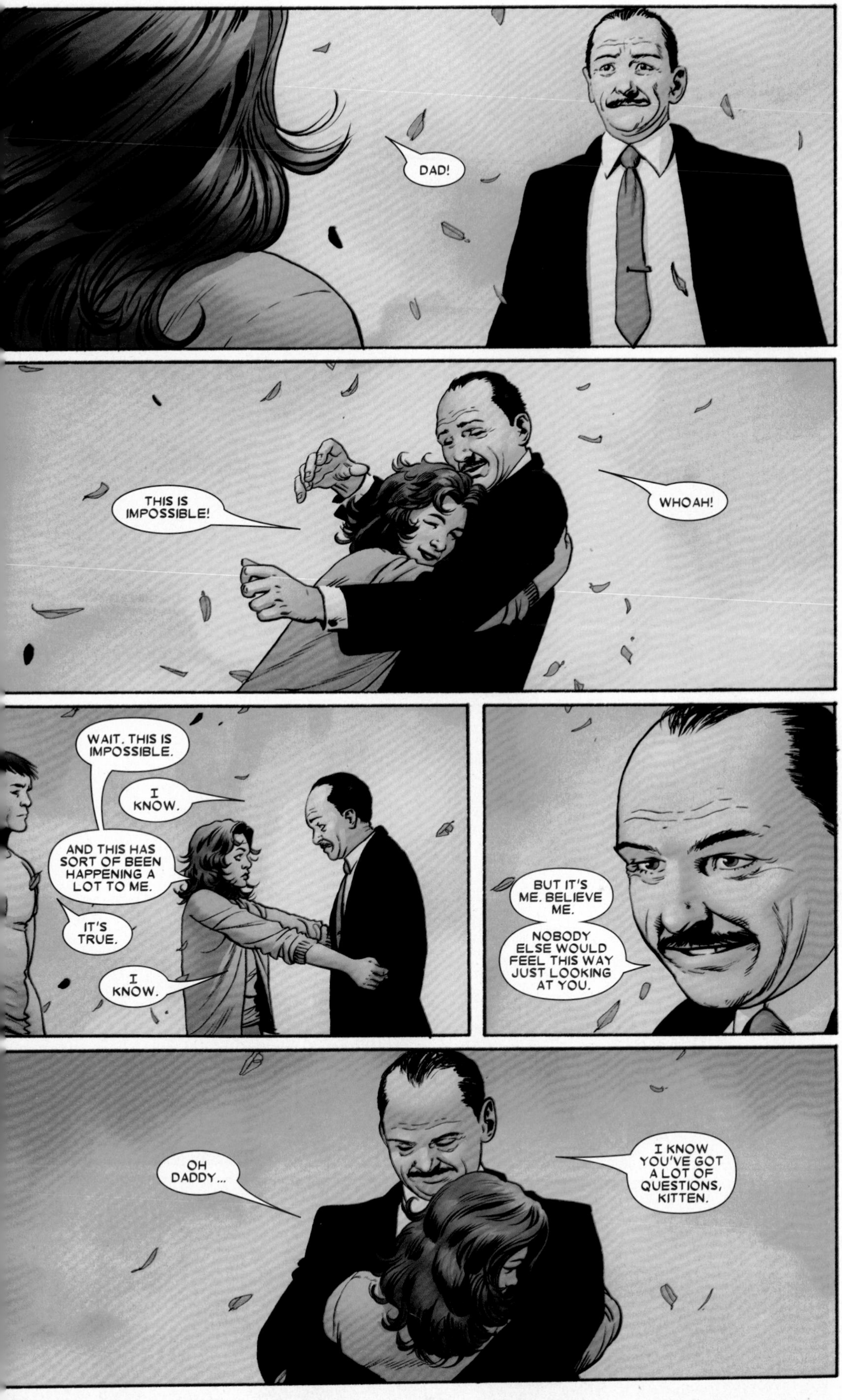

DAD!
THIS IS IMPOSSIBLE!
WHOAH!
WAIT. THIS IS IMPOSSIBLE.
I KNOW.
AND THIS HAS SORT OF BEEN HAPPENING A LOT TO ME.
IT'S TRUE.
I KNOW.
BUT IT'S ME. BELIEVE ME.
NOBODY ELSE WOULD FEEL THIS WAY JUST LOOKING AT YOU.
OH DADDY...
I KNOW YOU'VE GOT A LOT OF QUESTIONS, KITTEN.

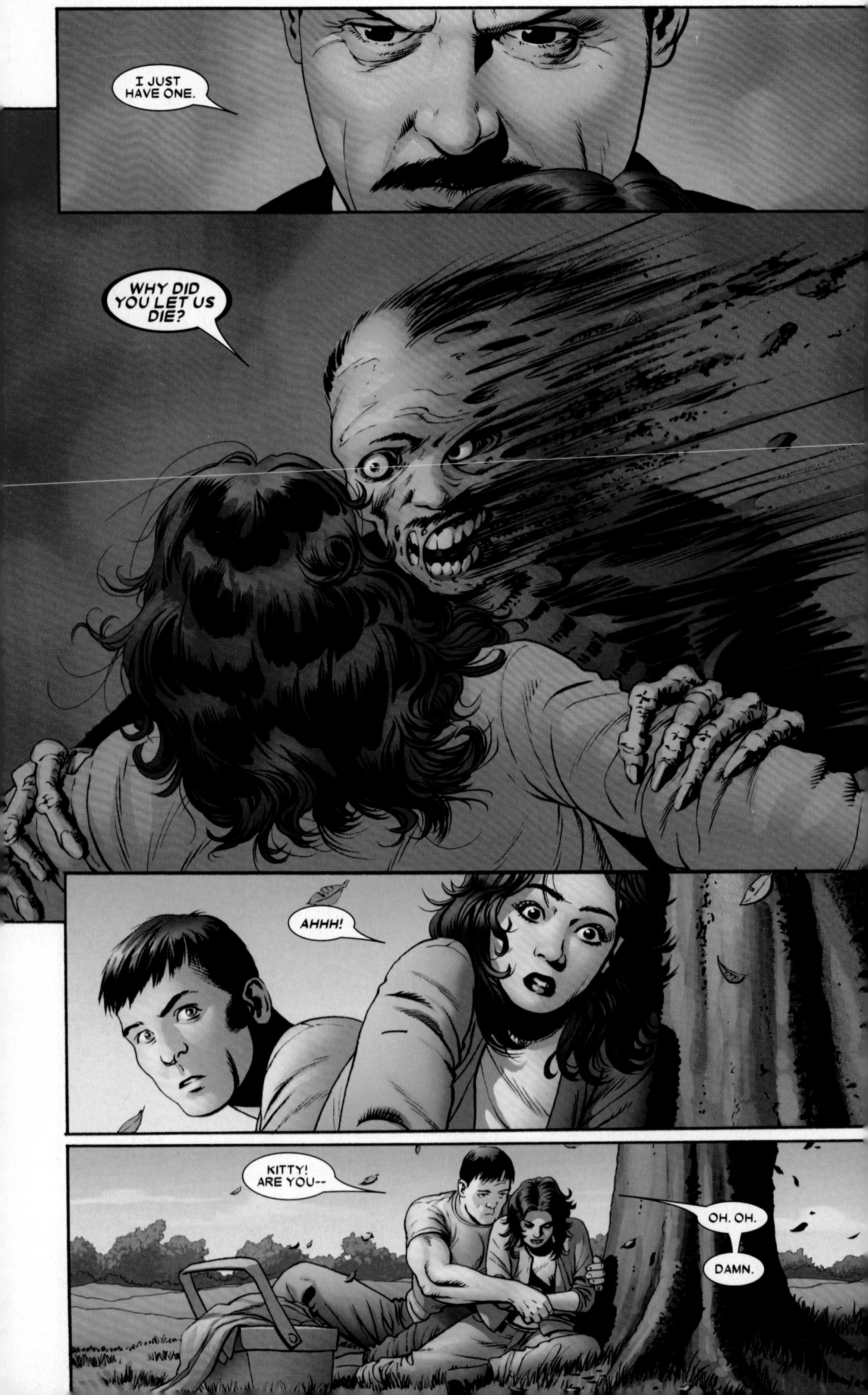

I JUST HAVE ONE.
WHY DID YOU LET US DIE?
AHHH!
KITTY! ARE YOU--
OH, OH.
DAMN.

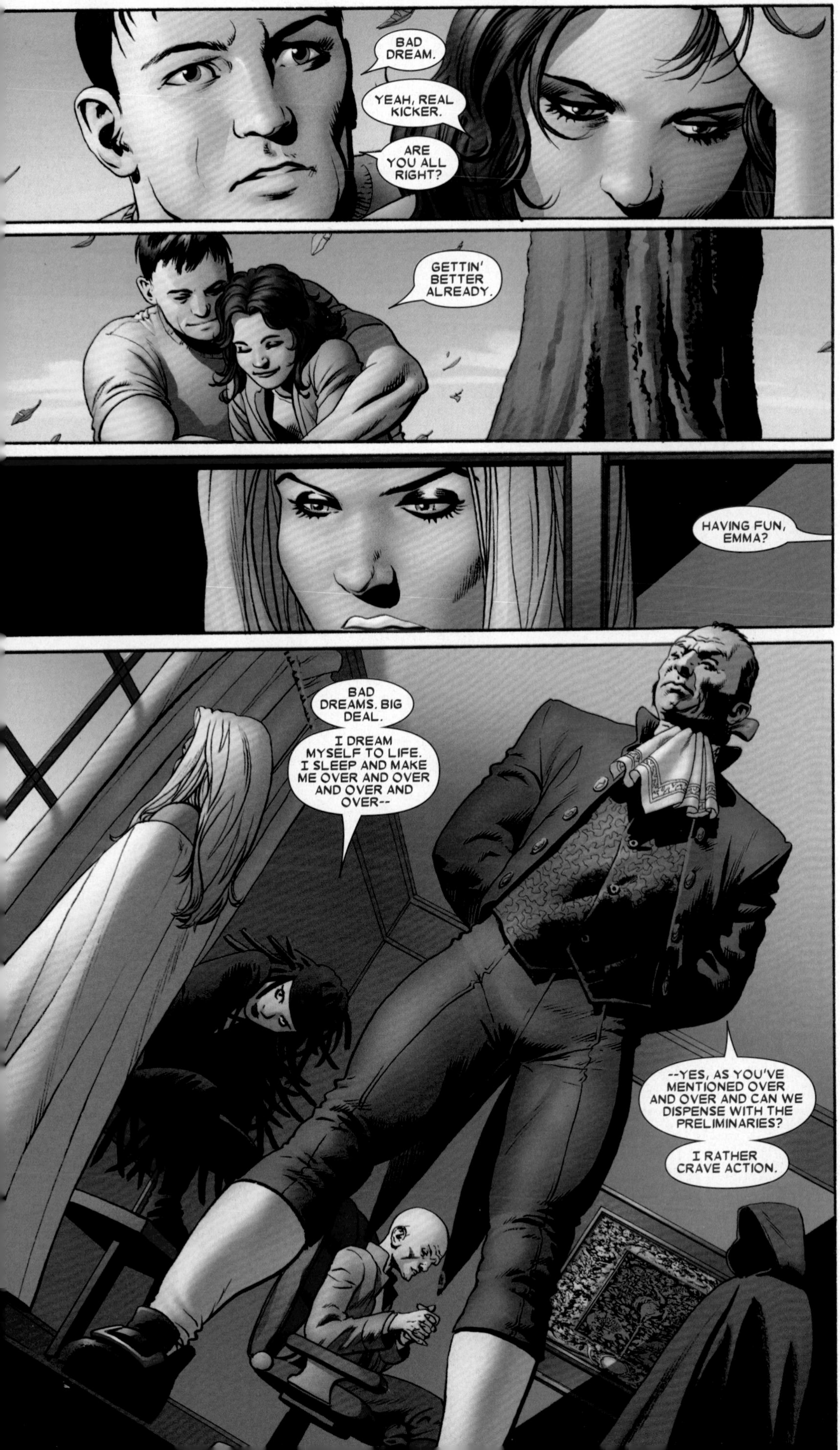
BAD DREAM.
YEAH, REAL KICKER.
ARE YOU ALL RIGHT?
GETTIN' BETTER ALREADY.
HAVING FUN, EMMA?
BAD DREAMS. BIG DEAL.
I DREAM MYSELF TO LIFE. I SLEEP AND MAKE ME OVER AND OVER AND OVER AND OVER--
--YES, AS YOU'VE MENTIONED OVER AND OVER AND CAN WE DISPENSE WITH THE PRELIMINARIES?
I RATHER CRAVE ACTION.

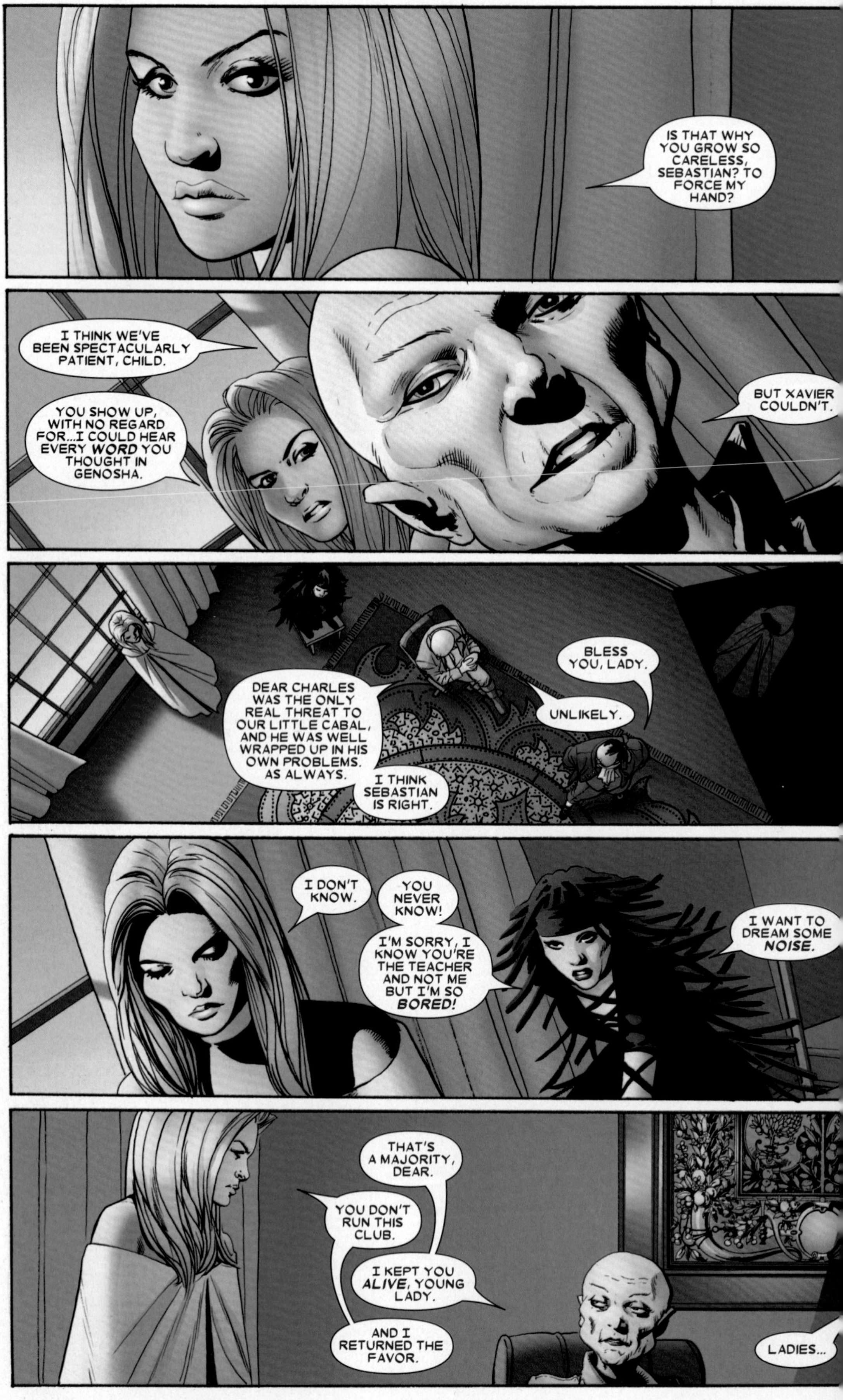

IS THAT WHY YOU GROW SO CARELESS, SEBASTIAN? TO FORCE MY HAND?
I THINK WE'VE BEEN SPECTACULARLY PATIENT, CHILD.
YOU SHOW UP, WITH NO REGARD FOR...I COULD HEAR EVERY WORD YOU THOUGHT IN GENOSHA.
BUT XAVIER COULDN'T.
DEAR CHARLES WAS THE ONLY REAL THREAT TO OUR LITTLE CABAL, AND HE WAS WELL WRAPPED UP IN HIS OWN PROBLEMS. AS ALWAYS.
BLESS YOU, LADY.
UNLIKELY.
I THINK SEBASTIAN IS RIGHT.
I DON'T KNOW.
YOU NEVER KNOW!
I'M SORRY, I KNOW YOU'RE THE TEACHER AND NOT ME BUT I'M SO BORED!
I WANT TO DREAM SOME NOISE.
THAT'S A MAJORITY, DEAR.
YOU DON'T RUN THIS CLUB.
I KEPT YOU ALIVE, YOUNG LADY.
AND I RETURNED THE FAVOR.
LADIES...

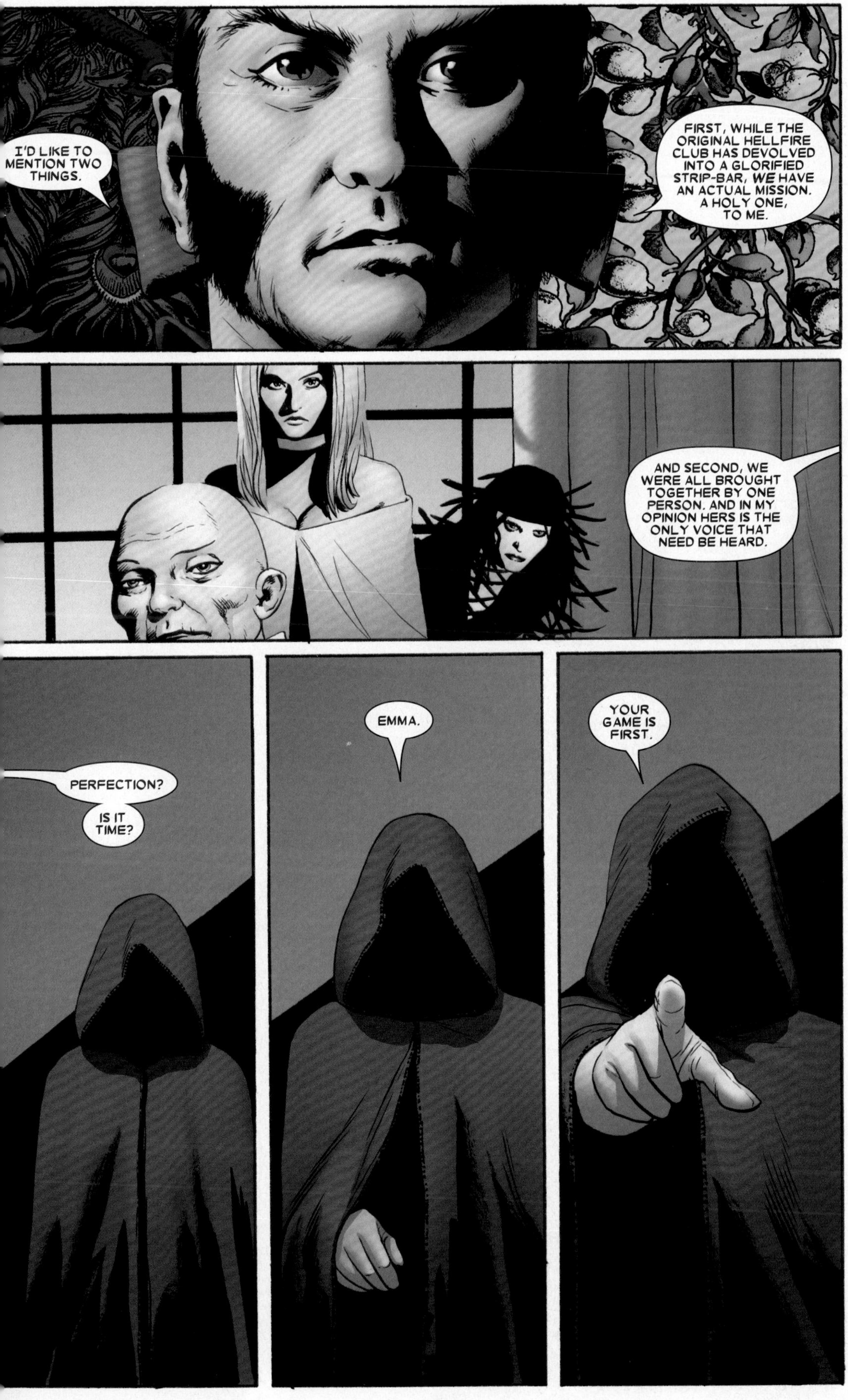
I'D LIKE TO MENTION TWO THINGS.
FIRST, WHILE THE ORIGINAL HELLFIRE CLUB HAS DEVOLVED INTO A GLORIFIED STRIP-BAR, *WE* HAVE AN ACTUAL MISSION. A HOLY ONE, TO ME.
AND SECOND, WE WERE ALL BROUGHT TOGETHER BY ONE PERSON. AND IN MY OPINION HERS IS THE ONLY VOICE THAT NEED BE HEARD.
PERFECTION?
IS IT TIME?
EMMA.
YOUR GAME IS FIRST.

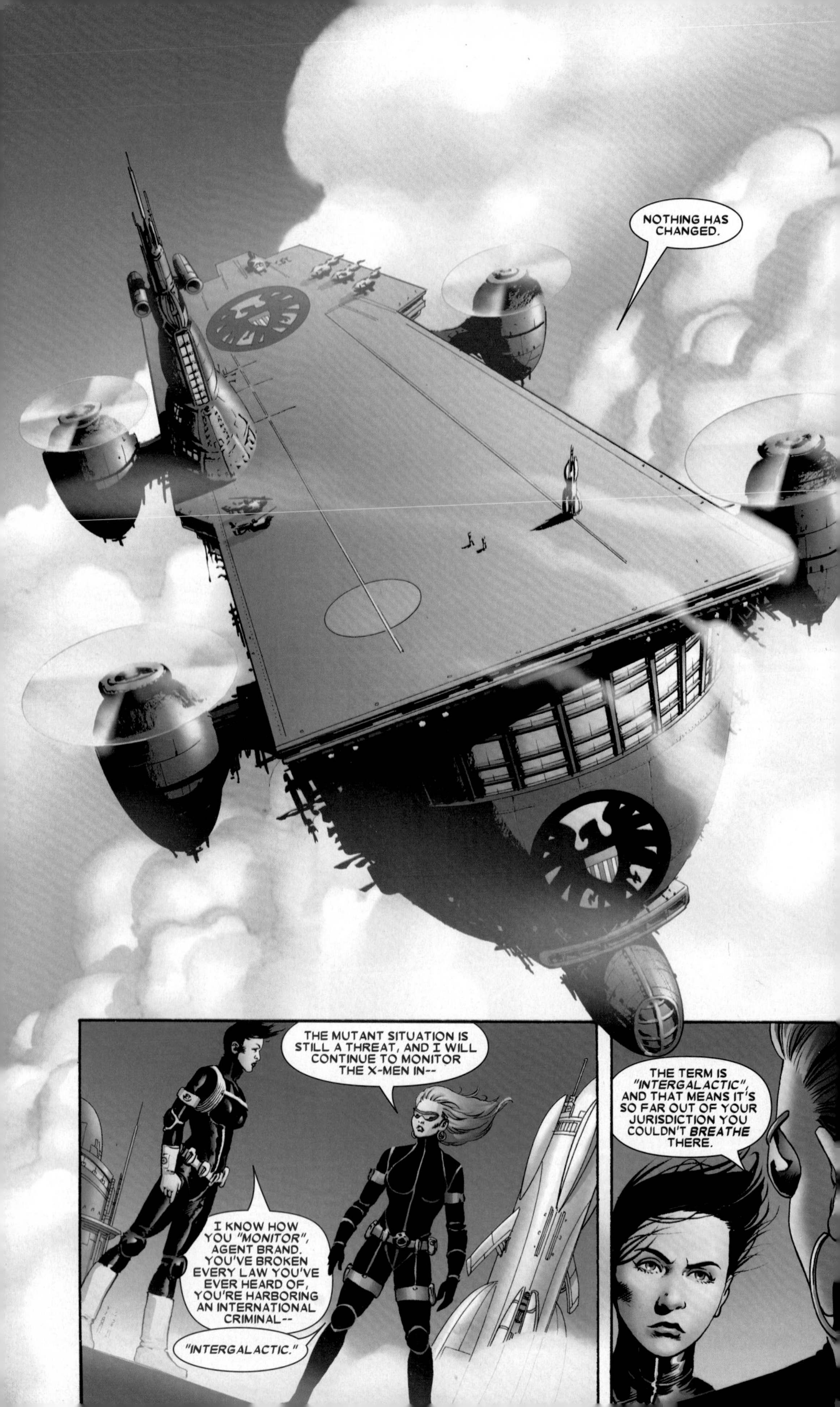
NOTHING HAS CHANGED.
THE MUTANT SITUATION IS STILL A THREAT, AND I WILL CONTINUE TO MONITOR THE X-MEN IN--
I KNOW HOW YOU "MONITOR", AGENT BRAND. YOU'VE BROKEN EVERY LAW YOU'VE EVER HEARD OF, YOU'RE HARBORING AN INTERNATIONAL CRIMINAL--
"INTERGALACTIC."
THE TERM IS "INTERGALACTIC", AND THAT MEANS IT'S SO FAR OUT OF YOUR JURISDICTION YOU COULDN'T BREATHE THERE.

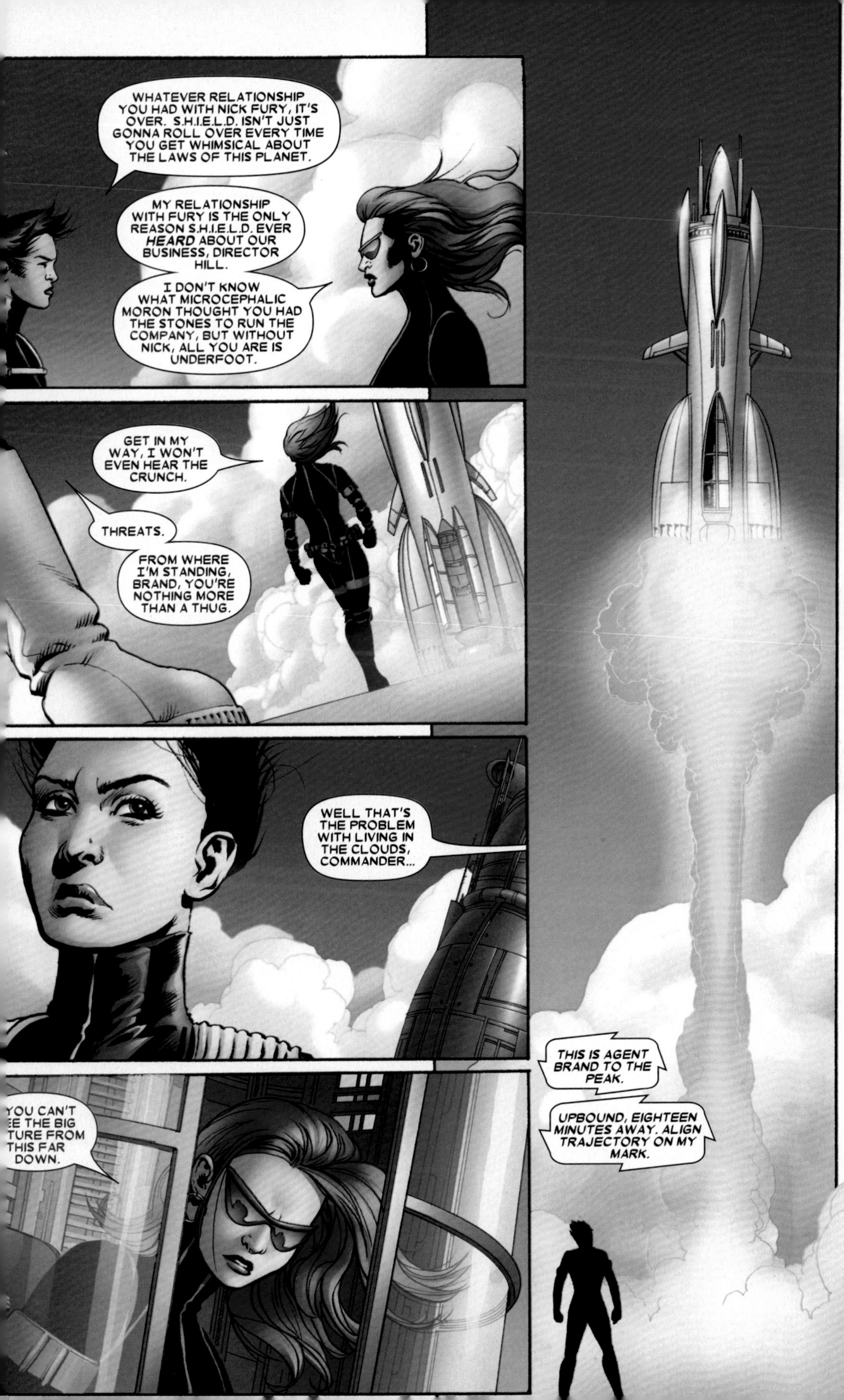

WHATEVER RELATIONSHIP YOU HAD WITH NICK FURY, IT'S OVER. S.H.I.E.L.D. ISN'T JUST GONNA ROLL OVER EVERY TIME YOU GET WHIMSICAL ABOUT THE LAWS OF THIS PLANET.
MY RELATIONSHIP WITH FURY IS THE ONLY REASON S.H.I.E.L.D. EVER *HEARD* ABOUT OUR BUSINESS, DIRECTOR HILL.
I DON'T KNOW WHAT MICROCEPHALIC MORON THOUGHT YOU HAD THE STONES TO RUN THE COMPANY, BUT WITHOUT NICK, ALL YOU ARE IS UNDERFOOT.
GET IN MY WAY, I WON'T EVEN HEAR THE CRUNCH.
THREATS.
FROM WHERE I'M STANDING, BRAND, YOU'RE NOTHING MORE THAN A THUG.
WELL THAT'S THE PROBLEM WITH LIVING IN THE CLOUDS, COMMANDER...
YOU CAN'T EE THE BIG TURE FROM THIS FAR DOWN.
THIS IS AGENT BRAND TO THE PEAK.
UPBOUND, EIGHTEEN MINUTES AWAY. ALIGN TRAJECTORY ON MY MARK.

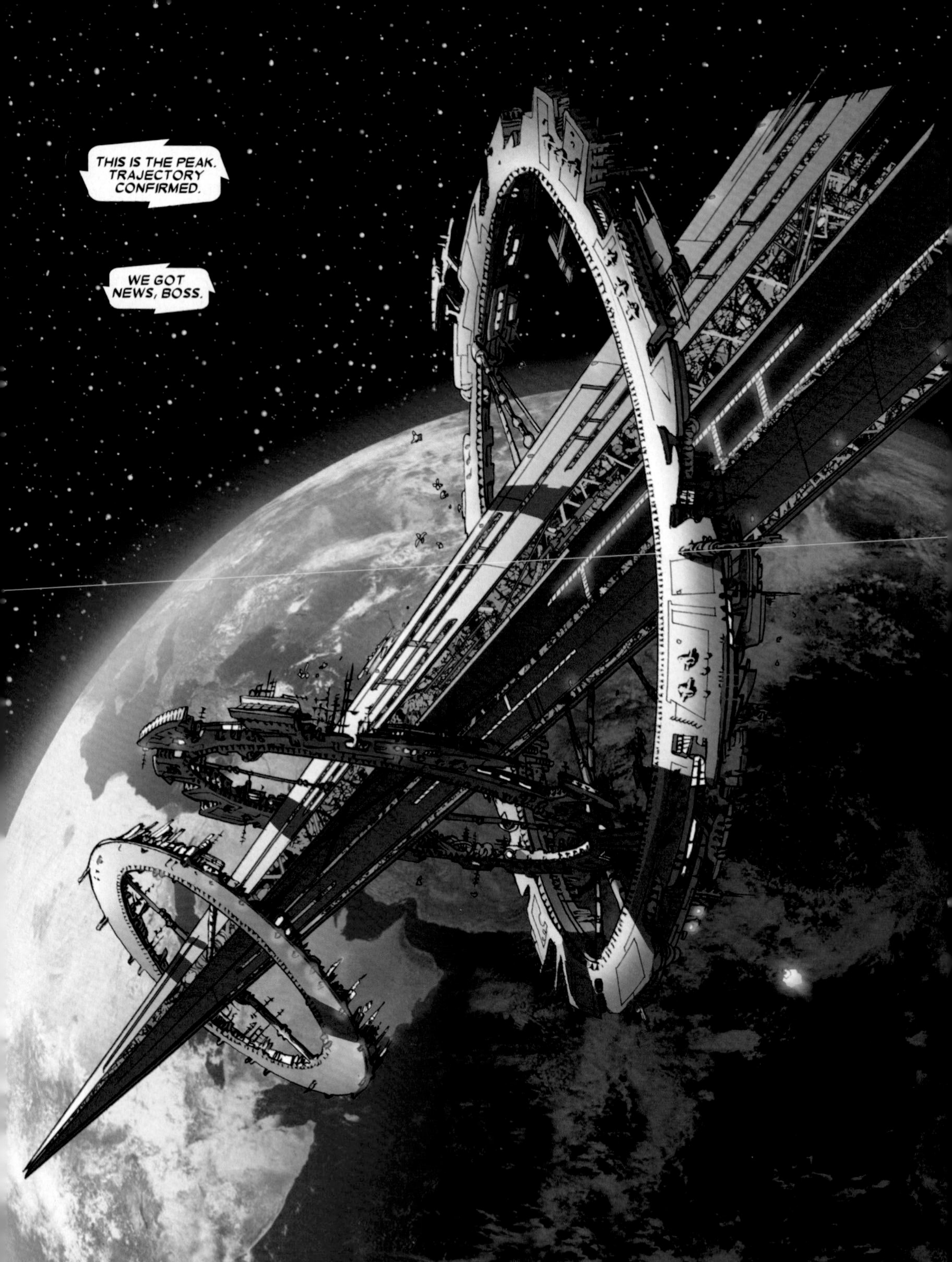
THIS IS THE PEAK. TRAJECTORY CONFIRMED.
WE GOT NEWS, BOSS.
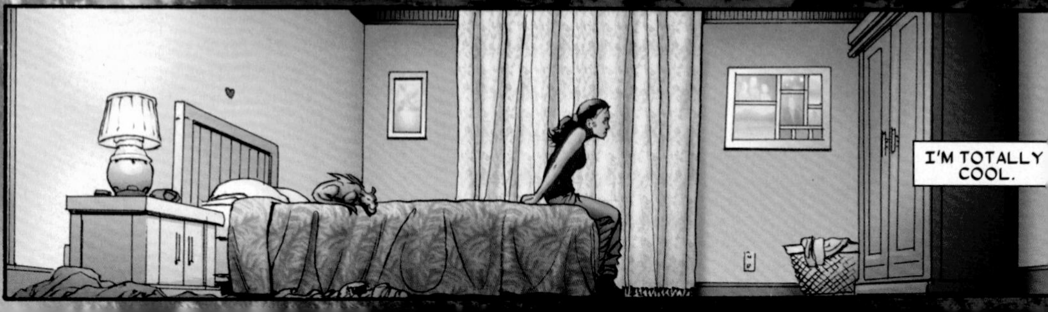
I'M TOTALLY COOL.

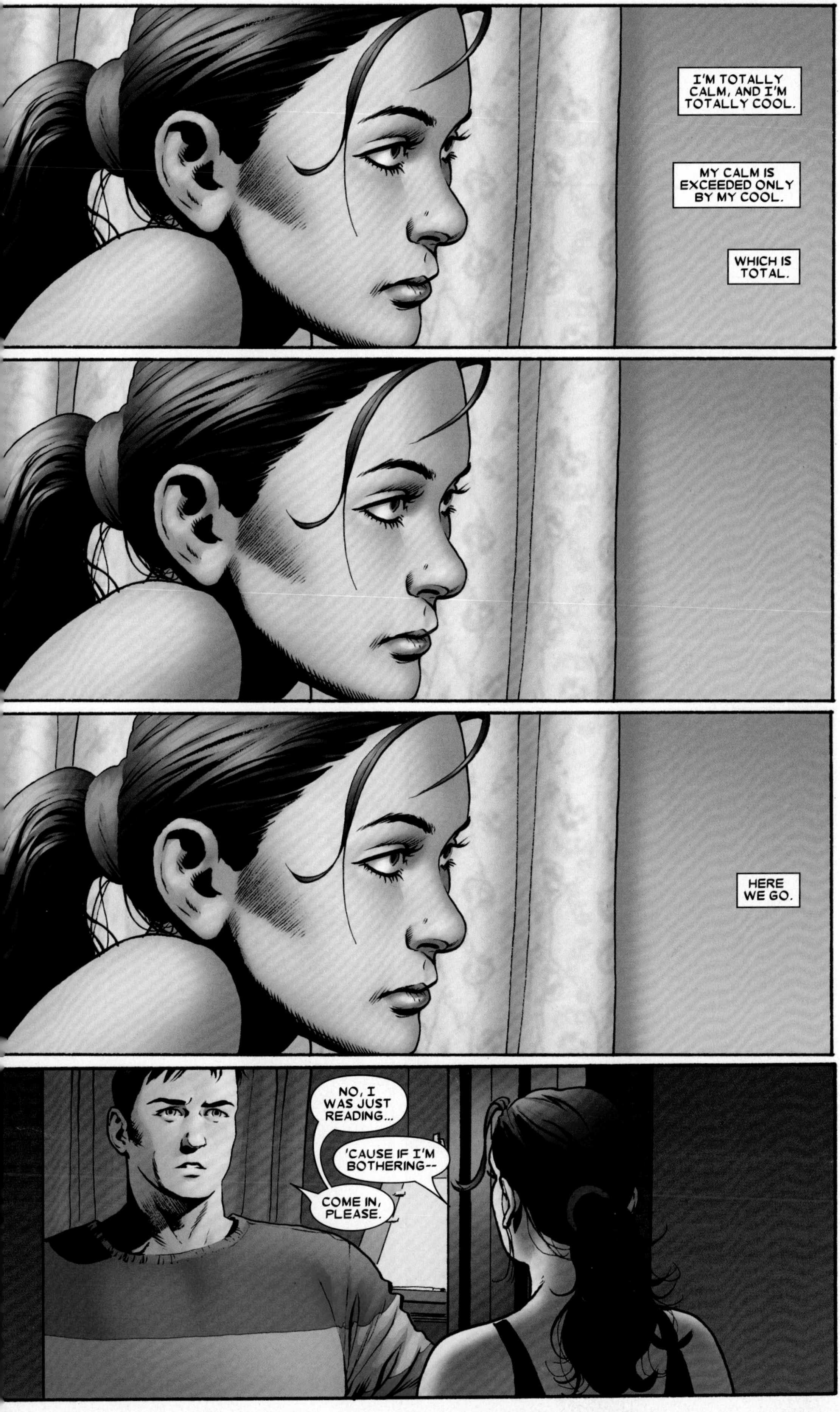

I'M TOTALLY CALM, AND I'M TOTALLY COOL.
MY CALM IS EXCEEDED ONLY BY MY COOL.
WHICH IS TOTAL.
HERE WE GO.
NO, I WAS JUST READING...
'CAUSE IF I'M BOTHERING--
COME IN, PLEASE.

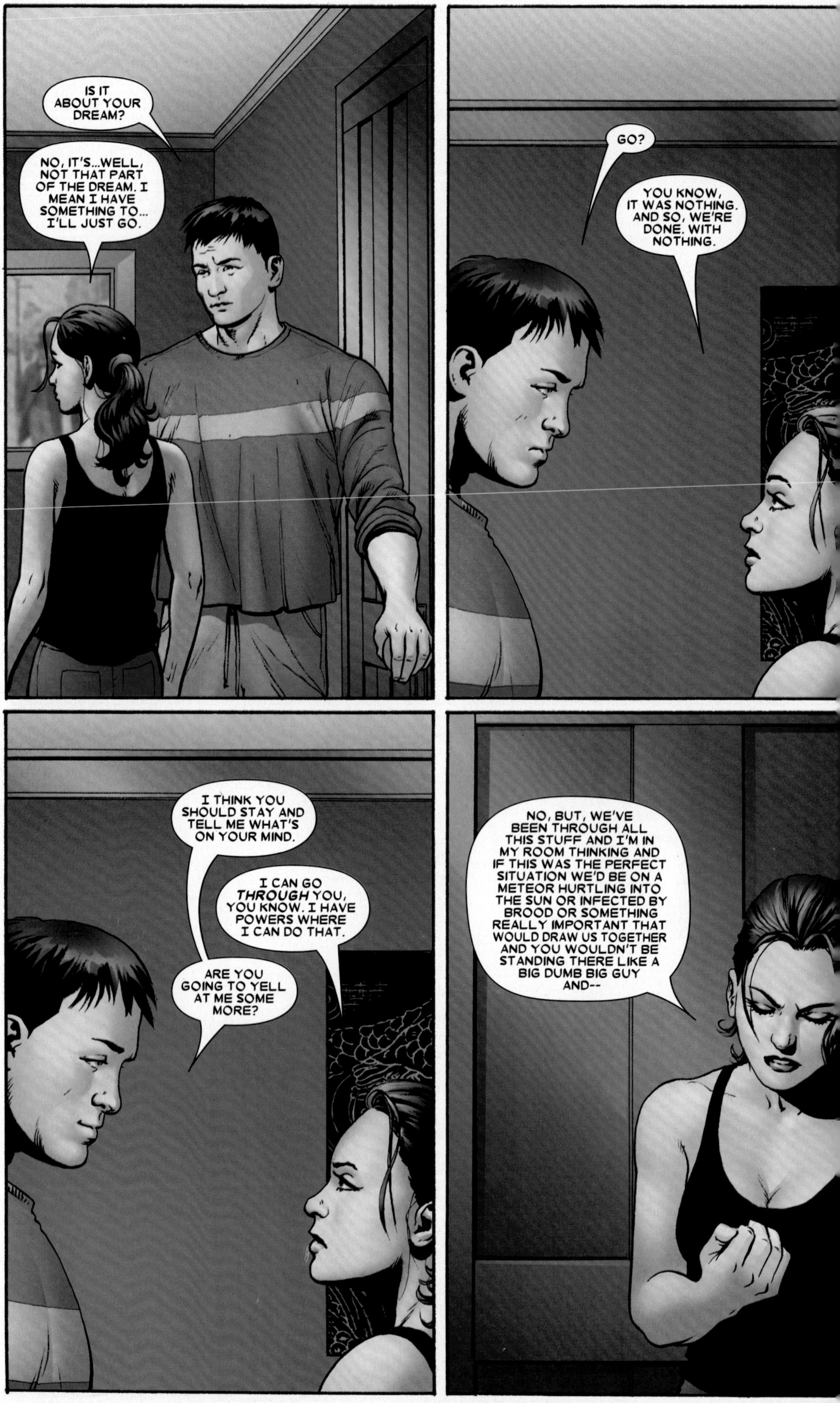
IS IT ABOUT YOUR DREAM?
NO, IT'S...WELL, NOT THAT PART OF THE DREAM. I MEAN I HAVE SOMETHING TO... I'LL JUST GO.
GO?
YOU KNOW, IT WAS NOTHING. AND SO, WE'RE DONE. WITH NOTHING.
I THINK YOU SHOULD STAY AND TELL ME WHAT'S ON YOUR MIND.
I CAN GO THROUGH YOU, YOU KNOW. I HAVE POWERS WHERE I CAN DO THAT.
ARE YOU GOING TO YELL AT ME SOME MORE?
NO, BUT, WE'VE BEEN THROUGH ALL THIS STUFF AND I'M IN MY ROOM THINKING AND IF THIS WAS THE PERFECT SITUATION WE'D BE ON A METEOR HURTLING INTO THE SUN OR INFECTED BY BROOD OR SOMETHING REALLY IMPORTANT THAT WOULD DRAW US TOGETHER AND YOU WOULDN'T BE STANDING THERE LIKE A BIG DUMB BIG GUY AND--

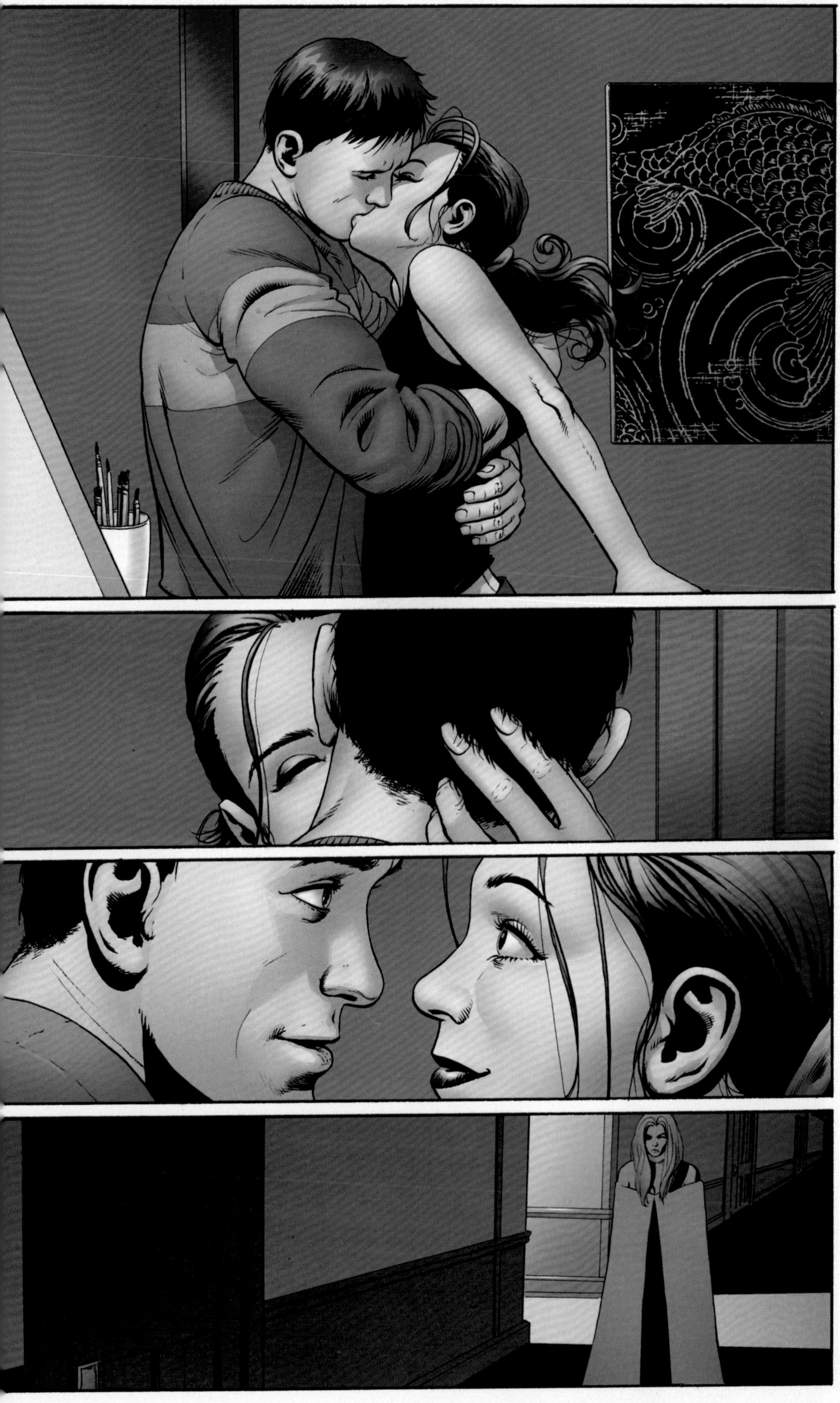

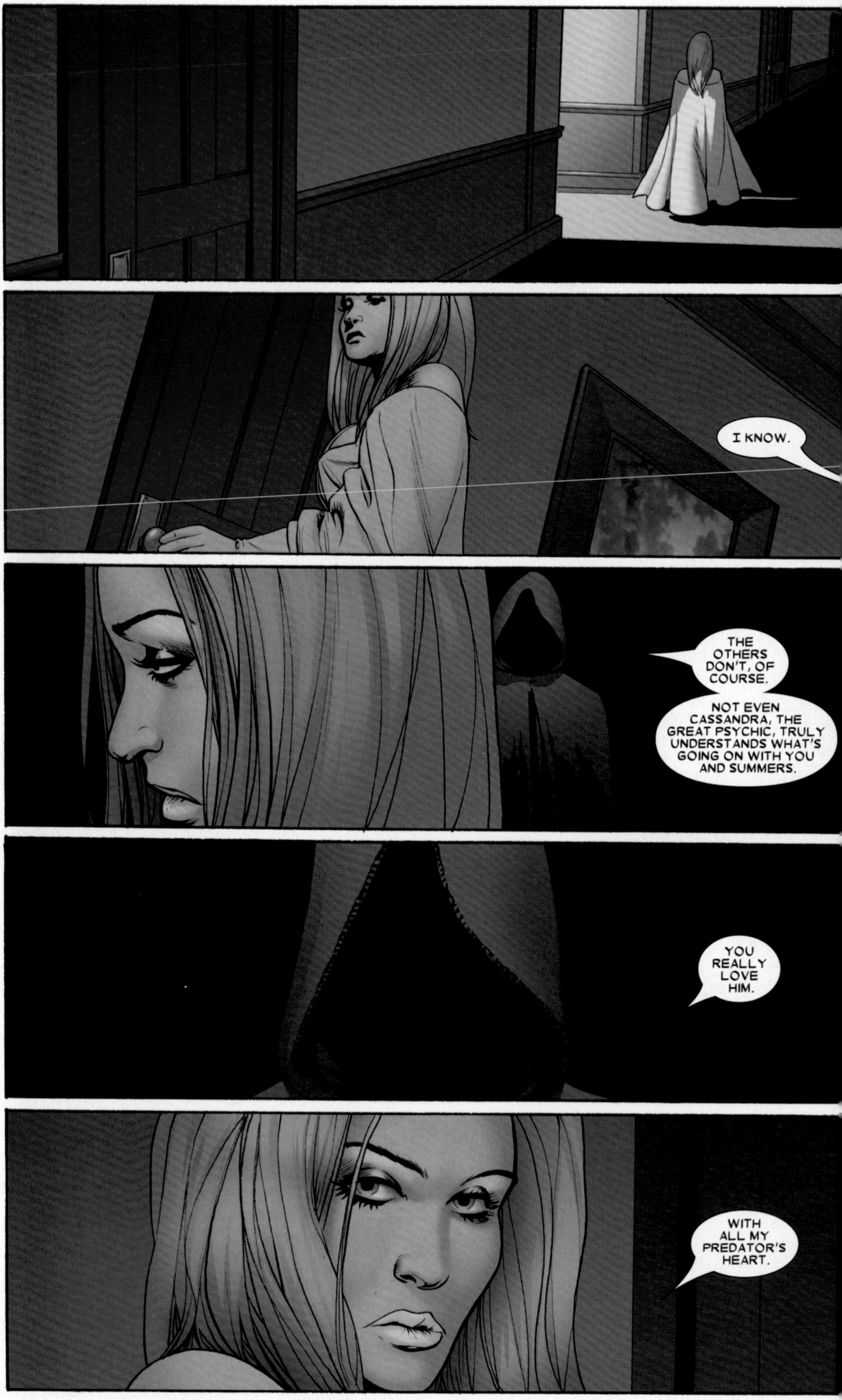
I KNOW.
THE OTHERS DON'T, OF COURSE.
NOT EVEN CASSANDRA, THE GREAT PSYCHIC, TRULY UNDERSTANDS WHAT'S GOING ON WITH YOU AND SUMMERS.
YOU REALLY LOVE HIM.
WITH ALL MY PREDATOR'S HEART.

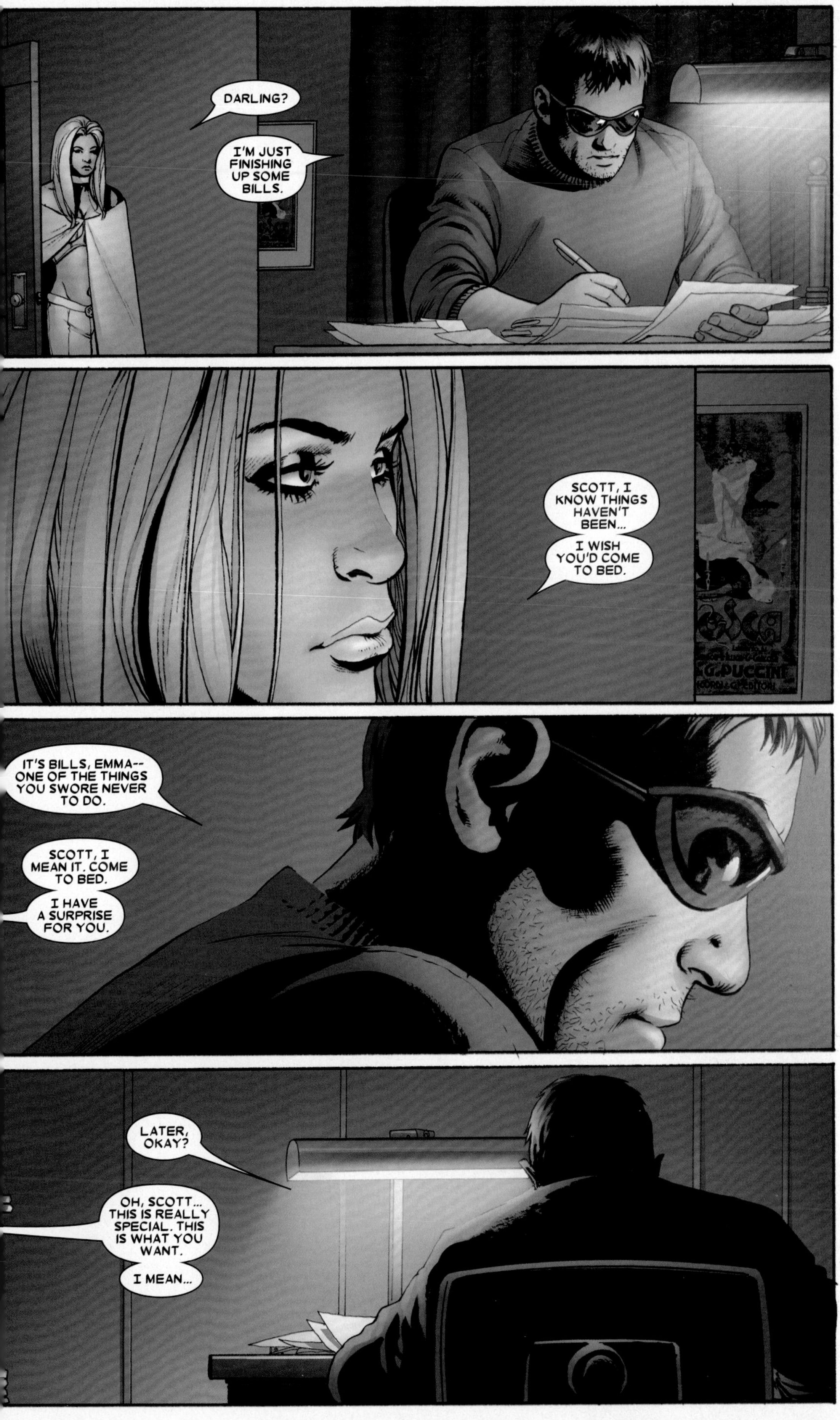
DARLING?
I'M JUST FINISHING UP SOME BILLS.
SCOTT, I KNOW THINGS HAVEN'T BEEN...
I WISH YOU'D COME TO BED.
G.PUCCINI
IT'S BILLS, EMMA-- ONE OF THE THINGS YOU SWORE NEVER TO DO.
SCOTT, I MEAN IT. COME TO BED.
I HAVE A SURPRISE FOR YOU.
LATER, OKAY?
OH, SCOTT... THIS IS REALLY SPECIAL. THIS IS WHAT YOU WANT.
I MEAN...

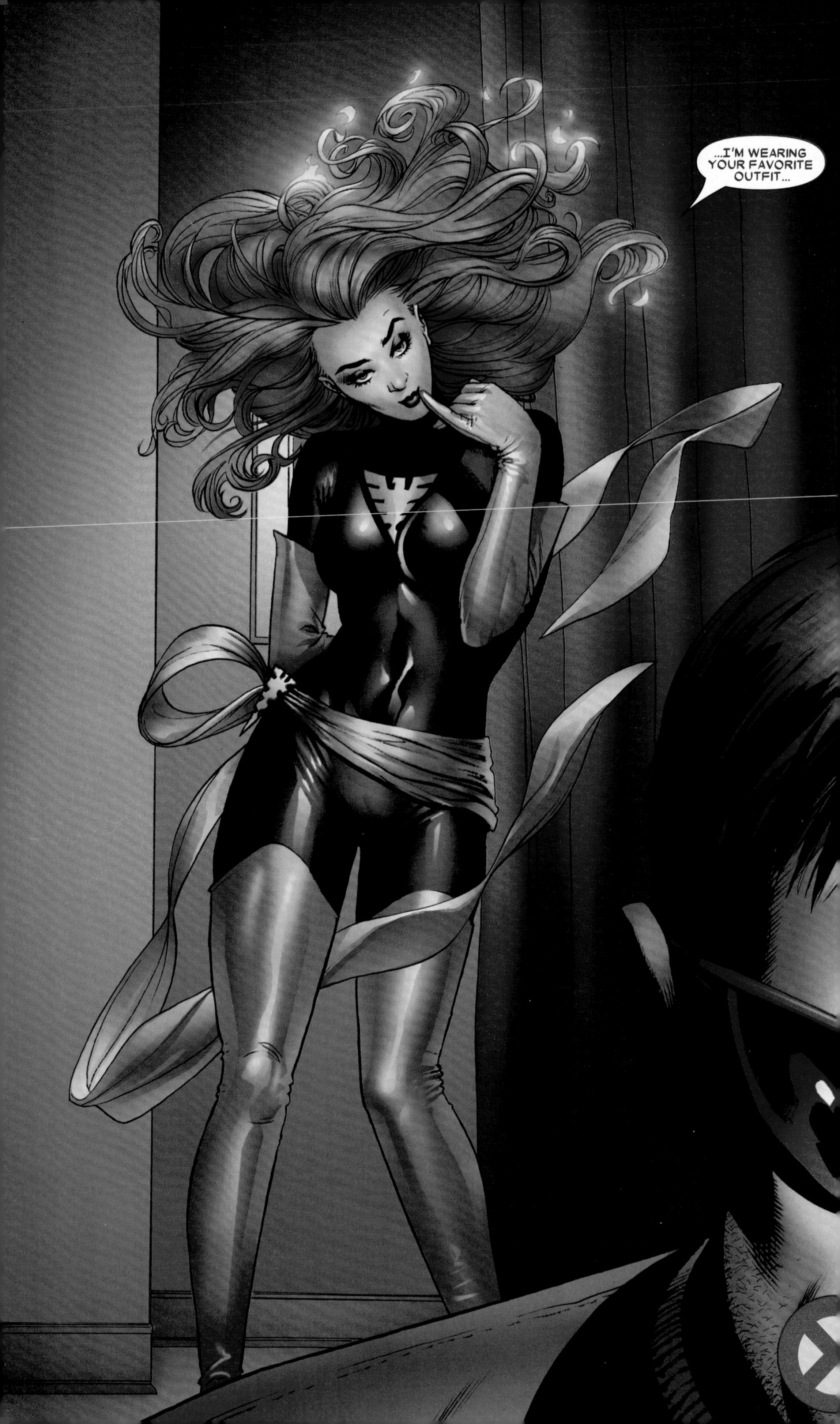
...I'M WEARING YOUR FAVORITE OUTFIT...

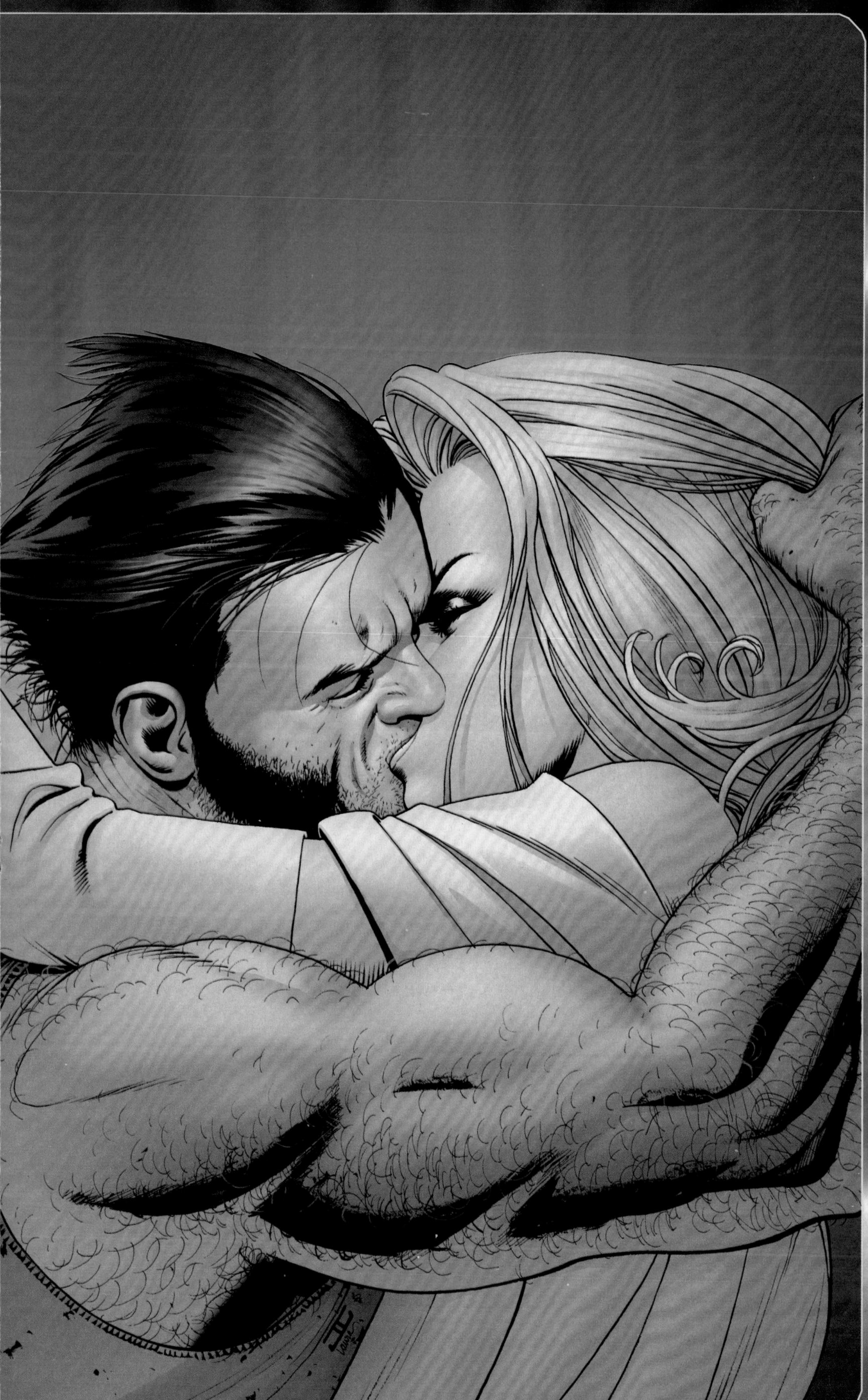

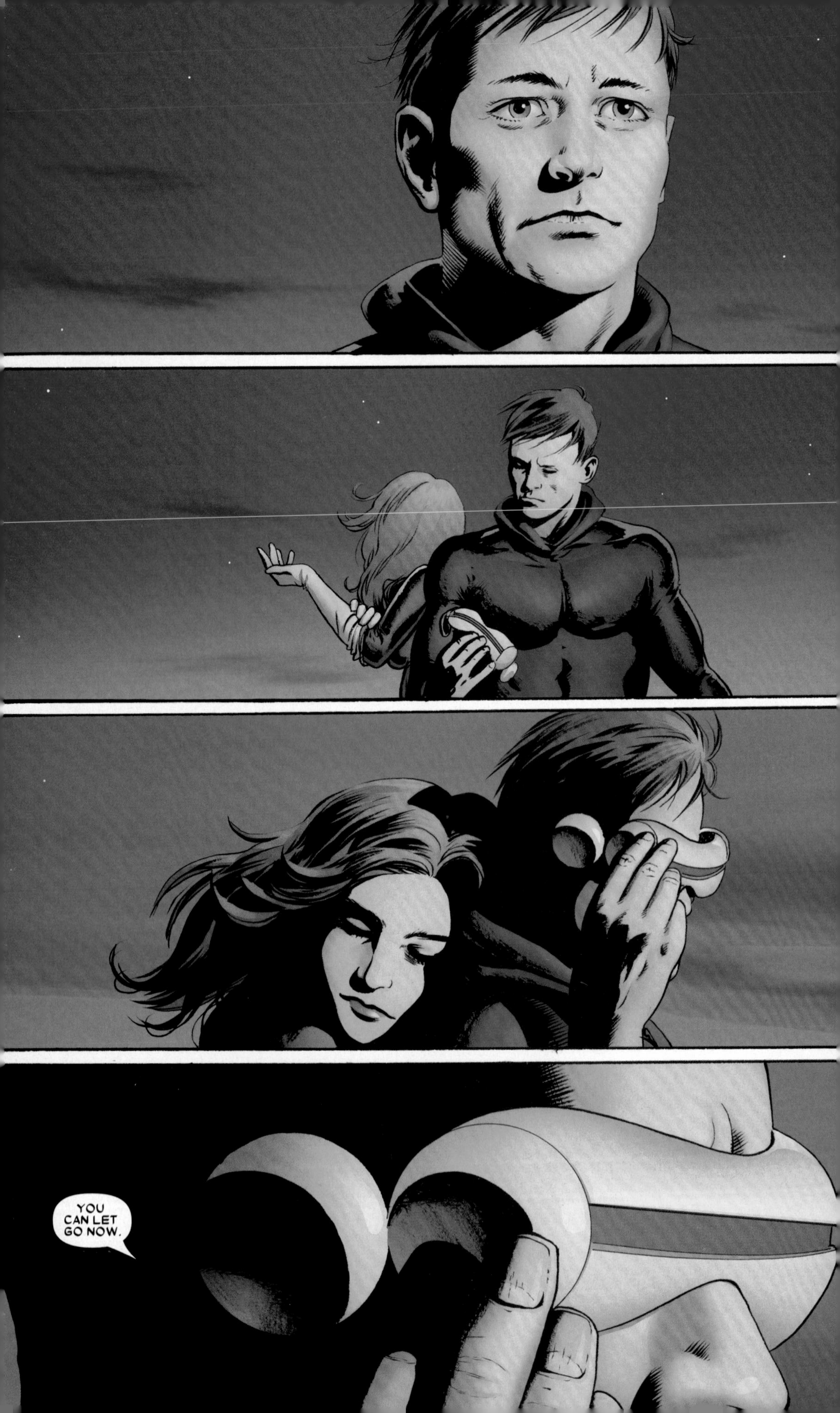
YOU CAN LET GO NOW.

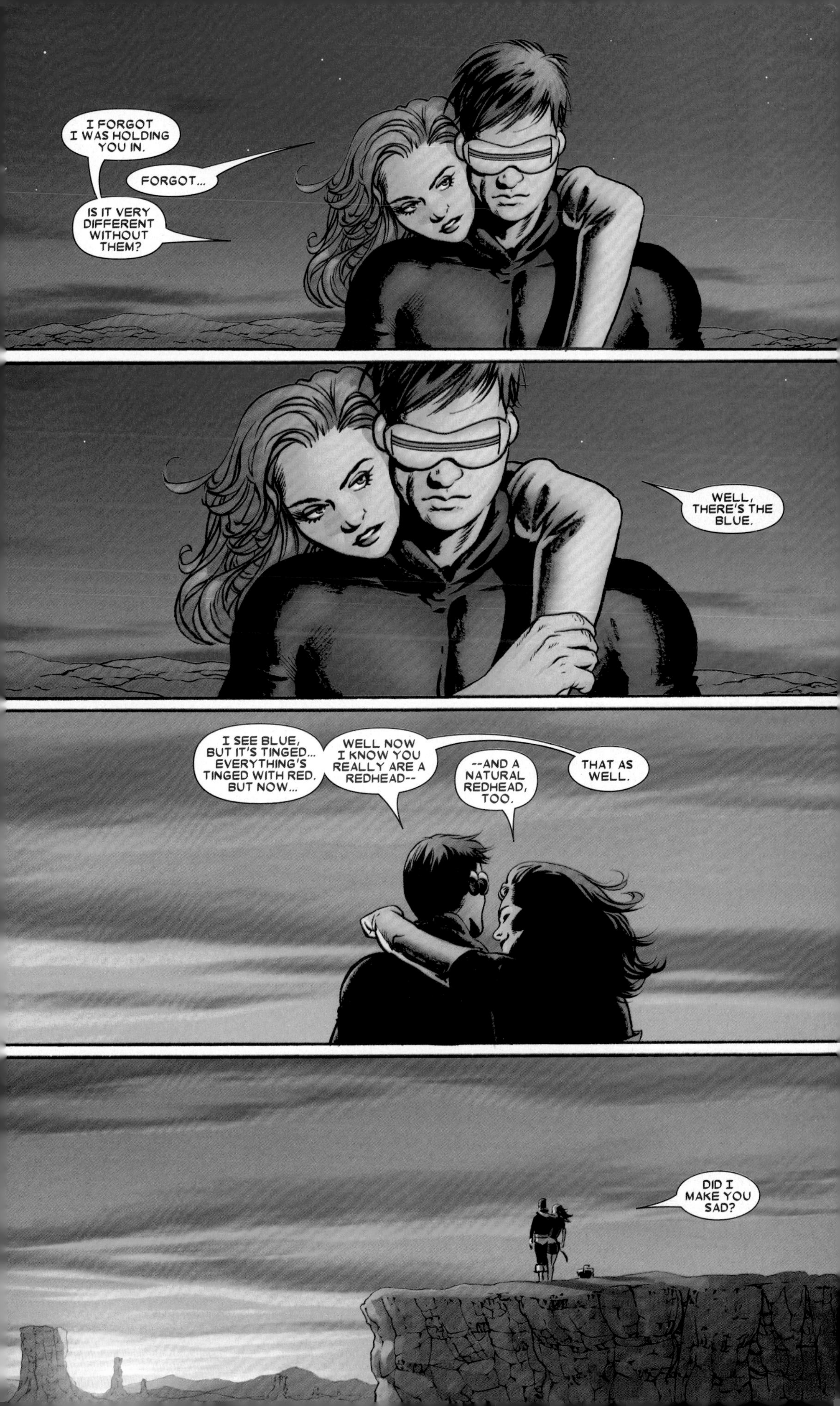
I FORGOT I WAS HOLDING YOU IN.
FORGOT...
IS IT VERY DIFFERENT WITHOUT THEM?
WELL, THERE'S THE BLUE.
I SEE BLUE, BUT IT'S TINGED... EVERYTHING'S TINGED WITH RED. BUT NOW...
WELL NOW I KNOW YOU REALLY ARE A REDHEAD--
--AND A NATURAL REDHEAD, TOO.
THAT AS WELL.
DID I MAKE YOU SAD?

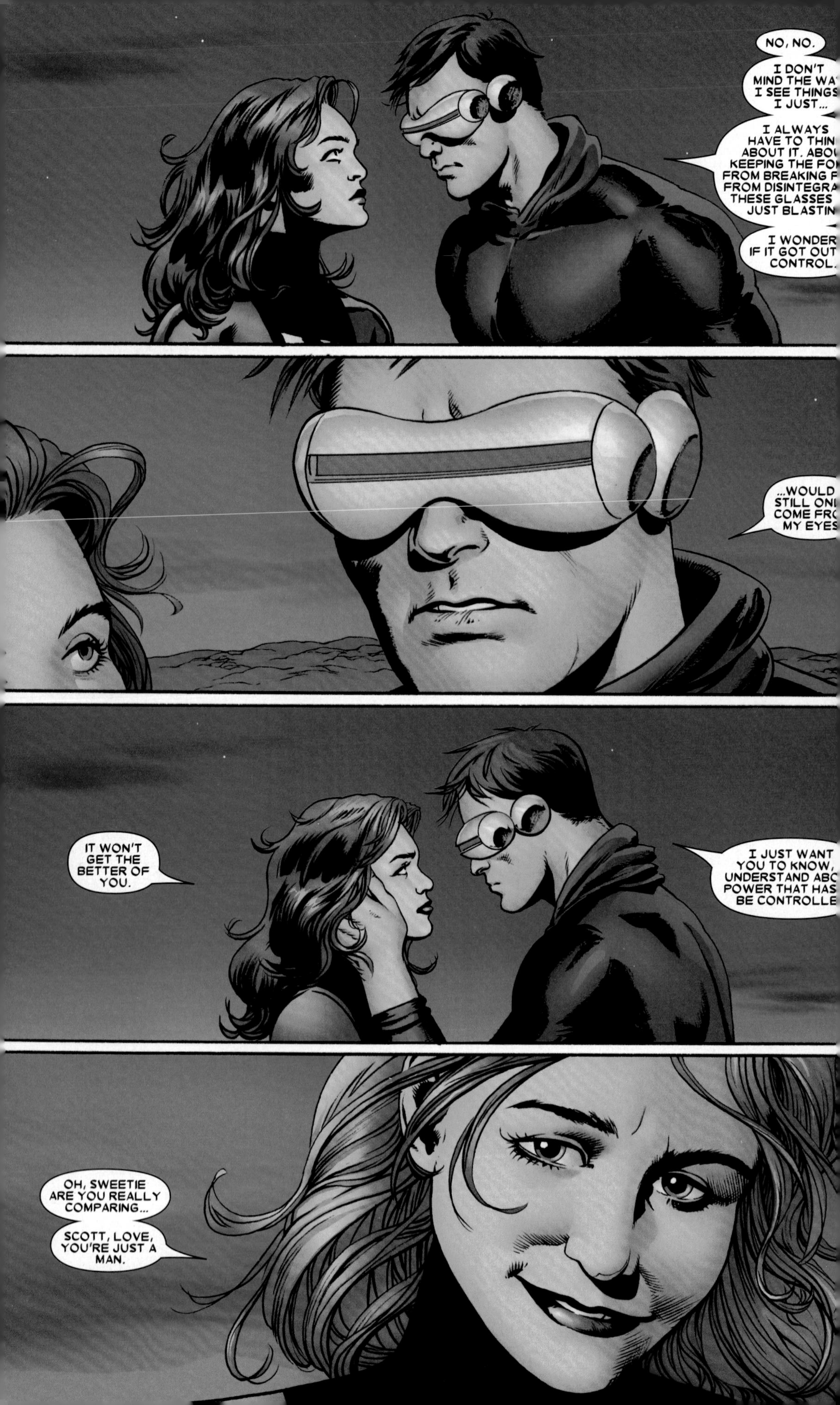
NO, NO.
I DON'T MIND THE WA I SEE THINGS I JUST...
I ALWAYS HAVE TO THIN ABOUT IT. ABOU KEEPING THE FO FROM BREAKING F FROM DISINTEGRA THESE GLASSES JUST BLASTIN
I WONDER IF IT GOT OUT CONTROL.
...WOULD STILL ONI COME FRO MY EYES
IT WON'T GET THE BETTER OF YOU.
I JUST WANT YOU TO KNOW, UNDERSTAND ABO POWER THAT HAS BE CONTROLLE
OH, SWEETIE ARE YOU REALLY COMPARING...
SCOTT, LOVE, YOU'RE JUST A MAN.

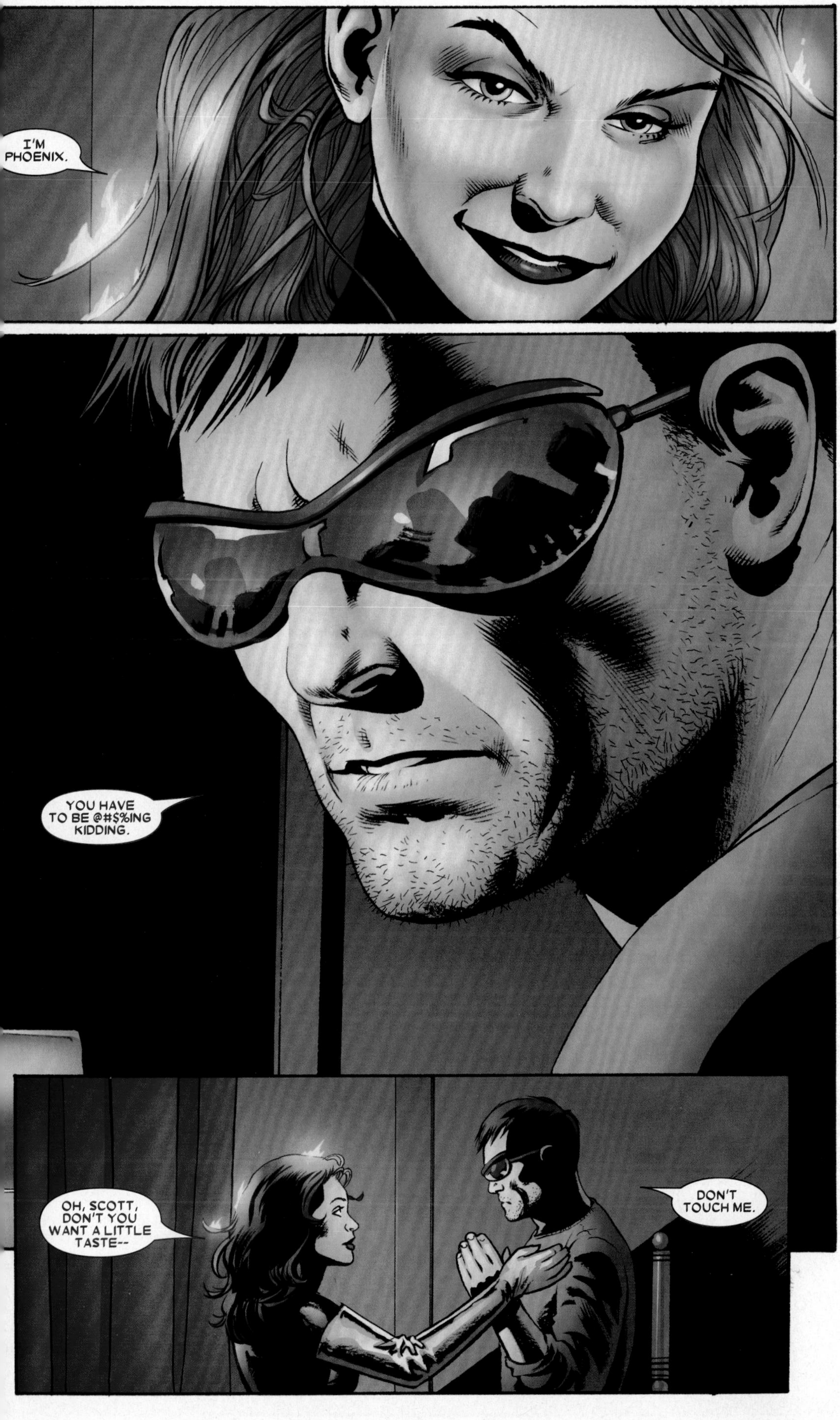
I'M PHOENIX.
YOU HAVE TO BE @#$%ING KIDDING.
OH, SCOTT, DON'T YOU WANT A LITTLE TASTE--
DON'T TOUCH ME.

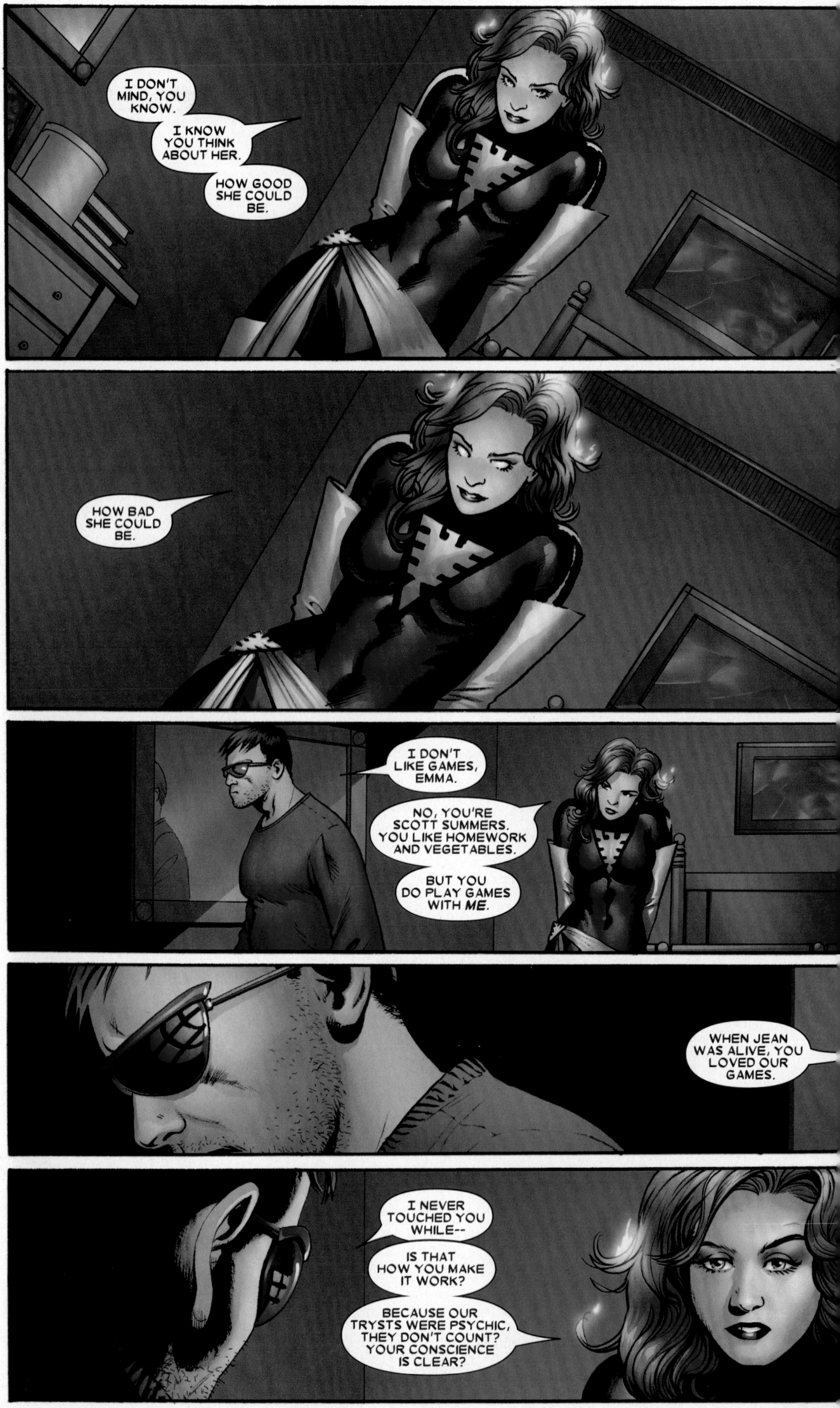
I DON'T MIND, YOU KNOW.
I KNOW YOU THINK ABOUT HER.
HOW GOOD SHE COULD BE.
HOW BAD SHE COULD BE.
I DON'T LIKE GAMES, EMMA.
NO, YOU'RE SCOTT SUMMERS. YOU LIKE HOMEWORK AND VEGETABLES.
BUT YOU DO PLAY GAMES WITH *ME*.
WHEN JEAN WAS ALIVE, YOU LOVED OUR GAMES.
I NEVER TOUCHED YOU WHILE--
IS THAT HOW YOU MAKE IT WORK?
BECAUSE OUR TRYSTS WERE PSYCHIC, THEY DON'T COUNT? YOUR CONSCIENCE IS CLEAR?

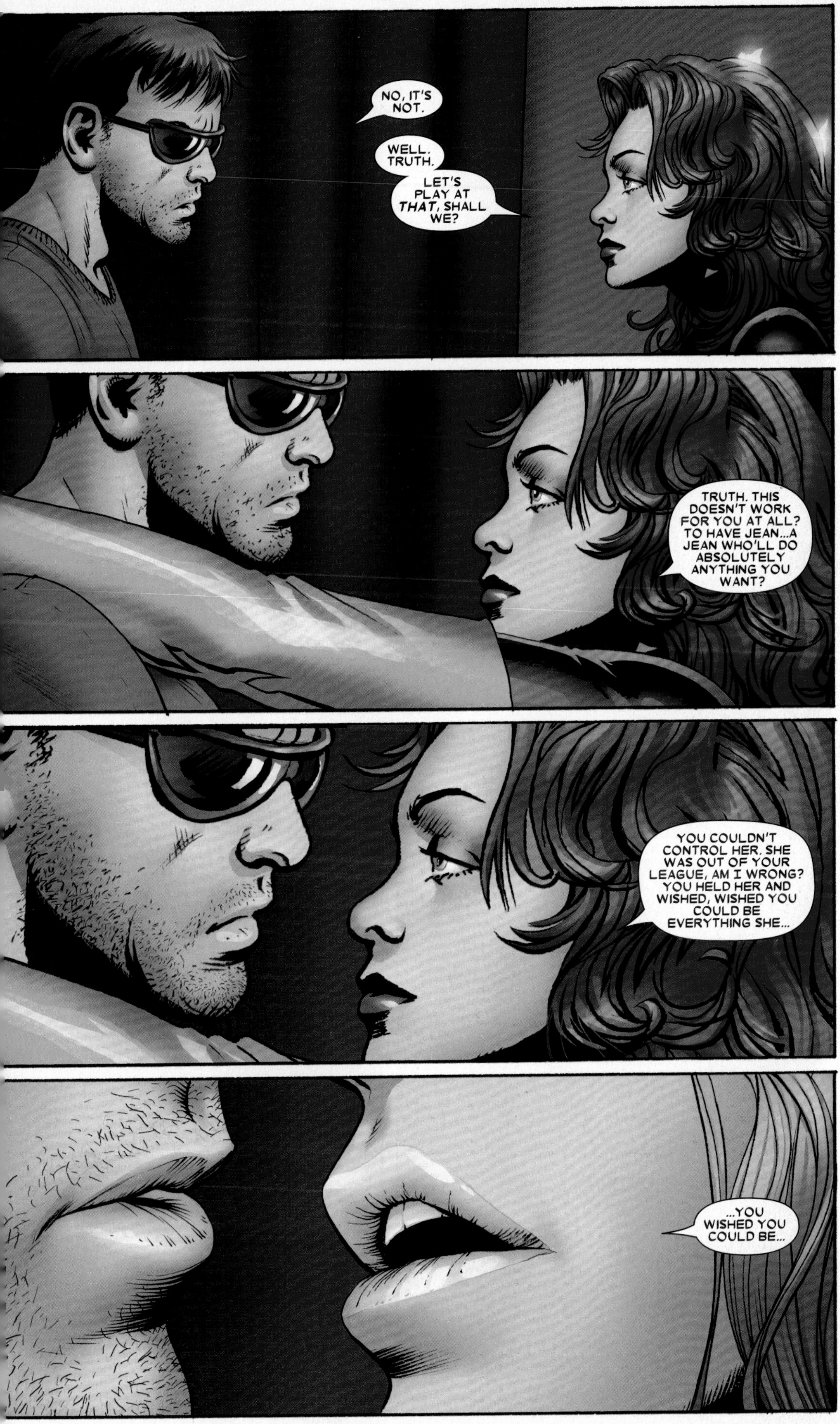
NO, IT'S NOT.
WELL. TRUTH.
LET'S PLAY AT *THAT*, SHALL WE?
TRUTH. THIS DOESN'T WORK FOR YOU AT ALL? TO HAVE JEAN...A JEAN WHO'LL DO ABSOLUTELY ANYTHING YOU WANT?
YOU COULDN'T CONTROL HER. SHE WAS OUT OF YOUR LEAGUE, AM I WRONG? YOU HELD HER AND WISHED, WISHED YOU COULD BE EVERYTHING SHE...
...YOU WISHED YOU COULD BE...

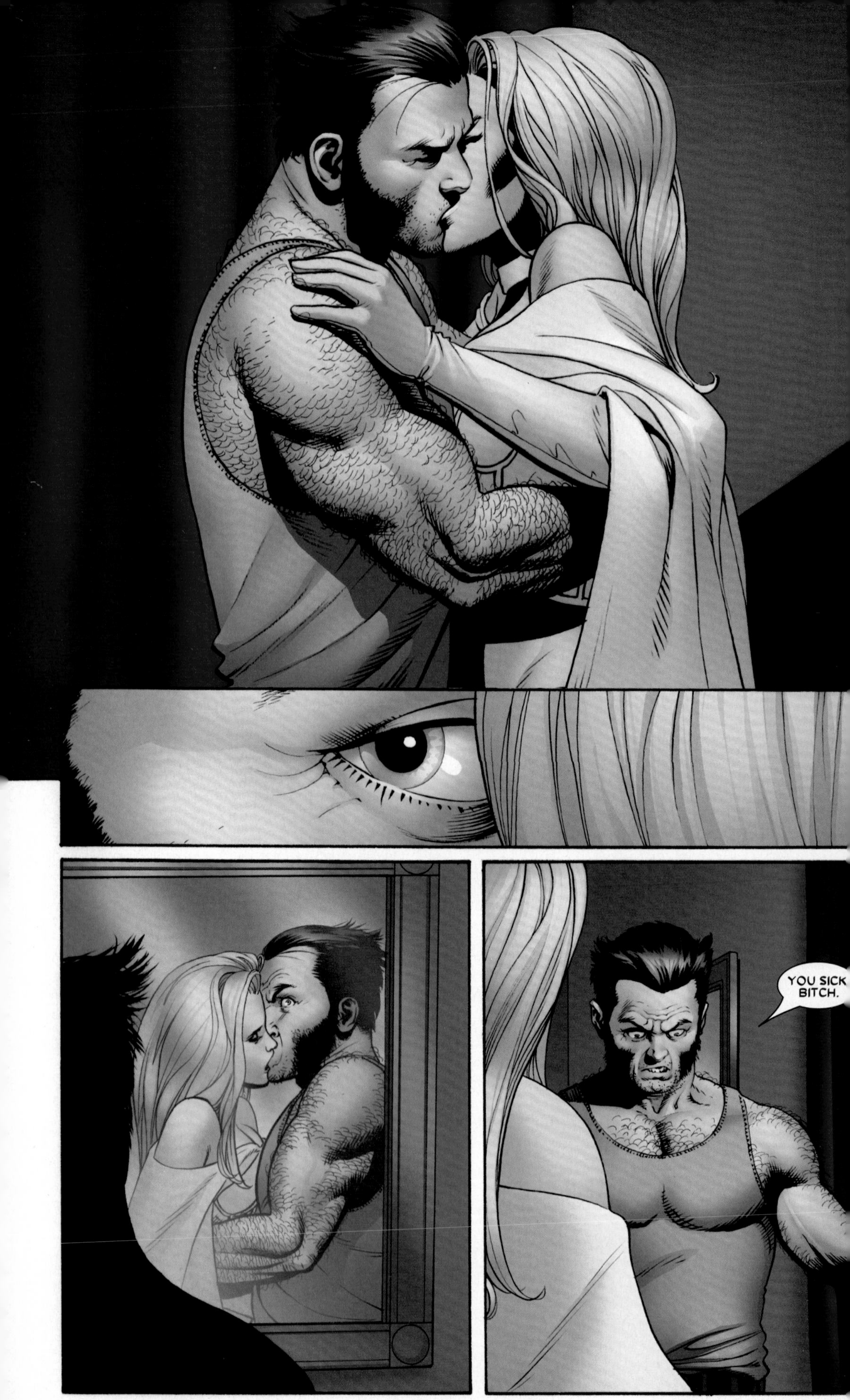
YOU SICK BITCH.

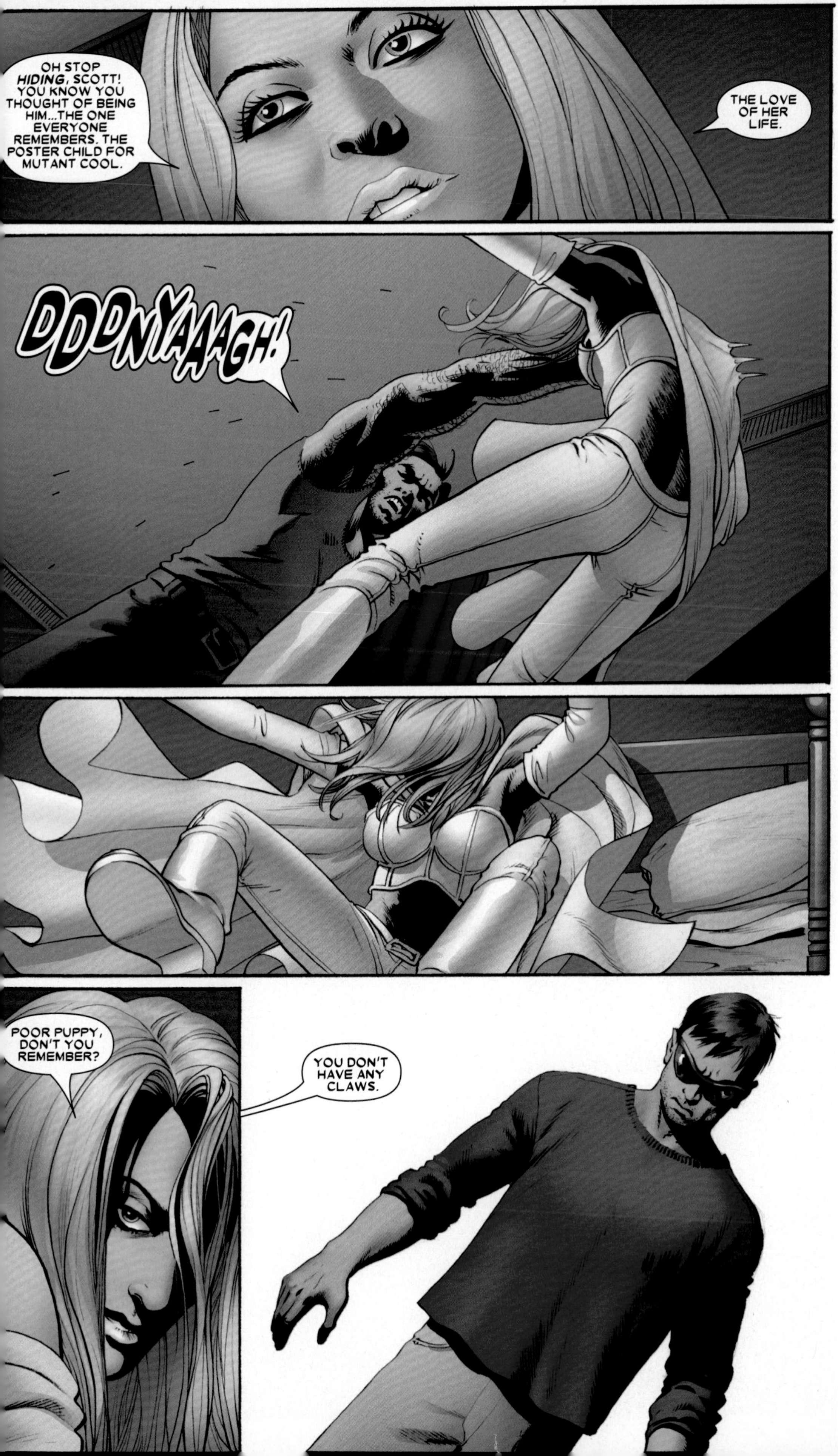
OH STOP HIDING, SCOTT! YOU KNOW YOU THOUGHT OF BEING HIM...THE ONE EVERYONE REMEMBERS. THE POSTER CHILD FOR MUTANT COOL.
THE LOVE OF HER LIFE.
DDDNYAAAGH!
POOR PUPPY, DON'T YOU REMEMBER?
YOU DON'T HAVE ANY CLAWS.

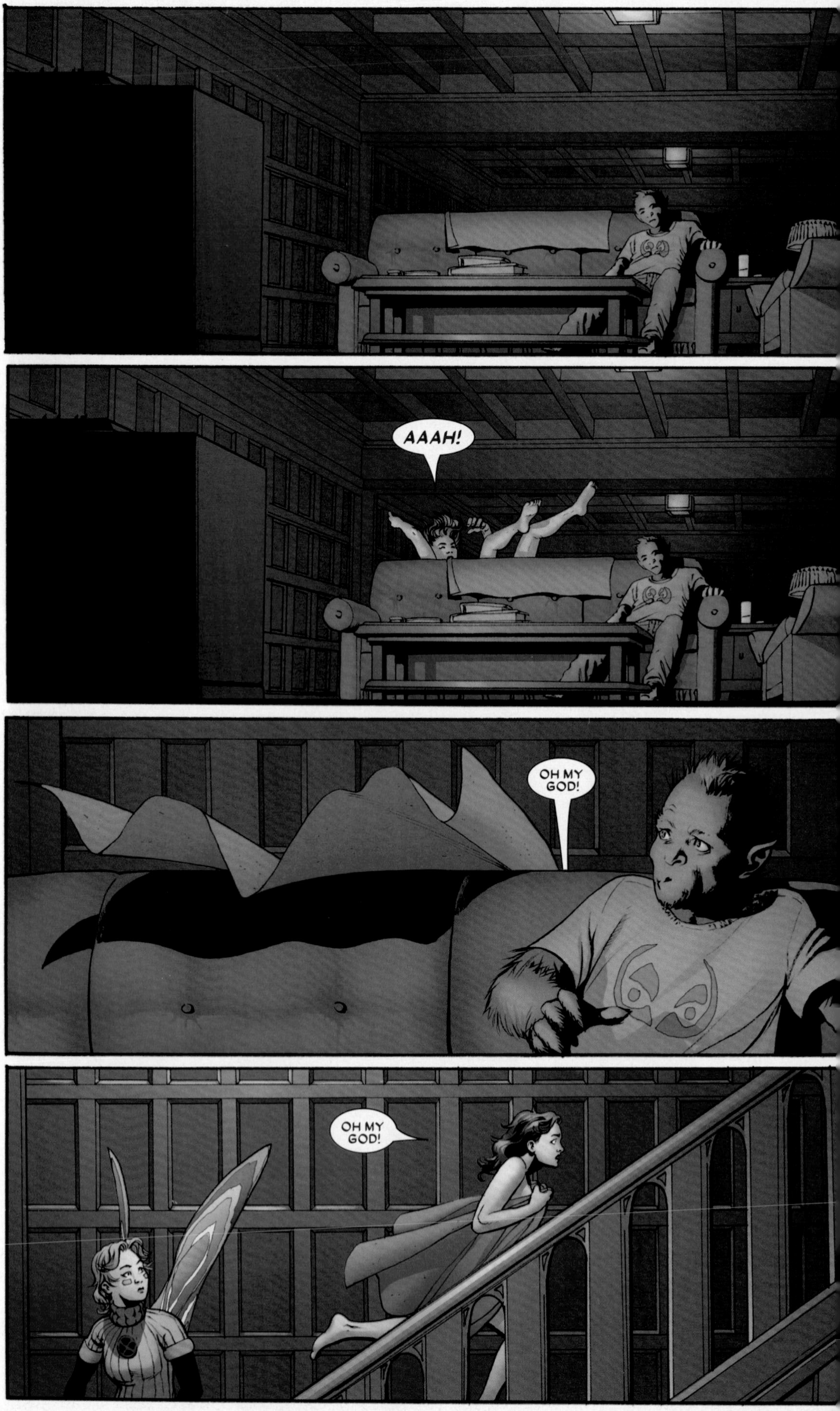
AAAH!
OH MY GOD!
OH MY GOD!

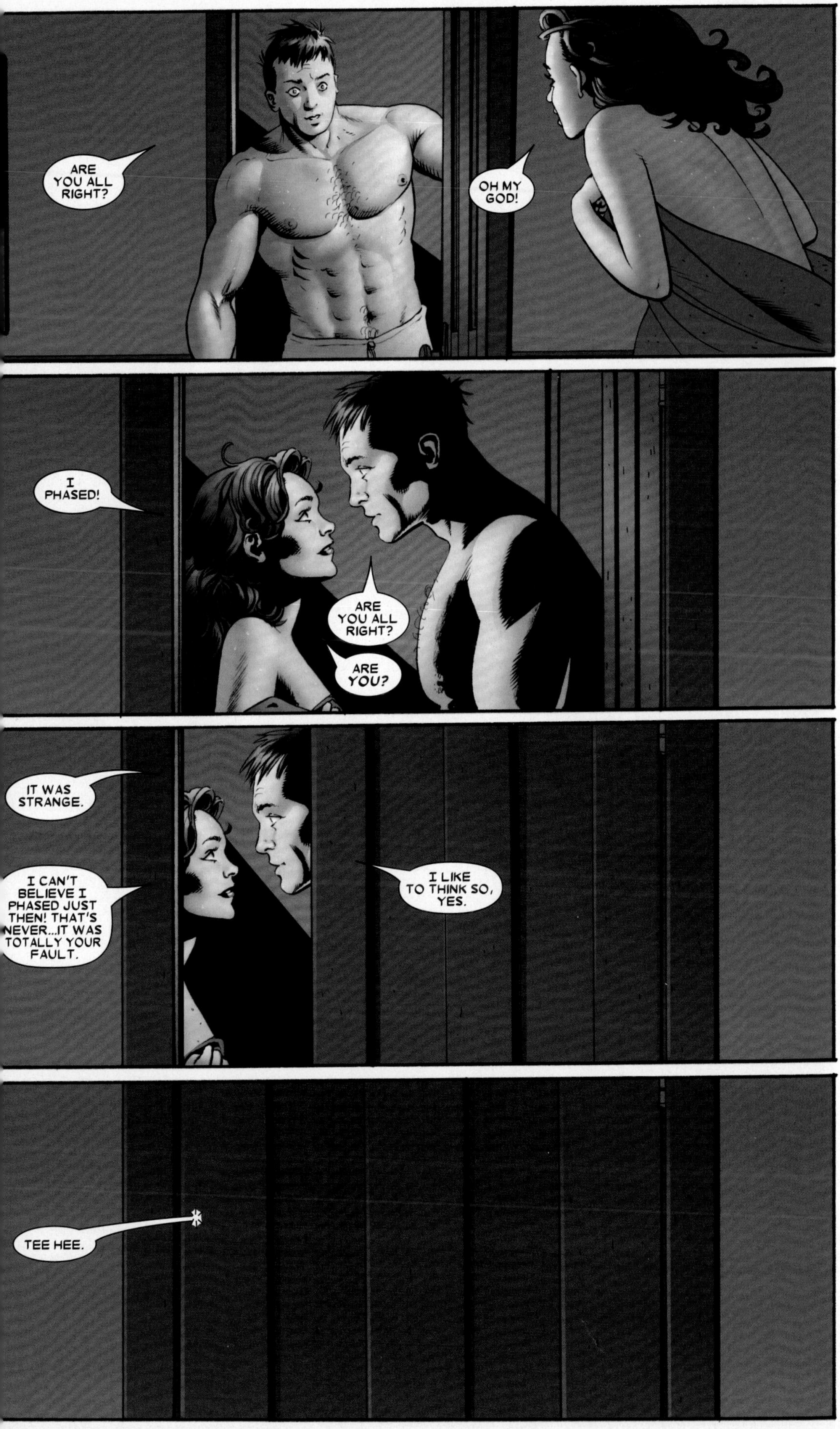
ARE YOU ALL RIGHT?
OH MY GOD!
I PHASED!
ARE YOU ALL RIGHT?
ARE YOU?
IT WAS STRANGE.
I CAN'T BELIEVE I PHASED JUST THEN! THAT'S NEVER...IT WAS TOTALLY YOUR FAULT.
I LIKE TO THINK SO, YES.
TEE HEE.

IT'S A SIMPLE QUESTION, SCOTT.

JEAN WAS HIS FAVORITE. HE SENSED HER POTENTIAL, EVEN THEN. AND HE'S ALWAYS BEEN PARTIAL TO PSYCHICS.

HE'D NEVER ADMIT IT, BUT HE THINKS WE'RE A BIT...ABOVE.

HANK IS A GENIUS, AND TERRIBLY GOOD WITH PEOPLE.

WARREN LOOKED LIKE A GOD.

AND XAVIER PICKS YOU?

TO LEAD.

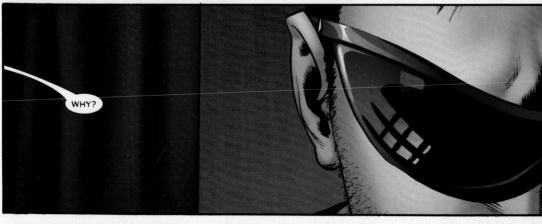

WHY?

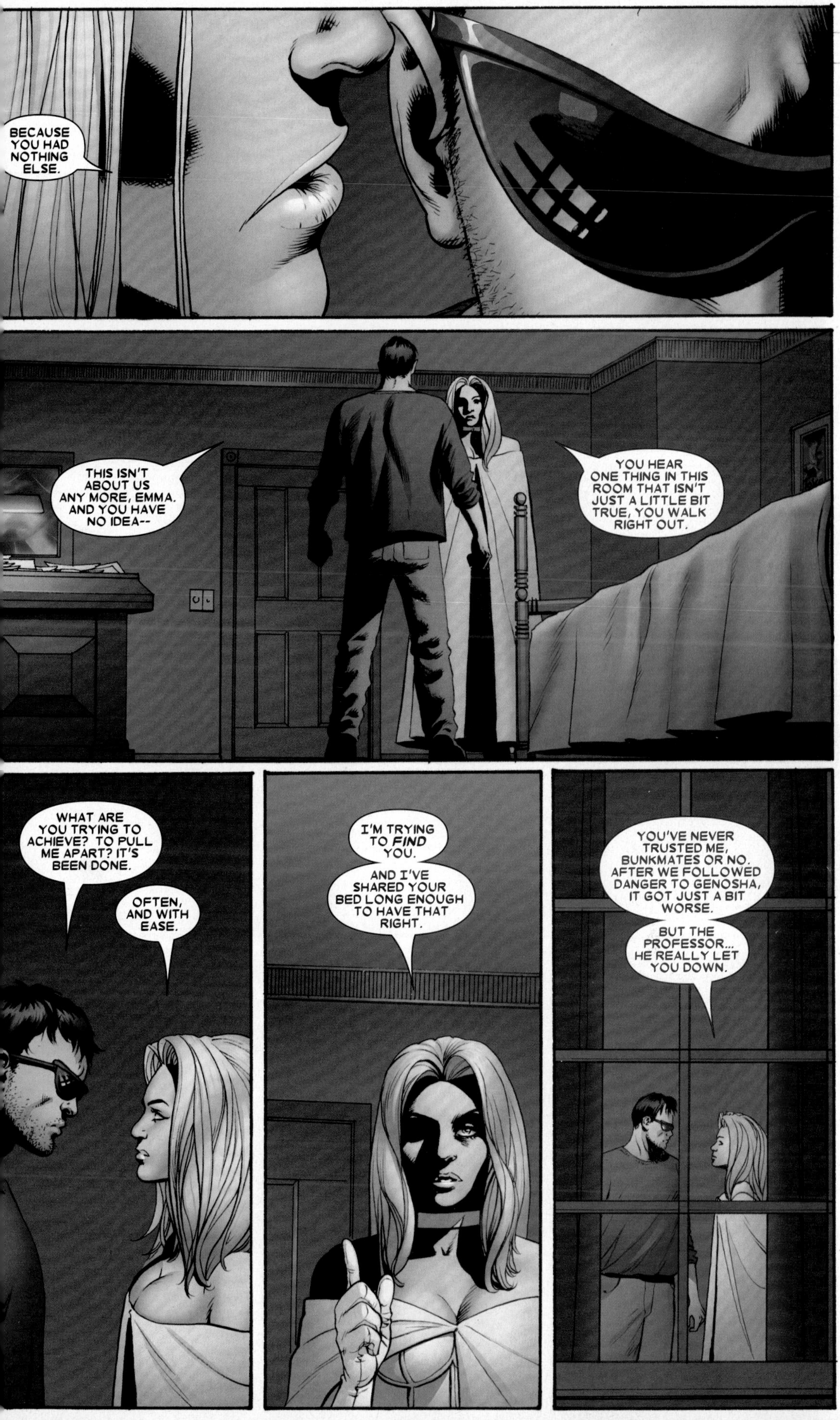
BECAUSE YOU HAD NOTHING ELSE.
THIS ISN'T ABOUT US ANY MORE, EMMA. AND YOU HAVE NO IDEA--
YOU HEAR ONE THING IN THIS ROOM THAT ISN'T JUST A LITTLE BIT TRUE, YOU WALK RIGHT OUT.
WHAT ARE YOU TRYING TO ACHIEVE? TO PULL ME APART? IT'S BEEN DONE.
OFTEN, AND WITH EASE.
I'M TRYING TO *FIND* YOU.
AND I'VE SHARED YOUR BED LONG ENOUGH TO HAVE THAT RIGHT.
YOU'VE NEVER TRUSTED ME, BUNKMATES OR NO. AFTER WE FOLLOWED DANGER TO GENOSHA, IT GOT JUST A BIT WORSE.
BUT THE PROFESSOR... HE REALLY LET YOU DOWN.

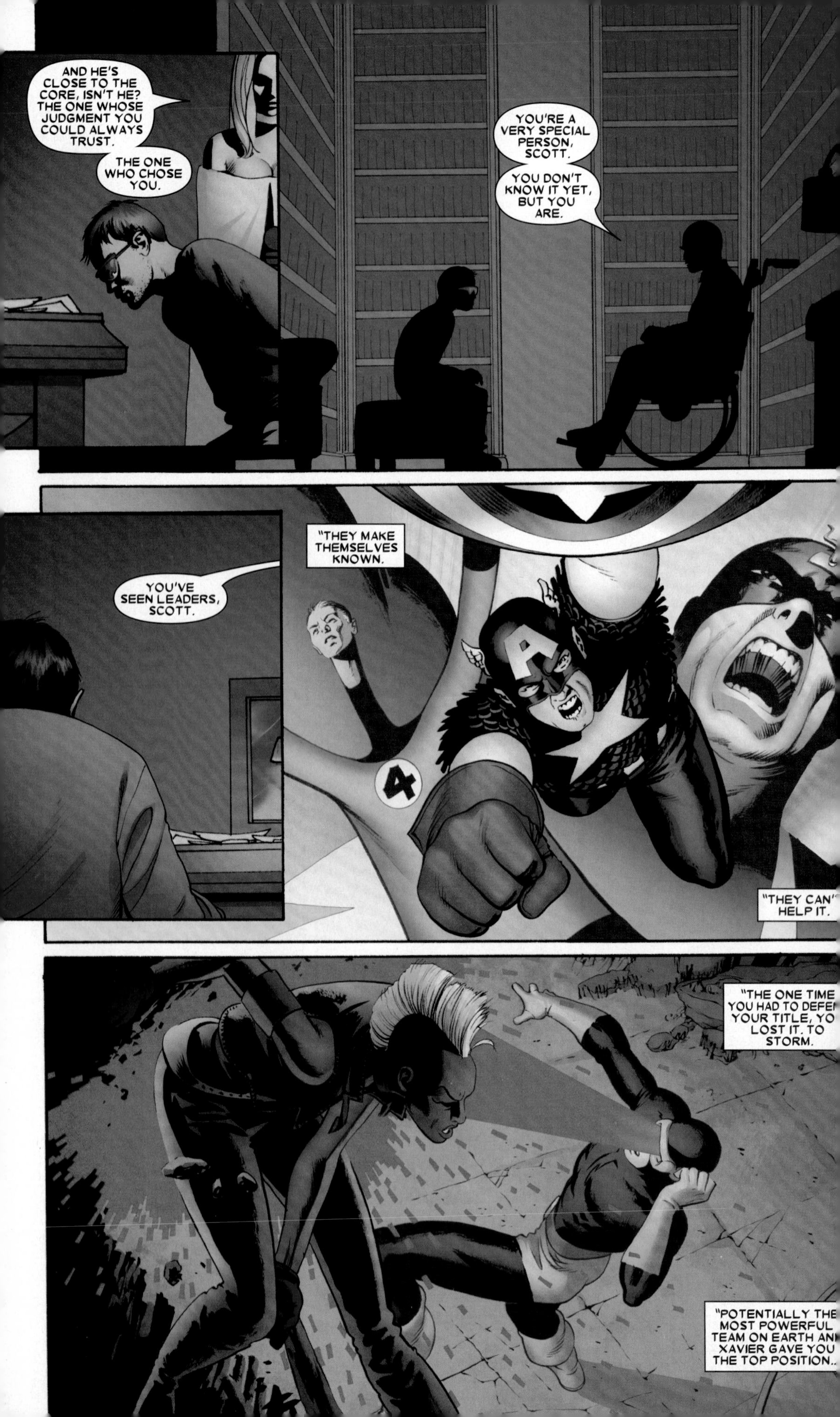
AND HE'S CLOSE TO THE CORE, ISN'T HE? THE ONE WHOSE JUDGMENT YOU COULD ALWAYS TRUST.
THE ONE WHO CHOSE YOU.
YOU'RE A VERY SPECIAL PERSON, SCOTT.
YOU DON'T KNOW IT YET, BUT YOU ARE.
YOU'VE SEEN LEADERS, SCOTT.
"THEY MAKE THEMSELVES KNOWN.
"THEY CAN' HELP IT.
"THE ONE TIME YOU HAD TO DEFE YOUR TITLE, YO LOST IT. TO STORM.
"POTENTIALLY THE MOST POWERFUL TEAM ON EARTH AN XAVIER GAVE YOU THE TOP POSITION..

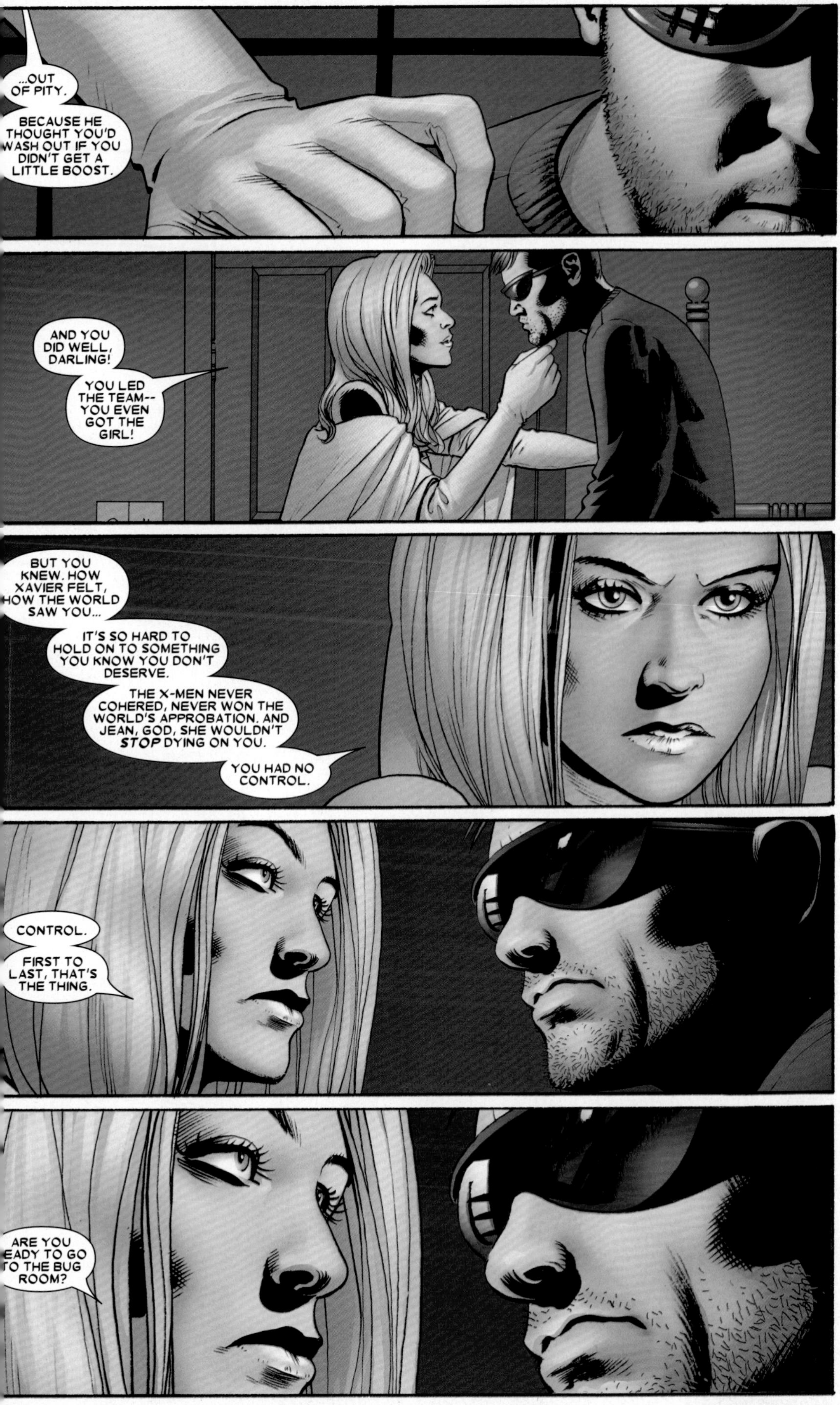
...OUT OF PITY.
BECAUSE HE THOUGHT YOU'D WASH OUT IF YOU DIDN'T GET A LITTLE BOOST.
AND YOU DID WELL, DARLING!
YOU LED THE TEAM-- YOU EVEN GOT THE GIRL!
BUT YOU KNEW. HOW XAVIER FELT, HOW THE WORLD SAW YOU...
IT'S SO HARD TO HOLD ON TO SOMETHING YOU KNOW YOU DON'T DESERVE.
THE X-MEN NEVER COHERED, NEVER WON THE WORLD'S APPROBATION. AND JEAN, GOD, SHE WOULDN'T *STOP* DYING ON YOU.
YOU HAD NO CONTROL.
CONTROL.
FIRST TO LAST, THAT'S THE THING.
ARE YOU EADY TO GO O THE BUG ROOM?

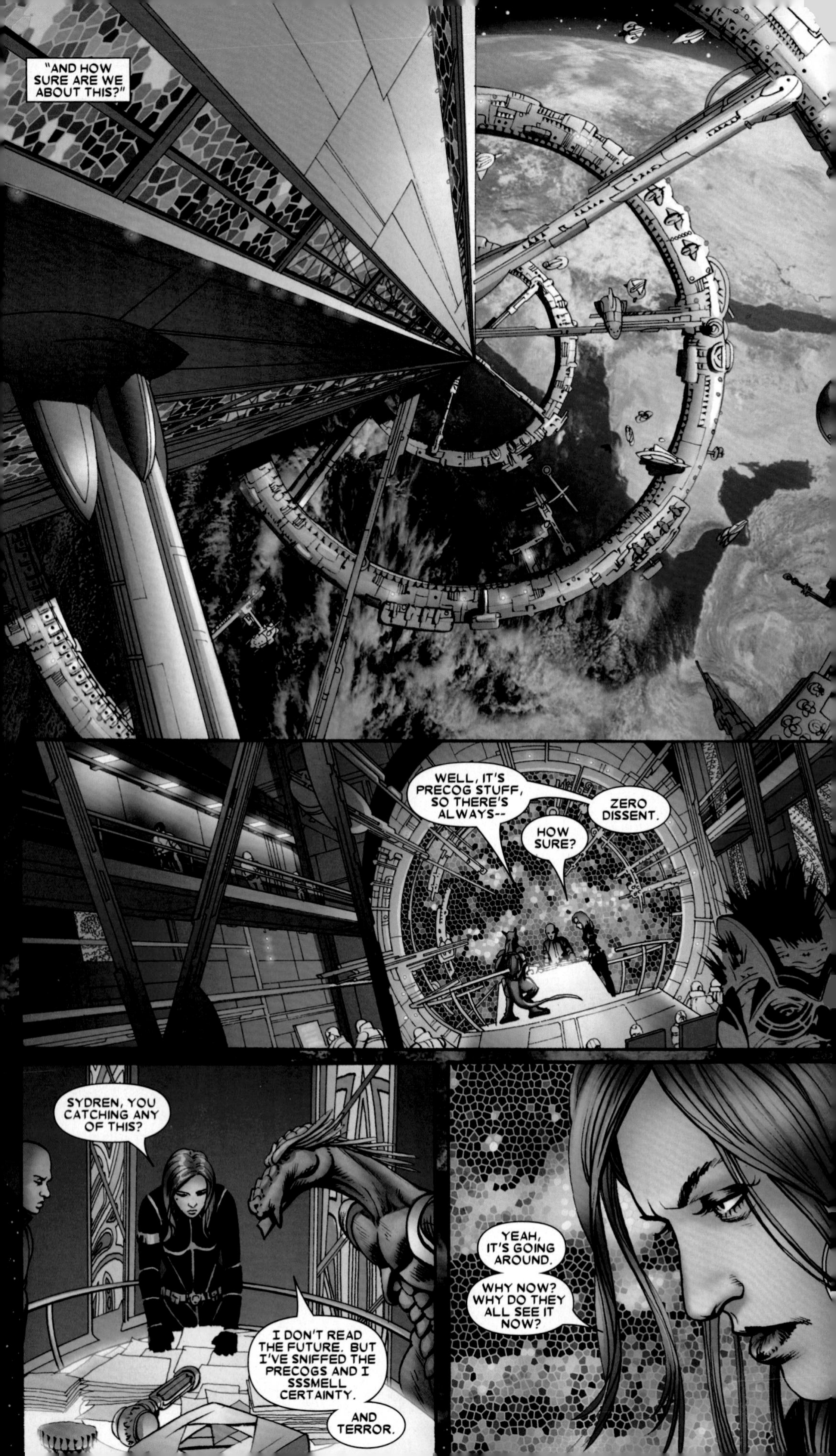
"AND HOW SURE ARE WE ABOUT THIS?"
WELL, IT'S PRECOG STUFF, SO THERE'S ALWAYS--
ZERO DISSENT.
HOW SURE?
SYDREN, YOU CATCHING ANY OF THIS?
I DON'T READ THE FUTURE. BUT I'VE SNIFFED THE PRECOGS AND I SSSMELL CERTAINTY.
AND TERROR.
YEAH, IT'S GOING AROUND.
WHY NOW? WHY DO THEY ALL SEE IT NOW?

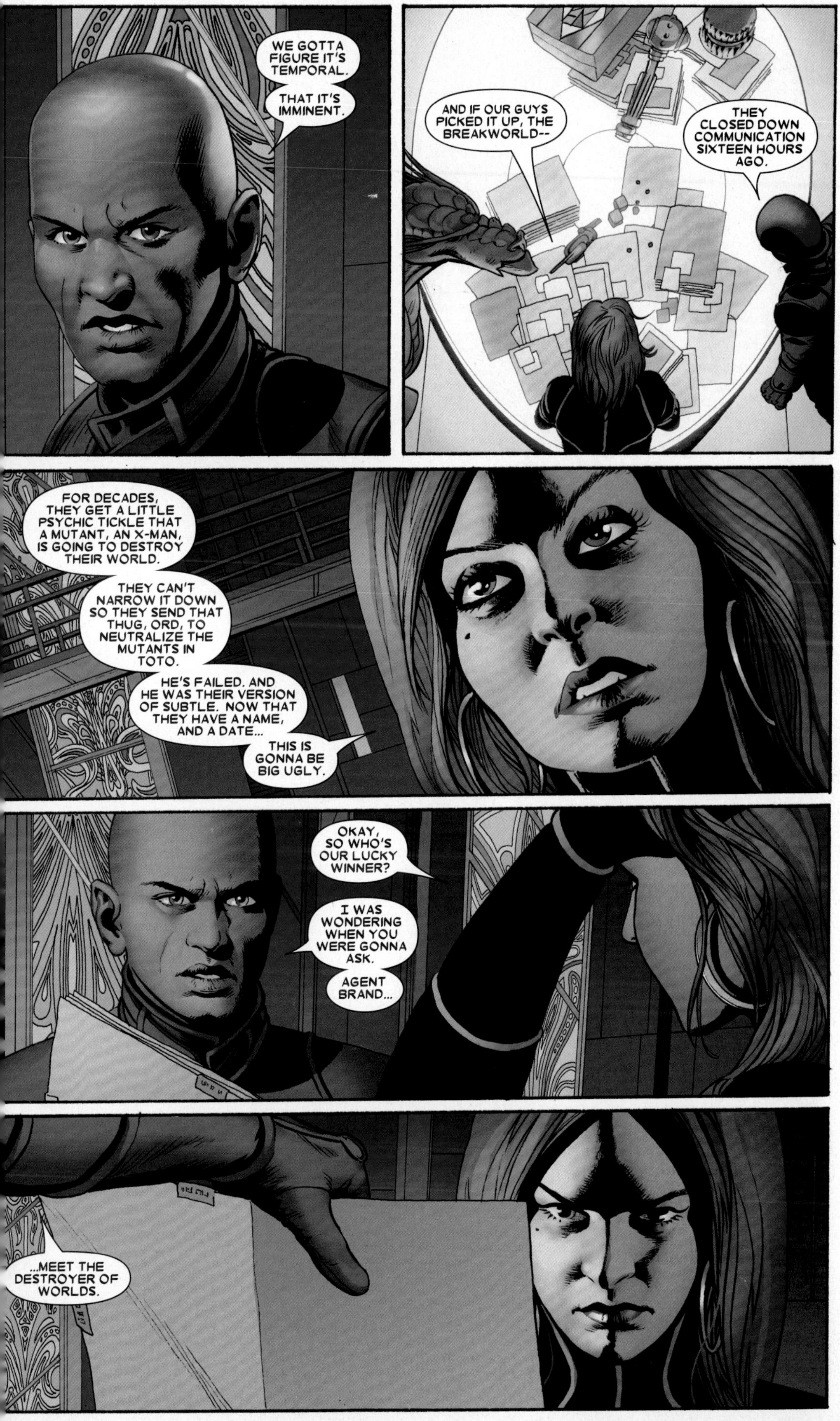

WE GOTTA FIGURE IT'S TEMPORAL.
THAT IT'S IMMINENT.
AND IF OUR GUYS PICKED IT UP, THE BREAKWORLD--
THEY CLOSED DOWN COMMUNICATION SIXTEEN HOURS AGO.
FOR DECADES, THEY GET A LITTLE PSYCHIC TICKLE THAT A MUTANT, AN X-MAN, IS GOING TO DESTROY THEIR WORLD.
THEY CAN'T NARROW IT DOWN SO THEY SEND THAT THUG, ORD, TO NEUTRALIZE THE MUTANTS IN TOTO.
HE'S FAILED. AND HE WAS THEIR VERSION OF SUBTLE. NOW THAT THEY HAVE A NAME, AND A DATE...
THIS IS GONNA BE BIG UGLY.
OKAY, SO WHO'S OUR LUCKY WINNER?
I WAS WONDERING WHEN YOU WERE GONNA ASK.
AGENT BRAND...
...MEET THE DESTROYER OF WORLDS.

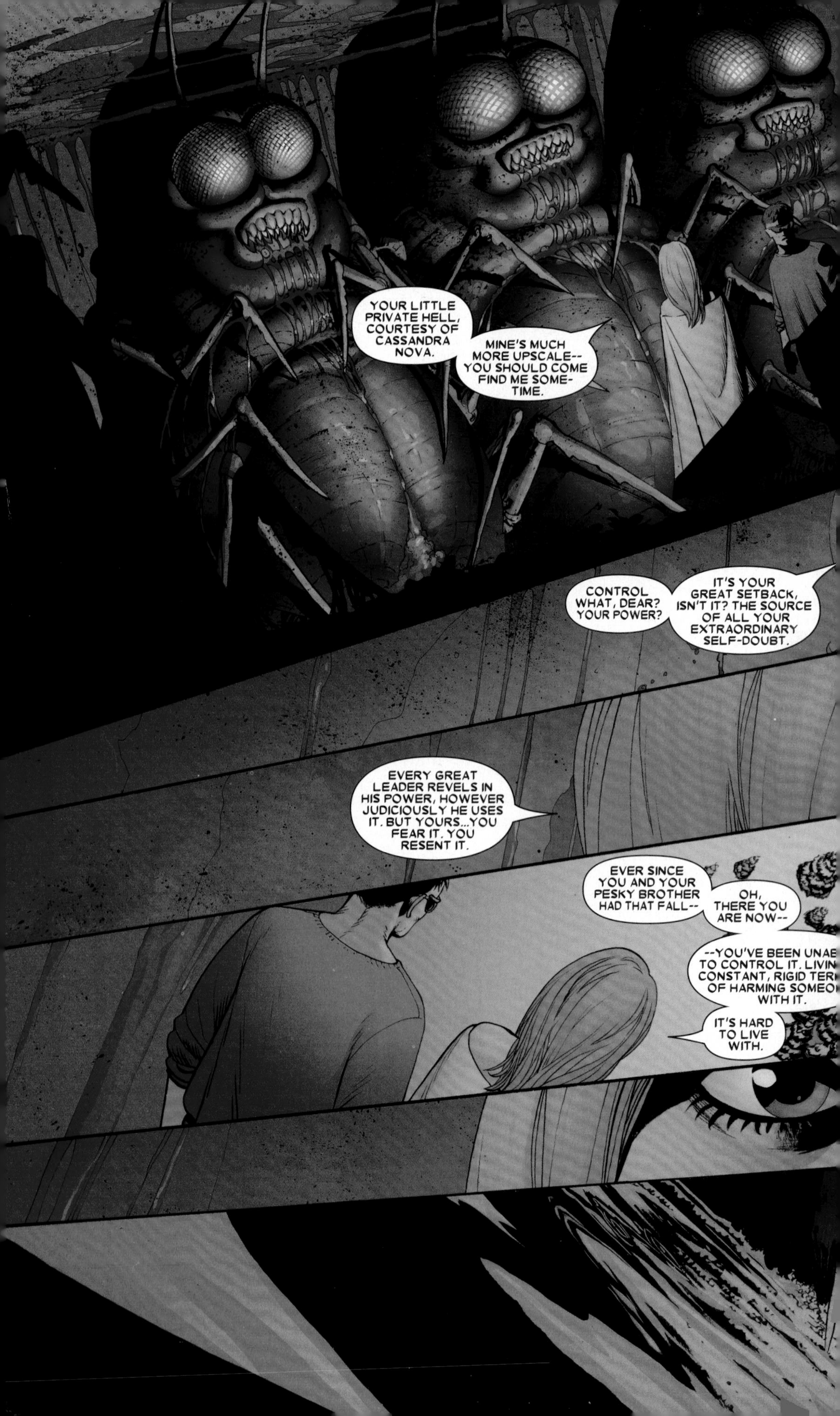
YOUR LITTLE PRIVATE HELL, COURTESY OF CASSANDRA NOVA.
MINE'S MUCH MORE UPSCALE-- YOU SHOULD COME FIND ME SOME-TIME.
CONTROL WHAT, DEAR? YOUR POWER?
IT'S YOUR GREAT SETBACK, ISN'T IT? THE SOURCE OF ALL YOUR EXTRAORDINARY SELF-DOUBT.
EVERY GREAT LEADER REVELS IN HIS POWER, HOWEVER JUDICIOUSLY HE USES IT. BUT YOURS...YOU FEAR IT. YOU RESENT IT.
EVER SINCE YOU AND YOUR PESKY BROTHER HAD THAT FALL--
OH, THERE YOU ARE NOW--
--YOU'VE BEEN UNAB TO CONTROL IT. LIVIN CONSTANT, RIGID TER OF HARMING SOMEO WITH IT.
IT'S HARD TO LIVE WITH.

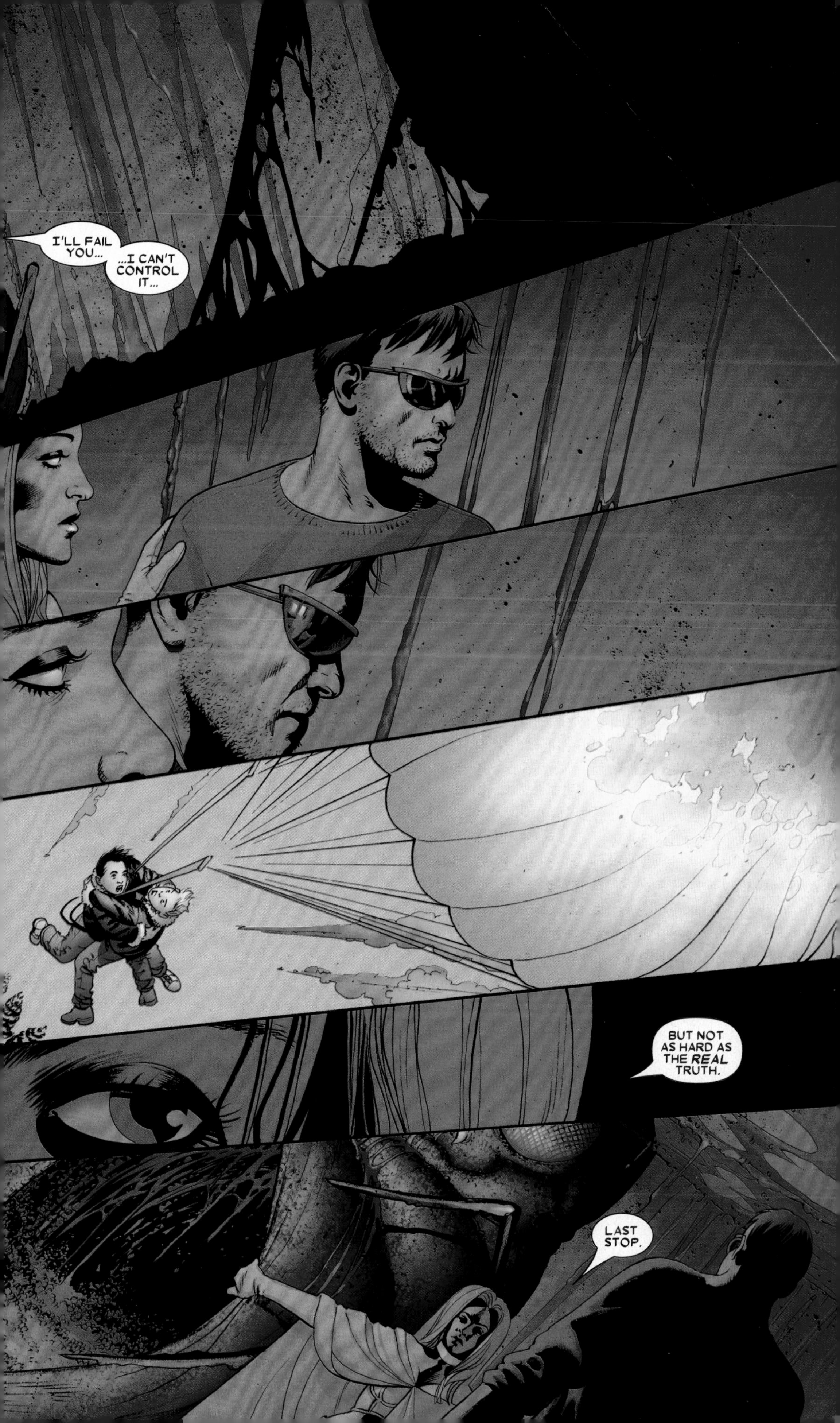
I'LL FAIL YOU...
...I CAN'T CONTROL IT...
BUT NOT AS HARD AS THE *REAL* TRUTH.
LAST STOP.

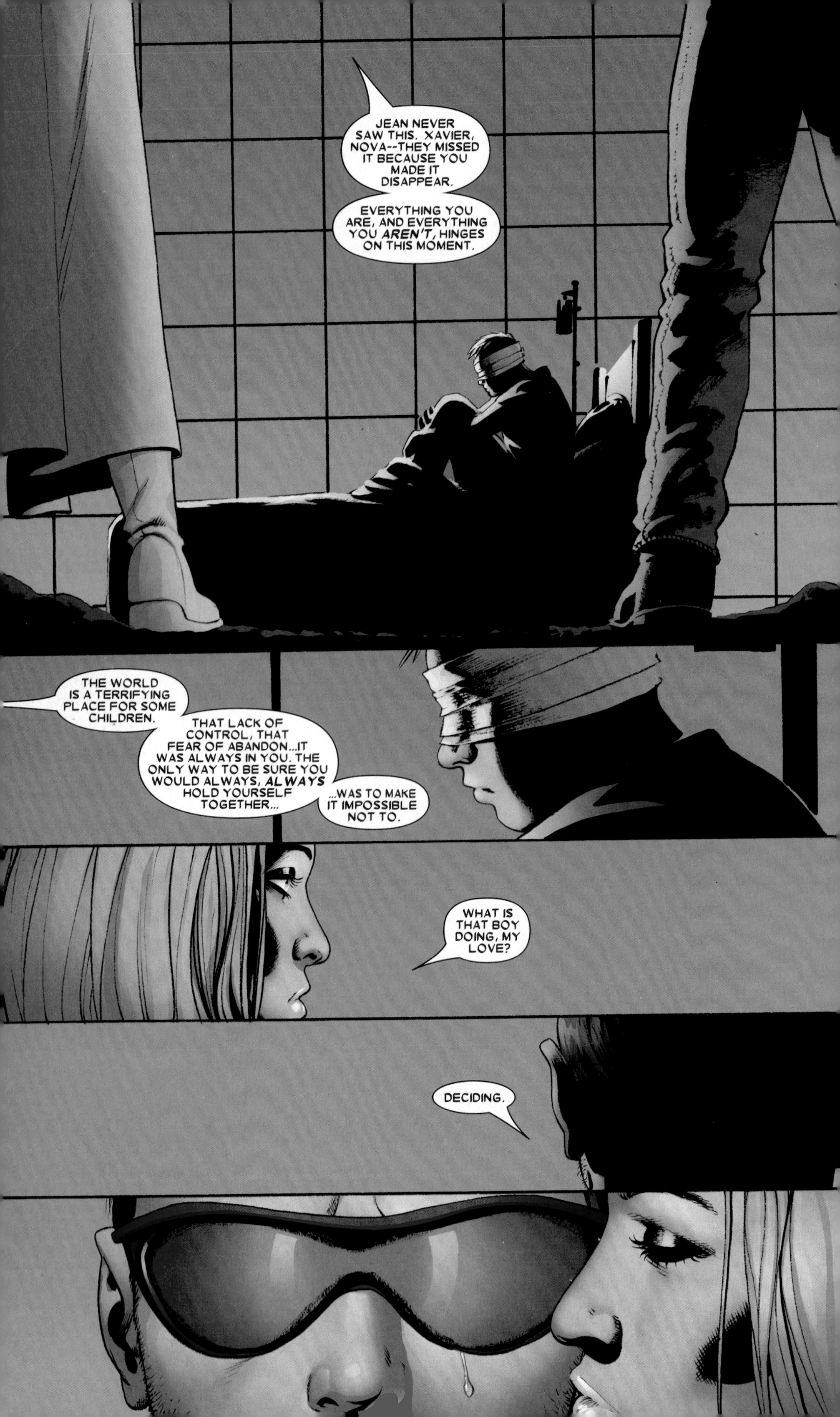

JEAN NEVER SAW THIS. XAVIER, NOVA--THEY MISSED IT BECAUSE YOU MADE IT DISAPPEAR.
EVERYTHING YOU ARE, AND EVERYTHING YOU *AREN'T*, HINGES ON THIS MOMENT.
THE WORLD IS A TERRIFYING PLACE FOR SOME CHILDREN.
THAT LACK OF CONTROL, THAT FEAR OF ABANDON...IT WAS ALWAYS IN YOU. THE ONLY WAY TO BE SURE YOU WOULD ALWAYS, *ALWAYS* HOLD YOURSELF TOGETHER...
...WAS TO MAKE IT IMPOSSIBLE NOT TO.
WHAT IS THAT BOY DOING, MY LOVE?
DECIDING.

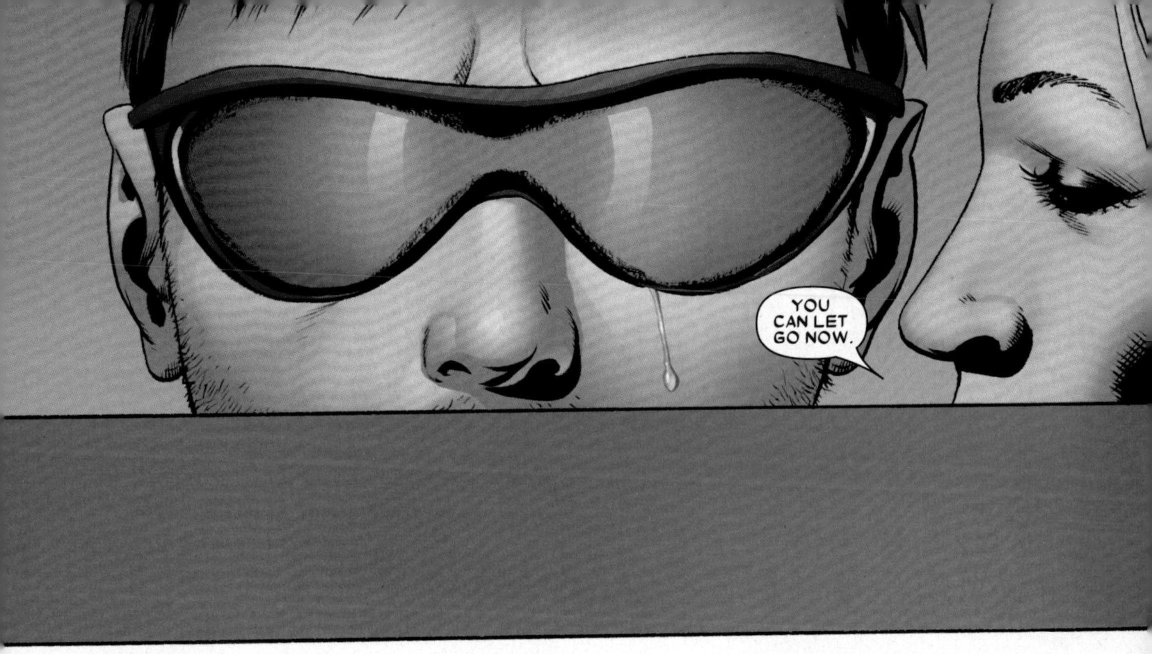
YOU CAN LET GO NOW.

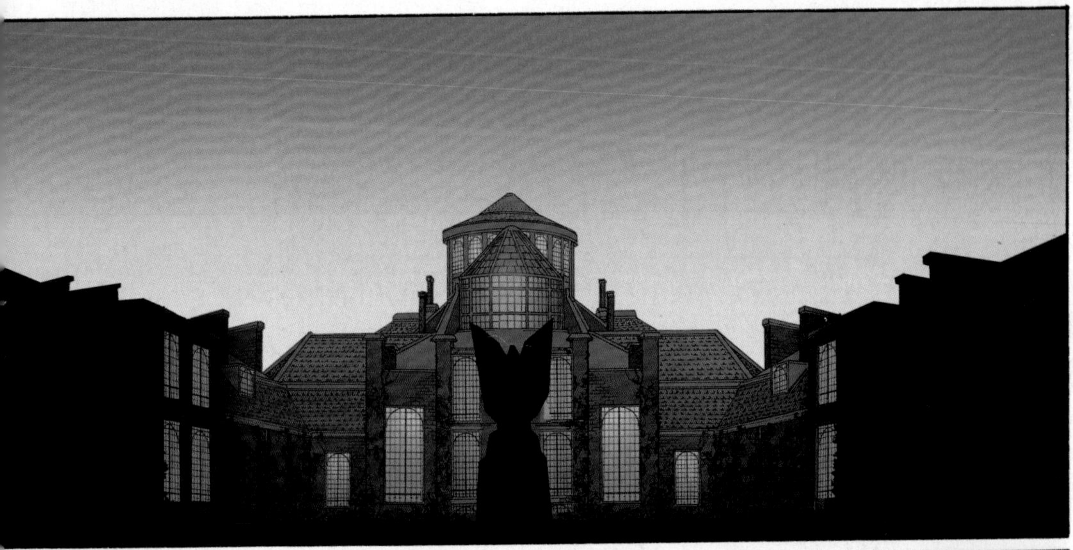

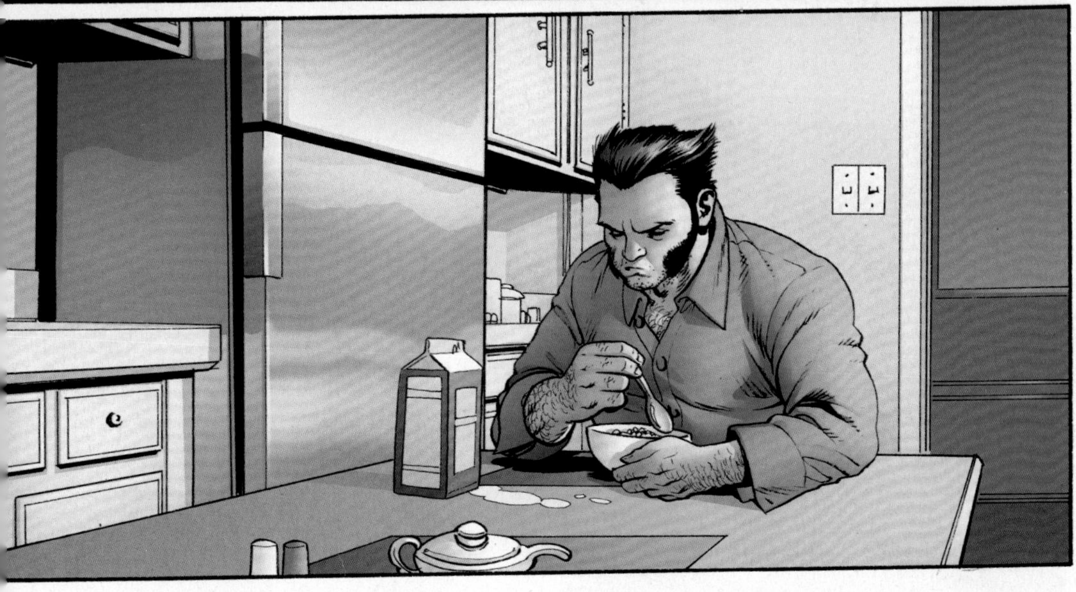

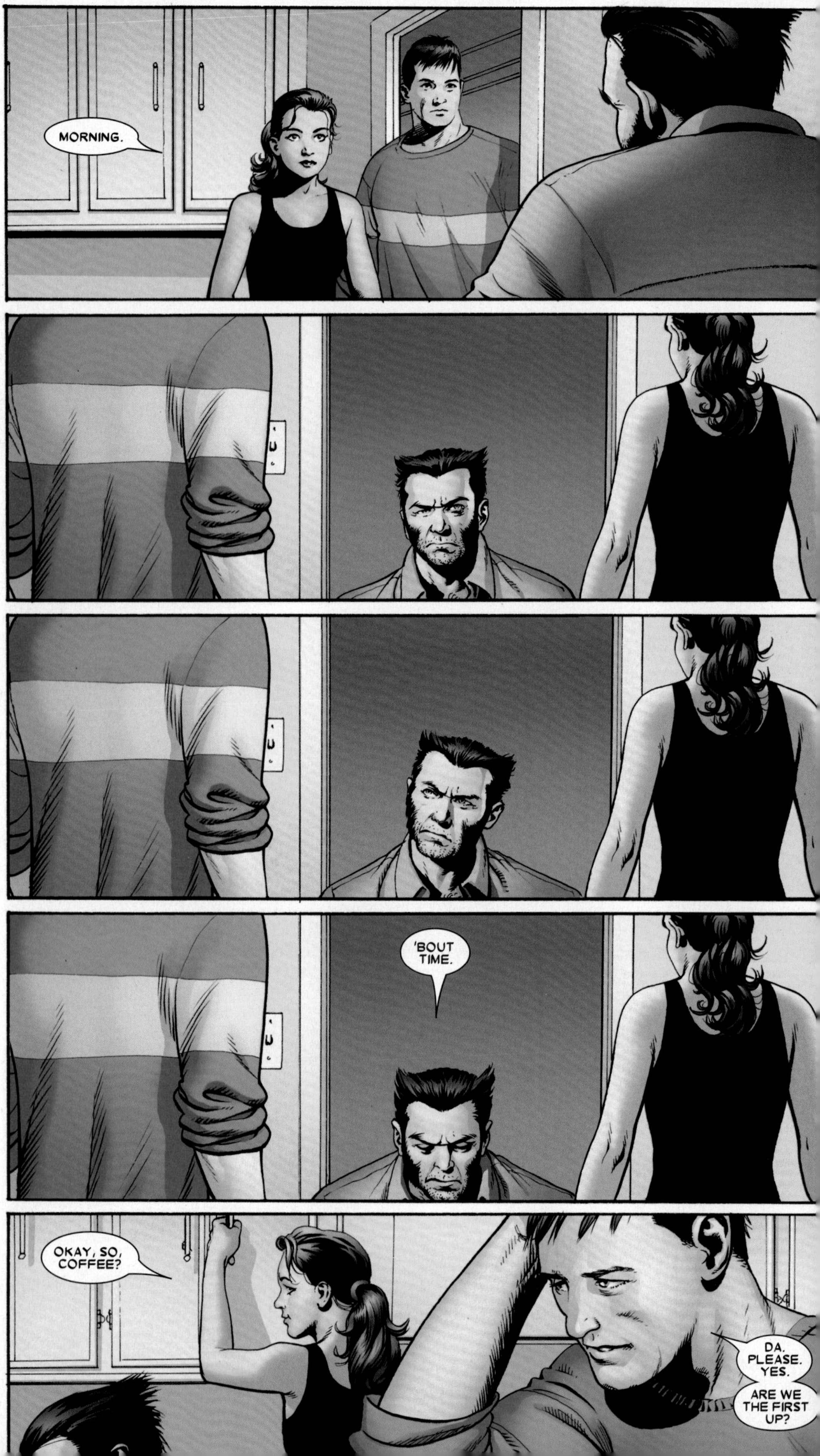
MORNING.
'BOUT TIME.
OKAY, SO, COFFEE?
DA. PLEASE. YES.
ARE WE THE FIRST UP?

HRRM.

EMMA, I'M GLAD YOU'RE UP. YOU MIGHT BE INTERESTED IN THIS...

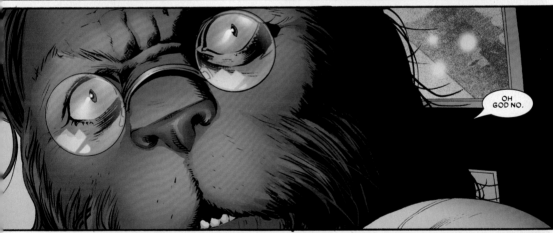

OH GOD NO.

"THERE'S SO MUCH YOU THOUGHT YOU COULD NEVER FACE."

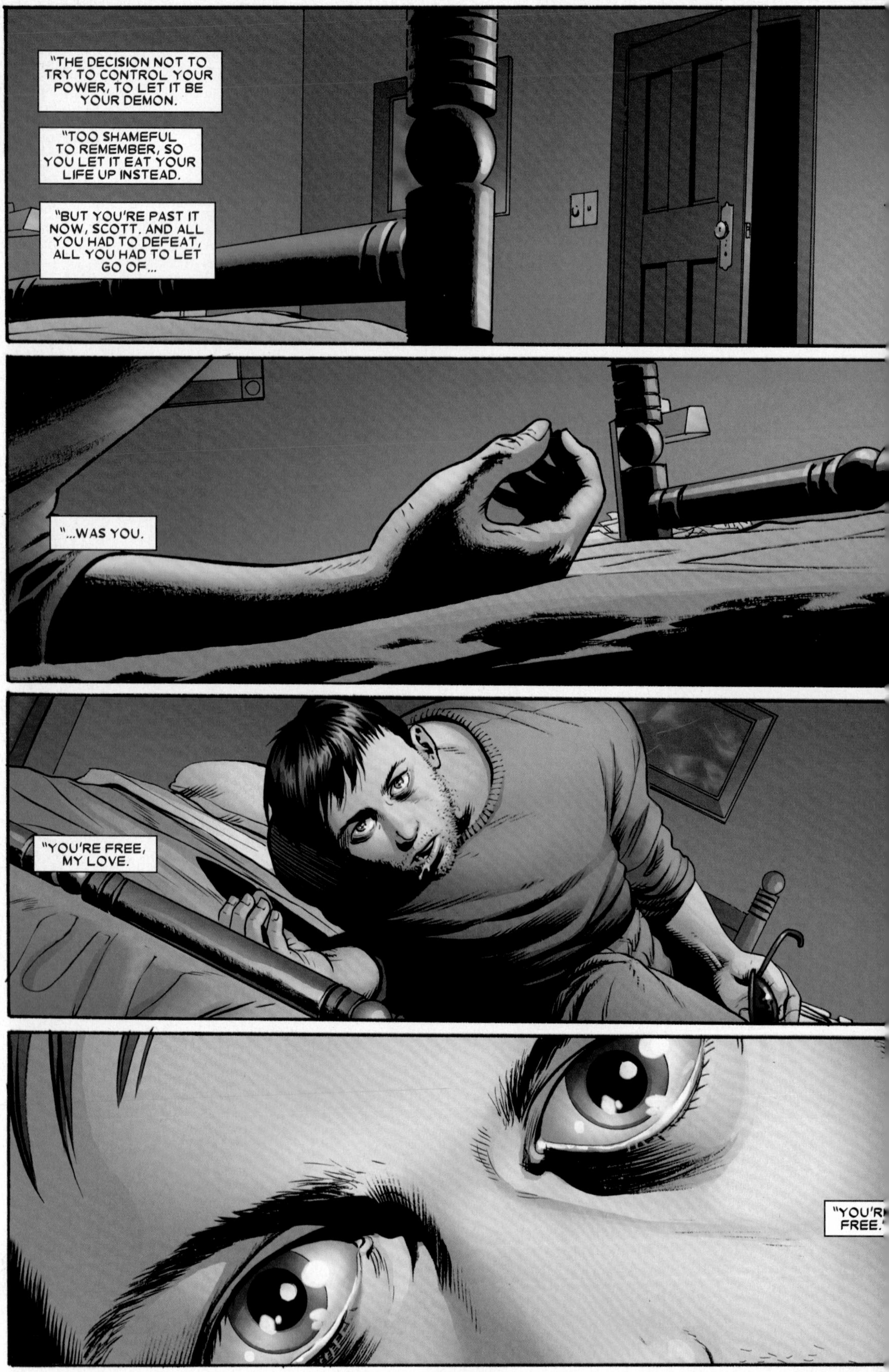
"THE DECISION NOT TO TRY TO CONTROL YOUR POWER, TO LET IT BE YOUR DEMON.
"TOO SHAMEFUL TO REMEMBER, SO YOU LET IT EAT YOUR LIFE UP INSTEAD.
"BUT YOU'RE PAST IT NOW, SCOTT. AND ALL YOU HAD TO DEFEAT, ALL YOU HAD TO LET GO OF...
"...WAS YOU.
"YOU'RE FREE, MY LOVE.
"YOU'R FREE."

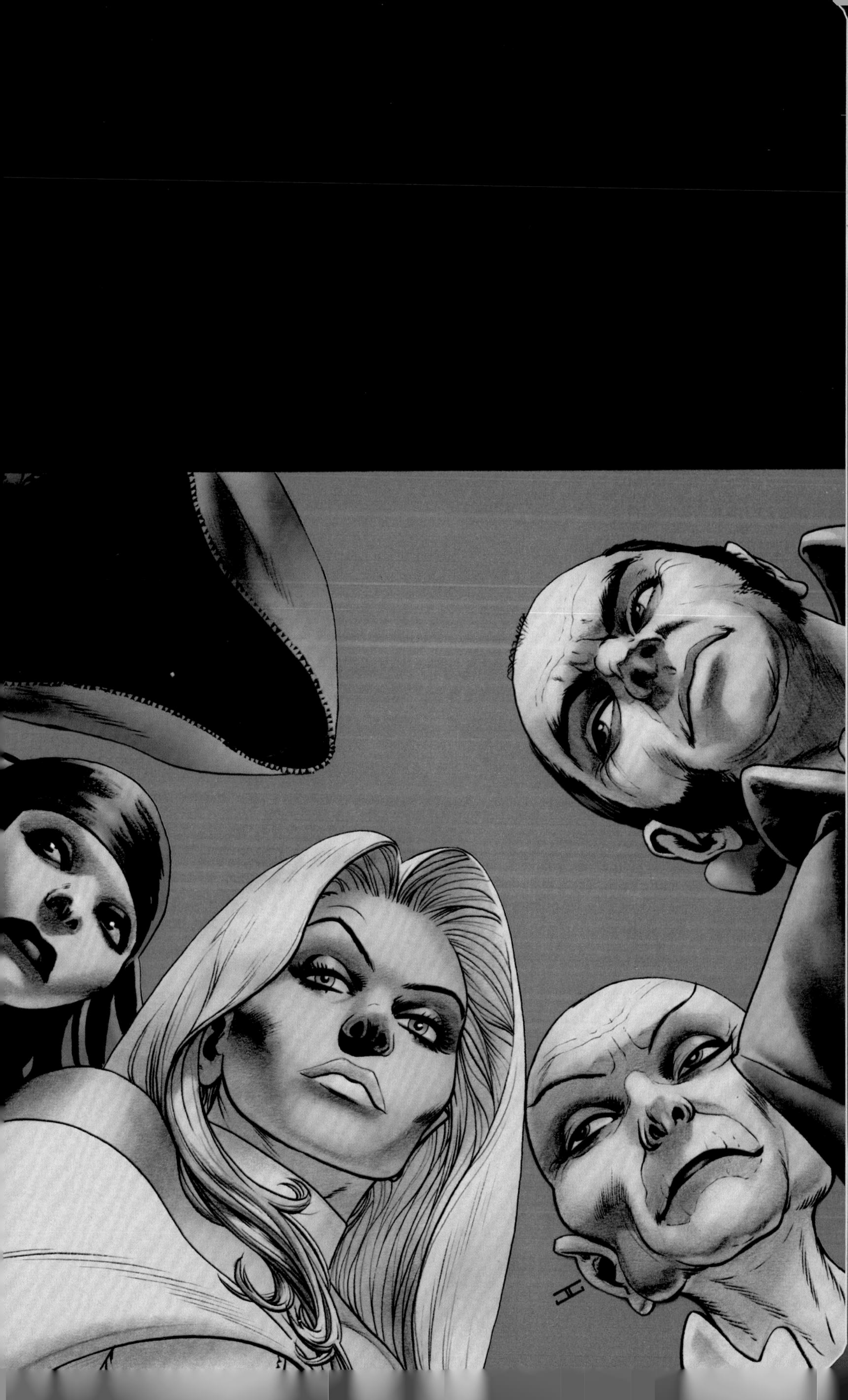

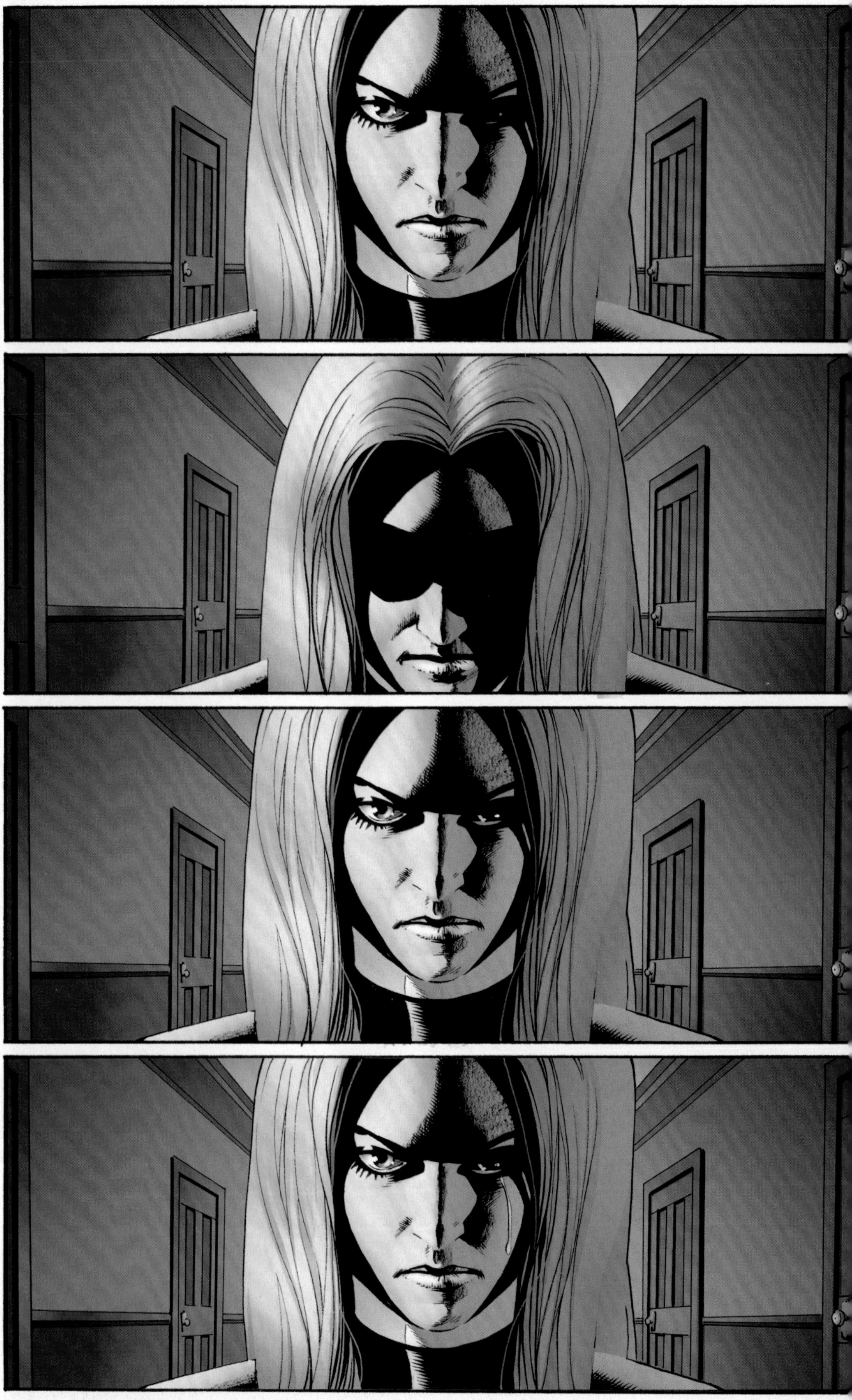

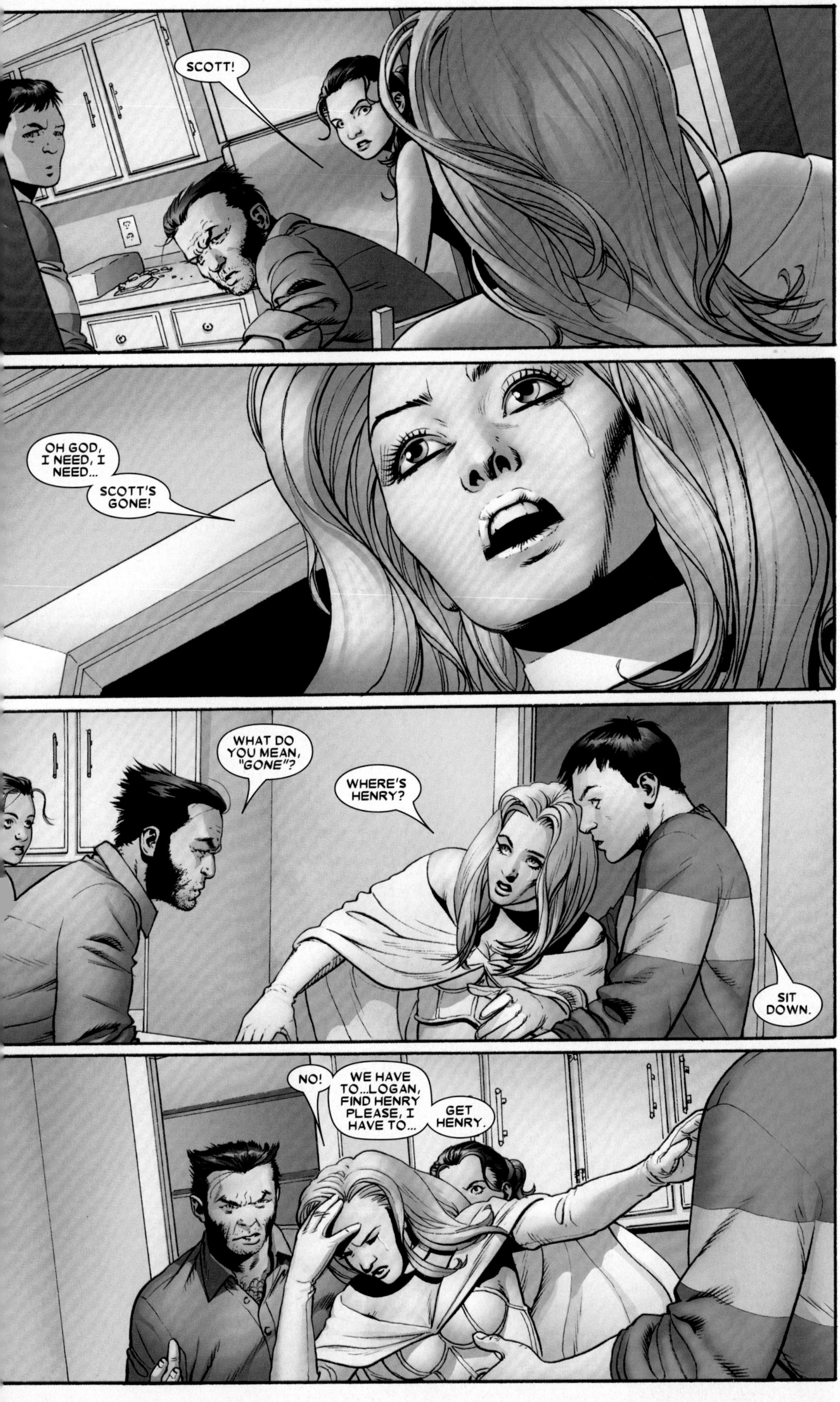
SCOTT!
OH GOD, I NEED, I NEED...
SCOTT'S GONE!
WHAT DO YOU MEAN, "GONE"?
WHERE'S HENRY?
SIT DOWN.
NO!
WE HAVE TO...LOGAN, FIND HENRY PLEASE, I HAVE TO...
GET HENRY.

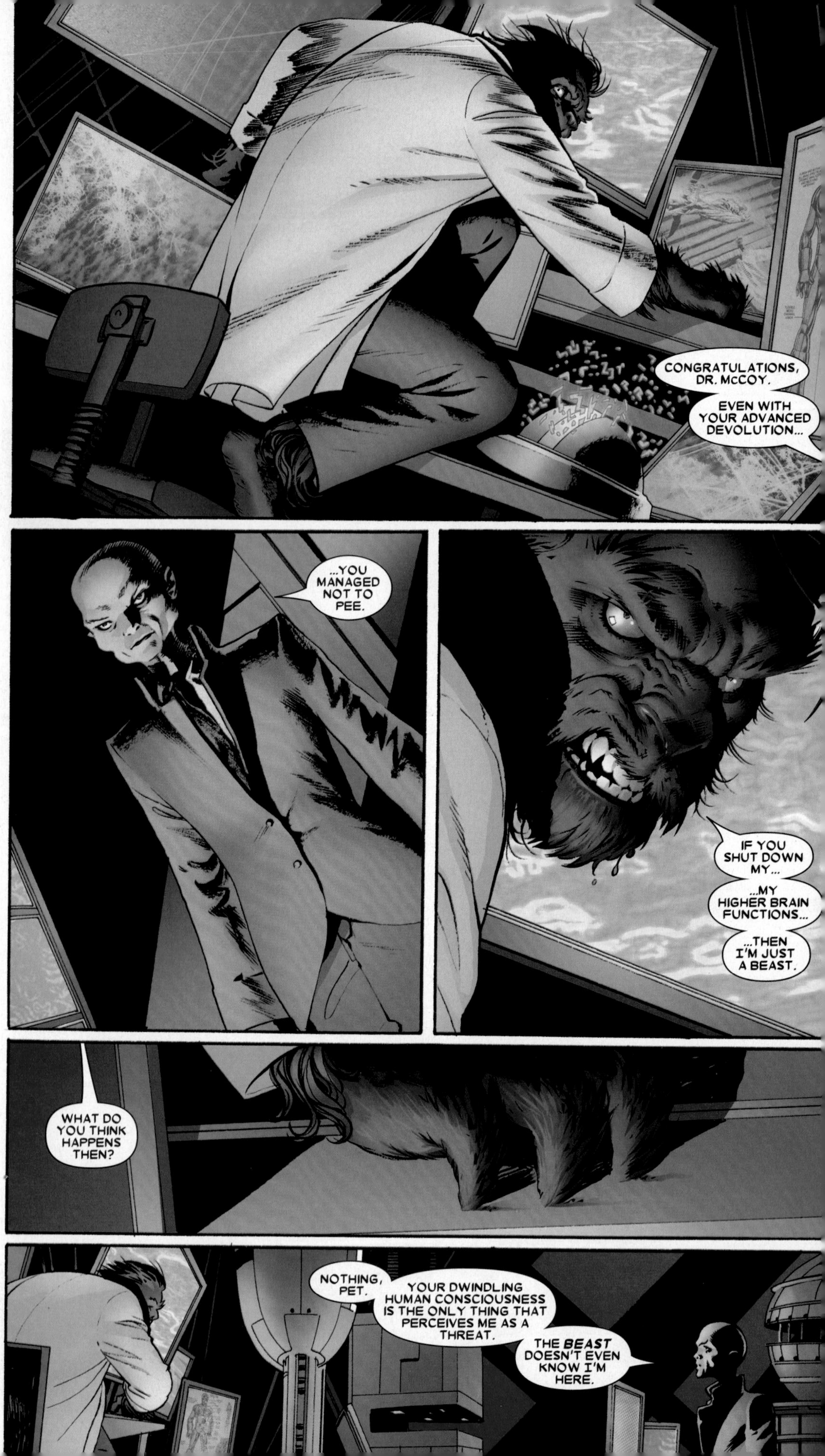

CONGRATULATIONS, DR. McCOY.
EVEN WITH YOUR ADVANCED DEVOLUTION...
...YOU MANAGED NOT TO PEE.
IF YOU SHUT DOWN MY...
...MY HIGHER BRAIN FUNCTIONS...
...THEN I'M JUST A BEAST.
WHAT DO YOU THINK HAPPENS THEN?
NOTHING, PET.
YOUR DWINDLING HUMAN CONSCIOUSNESS IS THE ONLY THING THAT PERCEIVES ME AS A THREAT.
THE BEAST DOESN'T EVEN KNOW I'M HERE.

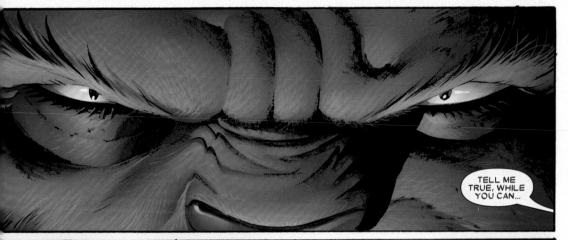

TELL ME TRUE, WHILE YOU CAN...

...DO YOU EVEN SMELL ANOTHER PERSON IN THIS ROOM?

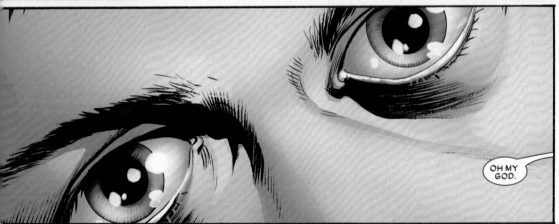

OH MY GOD.

SCOTT!

WHAT HAPPENED?

I JUST FOUND HIM--HE WAS FINE WHEN WE WENT TO BED...

I CAN'T GET IN HIS MIND!

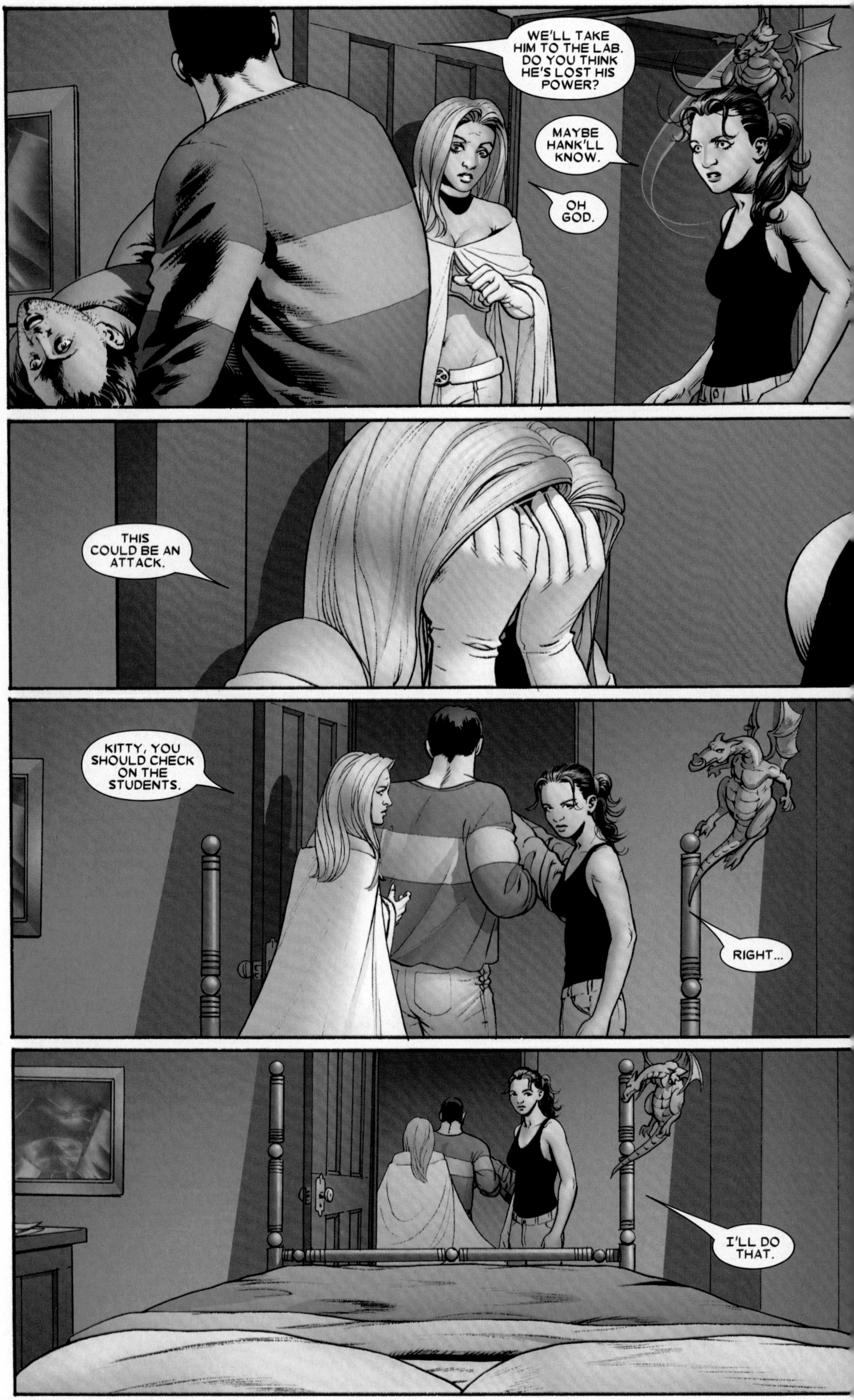
WE'LL TAKE HIM TO THE LAB. DO YOU THINK HE'S LOST HIS POWER?
MAYBE HANK'LL KNOW.
OH GOD.
THIS COULD BE AN ATTACK.
KITTY, YOU SHOULD CHECK ON THE STUDENTS.
RIGHT...
I'LL DO THAT.

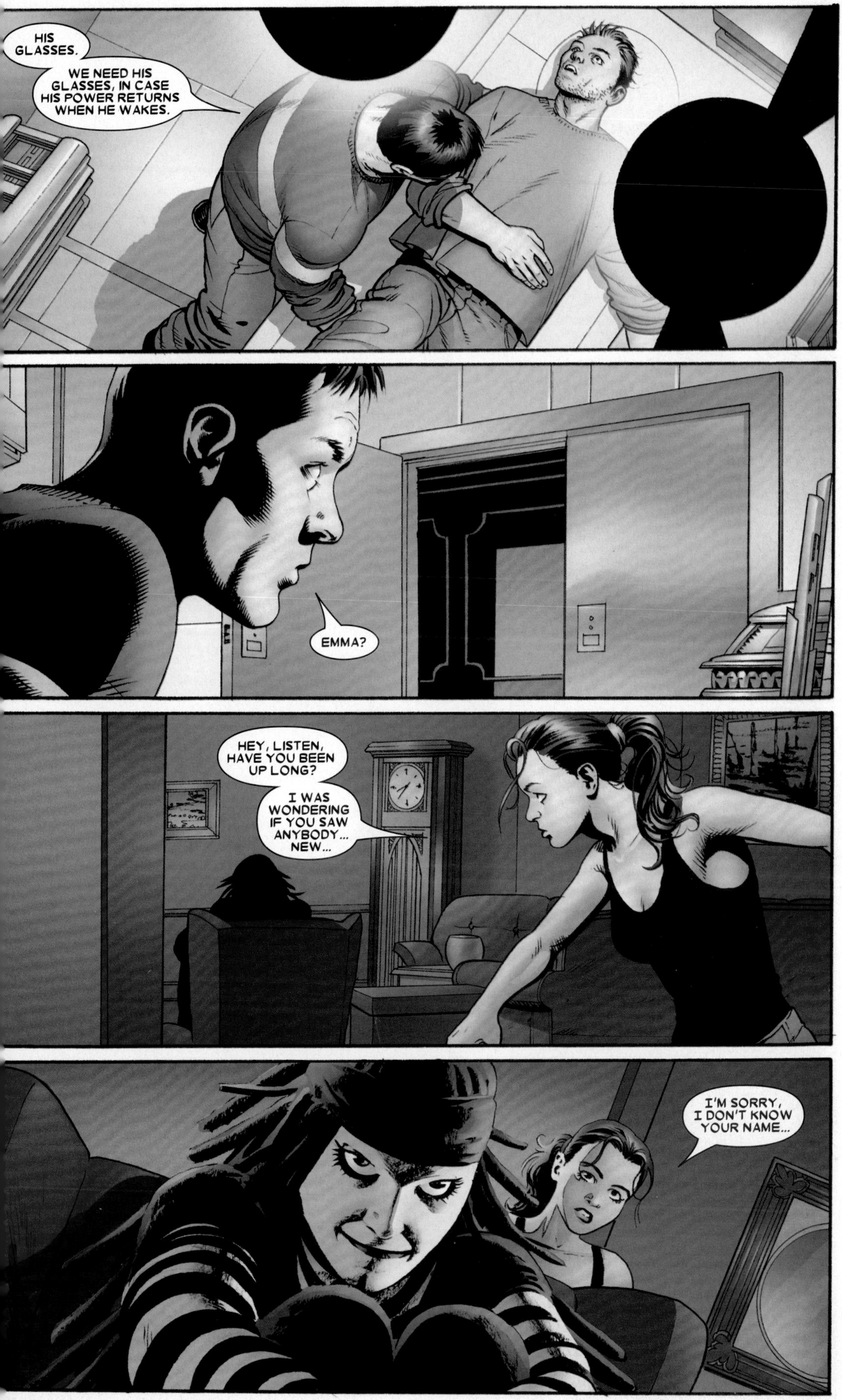

HIS GLASSES.
WE NEED HIS GLASSES, IN CASE HIS POWER RETURNS WHEN HE WAKES.
EMMA?
HEY, LISTEN, HAVE YOU BEEN UP LONG?
I WAS WONDERING IF YOU SAW ANYBODY... NEW...
I'M SORRY, I DON'T KNOW YOUR NAME...

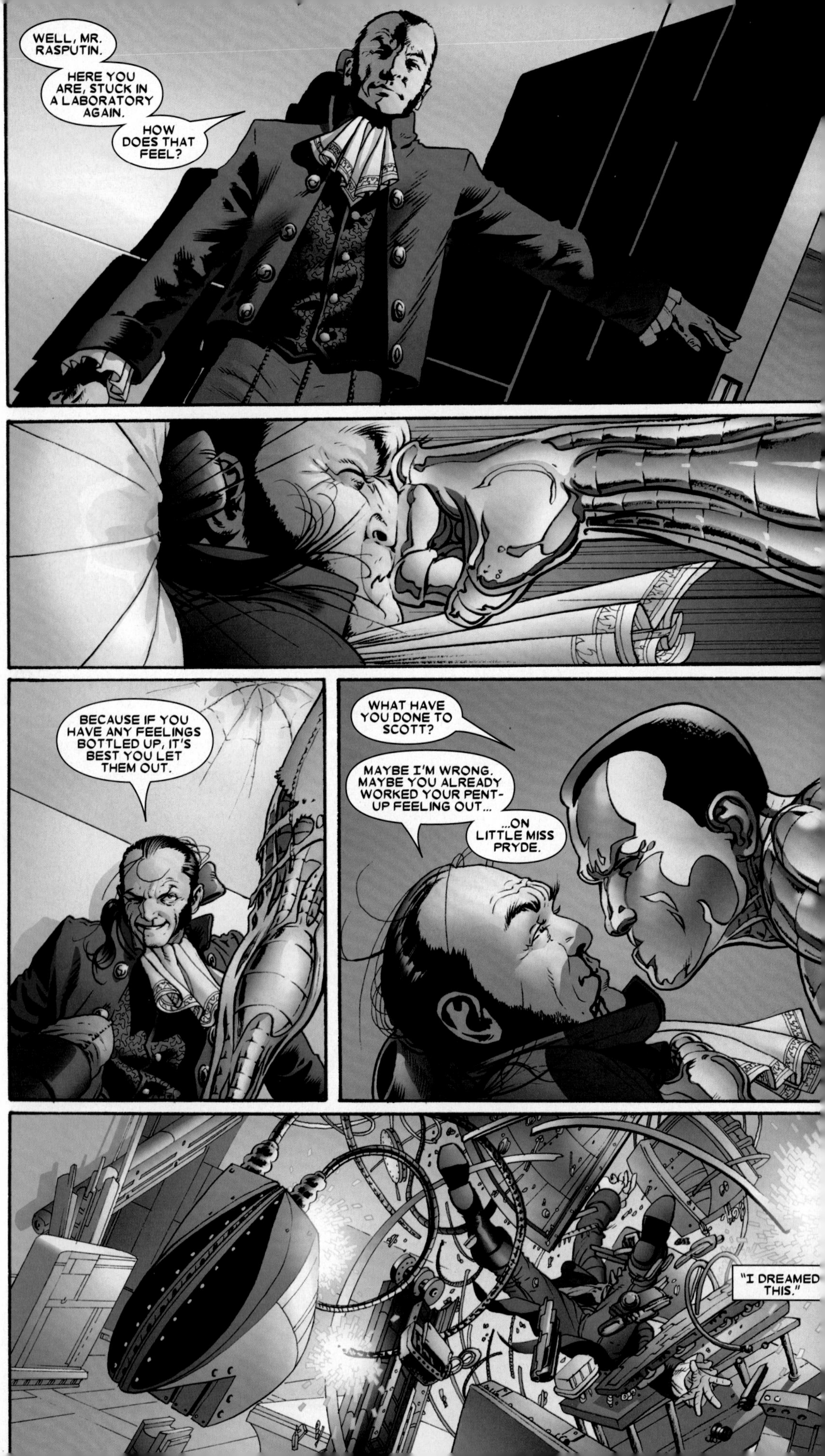
WELL, MR. RASPUTIN.
HERE YOU ARE, STUCK IN A LABORATORY AGAIN.
HOW DOES THAT FEEL?
BECAUSE IF YOU HAVE ANY FEELINGS BOTTLED UP, IT'S BEST YOU LET THEM OUT.
WHAT HAVE YOU DONE TO SCOTT?
MAYBE I'M WRONG. MAYBE YOU ALREADY WORKED YOUR PENT-UP FEELING OUT...
...ON LITTLE MISS PRYDE.
"I DREAMED THIS."

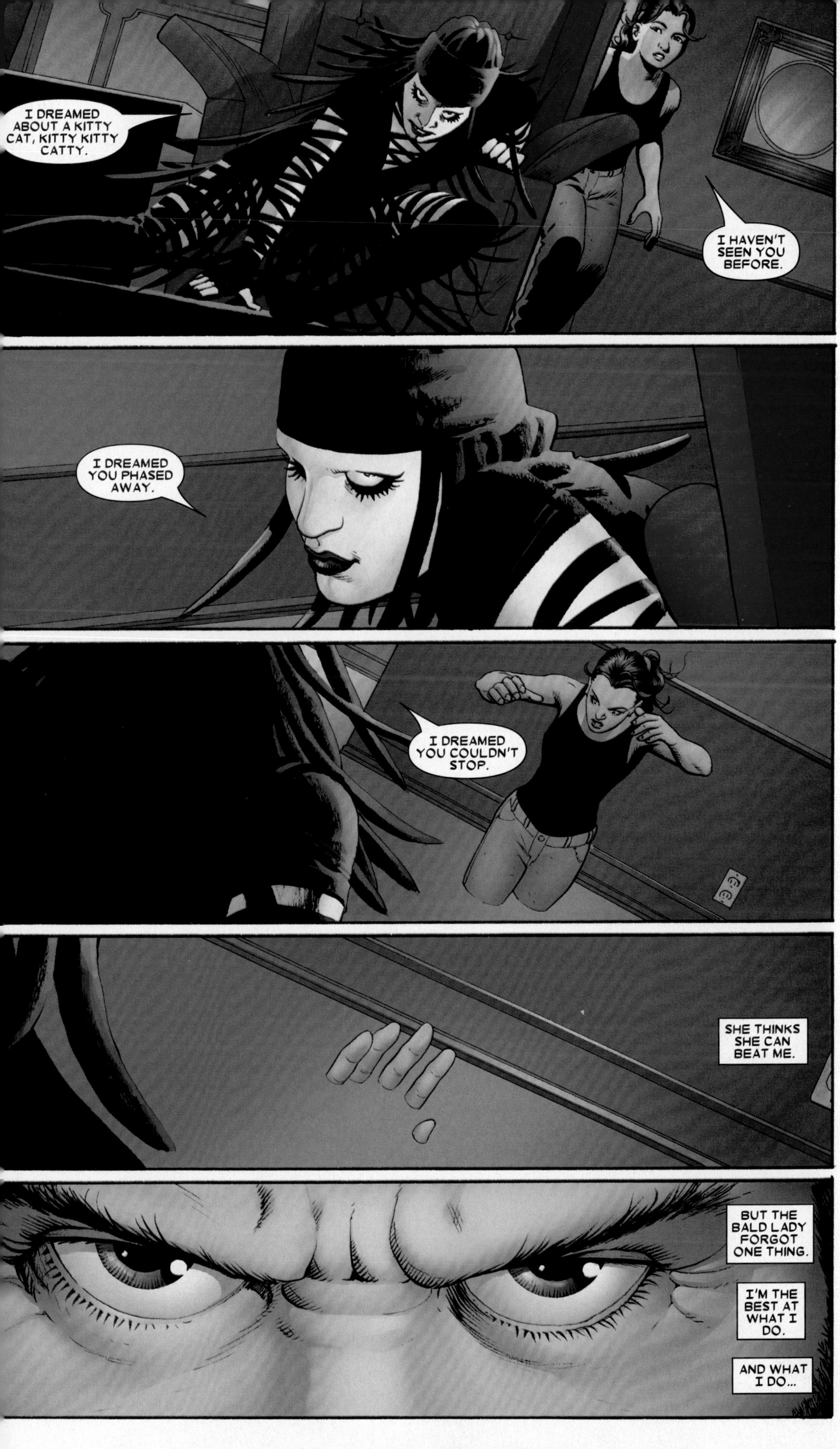
I DREAMED ABOUT A KITTY CAT, KITTY KITTY CATTY.
I HAVEN'T SEEN YOU BEFORE.
I DREAMED YOU PHASED AWAY.
I DREAMED YOU COULDN'T STOP.
SHE THINKS SHE CAN BEAT ME.
BUT THE BALD LADY FORGOT ONE THING.
I'M THE BEST AT WHAT I DO.
AND WHAT I DO...

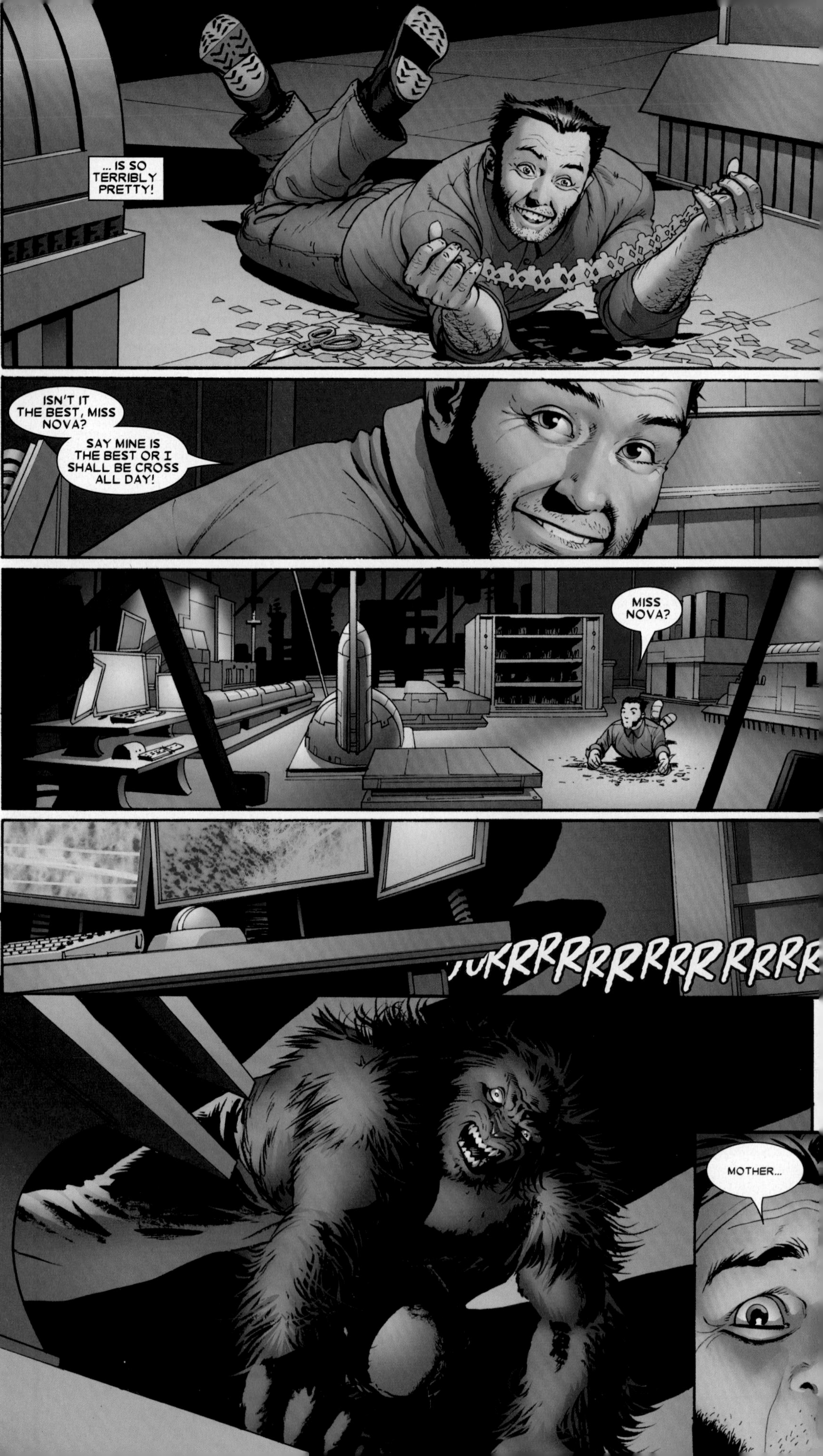

... IS SO TERRIBLY PRETTY!
ISN'T IT THE BEST, MISS NOVA?
SAY MINE IS THE BEST OR I SHALL BE CROSS ALL DAY!
MISS NOVA?
UKRRRRRRRRRRRRRR
MOTHER...

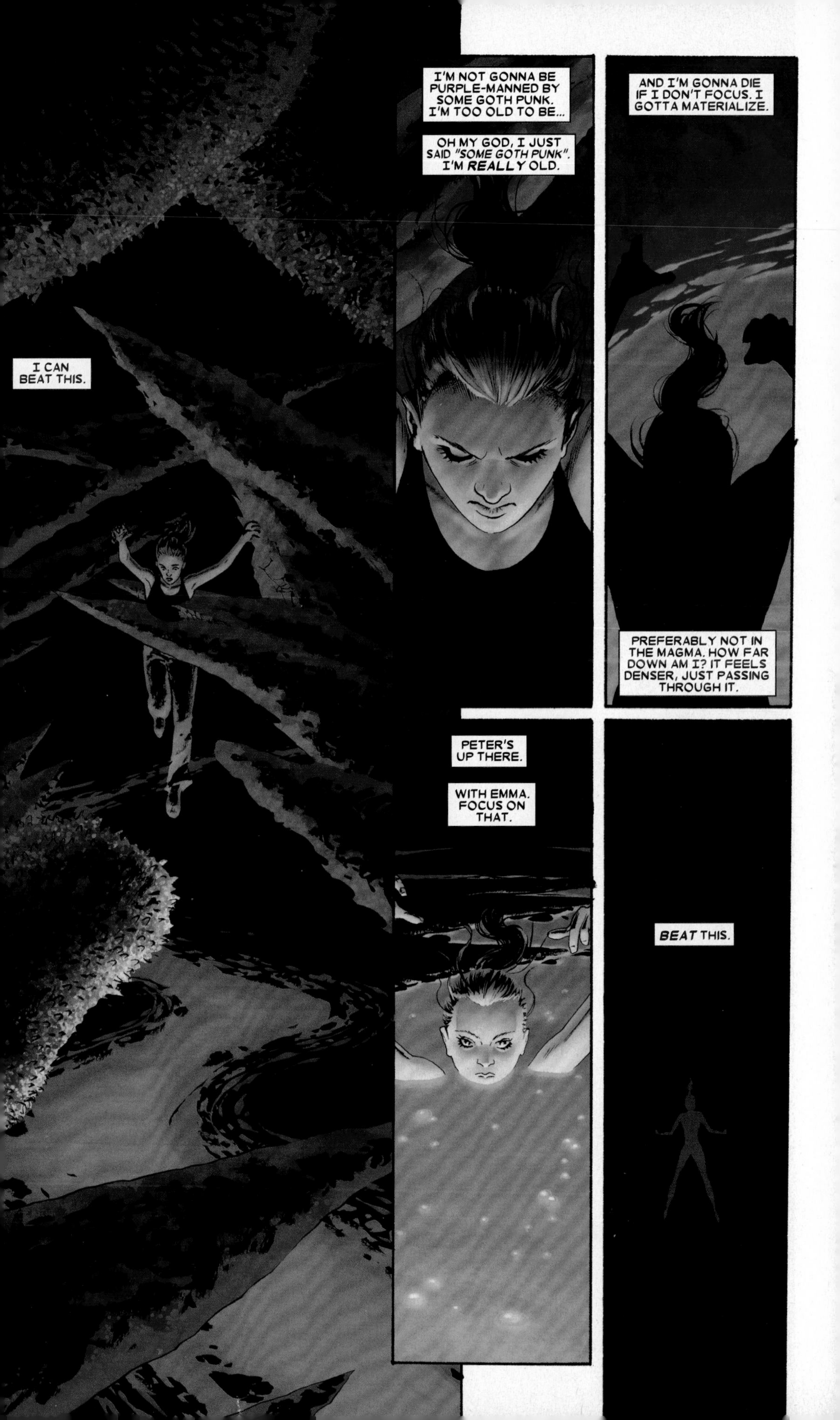
I CAN BEAT THIS.
I'M NOT GONNA BE PURPLE-MANNED BY SOME GOTH PUNK. I'M TOO OLD TO BE...
OH MY GOD, I JUST SAID "SOME GOTH PUNK". I'M REALLY OLD.
AND I'M GONNA DIE IF I DON'T FOCUS. I GOTTA MATERIALIZE.
PREFERABLY NOT IN THE MAGMA. HOW FAR DOWN AM I? IT FEELS DENSER, JUST PASSING THROUGH IT.
PETER'S UP THERE.
WITH EMMA. FOCUS ON THAT.
BEAT THIS.

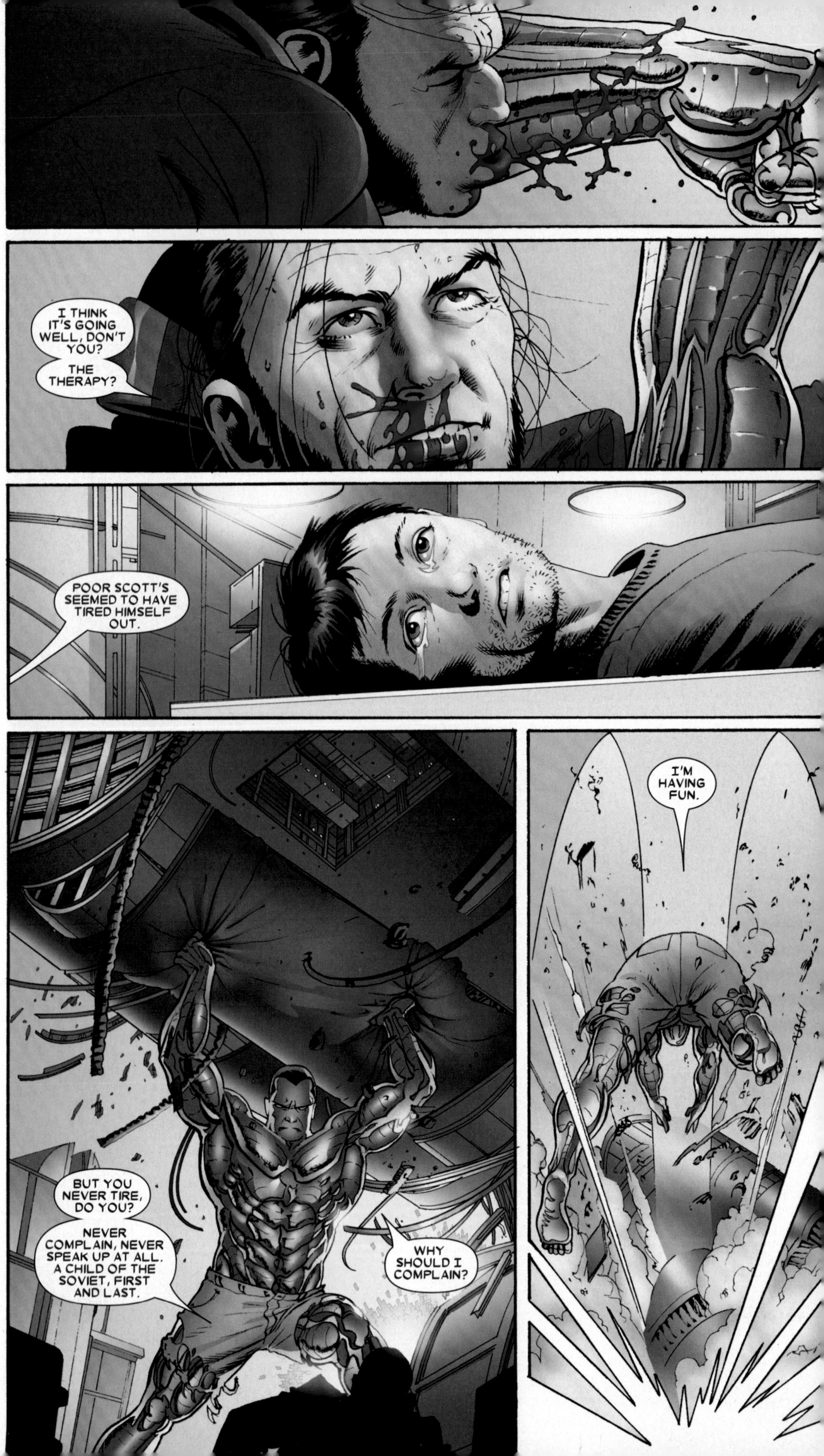
I THINK IT'S GOING WELL, DON'T YOU?
THE THERAPY?
POOR SCOTT'S SEEMED TO HAVE TIRED HIMSELF OUT.
BUT YOU NEVER TIRE, DO YOU?
NEVER COMPLAIN, NEVER SPEAK UP AT ALL. A CHILD OF THE SOVIET, FIRST AND LAST.
WHY SHOULD I COMPLAIN?
I'M HAVING FUN.

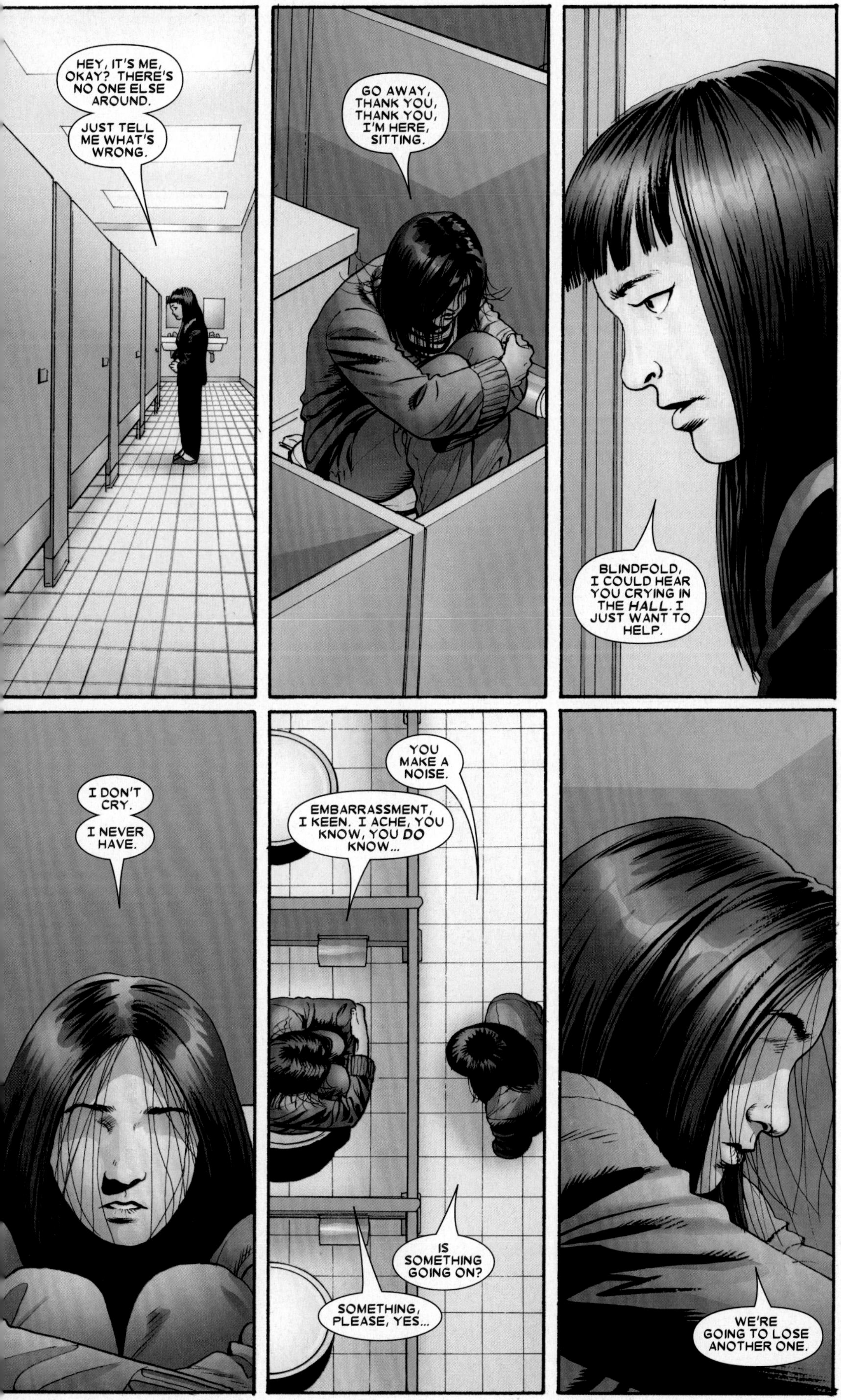
HEY, IT'S ME, OKAY? THERE'S NO ONE ELSE AROUND.
JUST TELL ME WHAT'S WRONG.
GO AWAY, THANK YOU, THANK YOU, I'M HERE, SITTING.
BLINDFOLD, I COULD HEAR YOU CRYING IN THE HALL. I JUST WANT TO HELP.
I DON'T CRY.
I NEVER HAVE.
YOU MAKE A NOISE.
EMBARRASSMENT, I KEEN. I ACHE, YOU KNOW, YOU DO KNOW...
IS SOMETHING GOING ON?
SOMETHING, PLEASE, YES...
WE'RE GOING TO LOSE ANOTHER ONE.

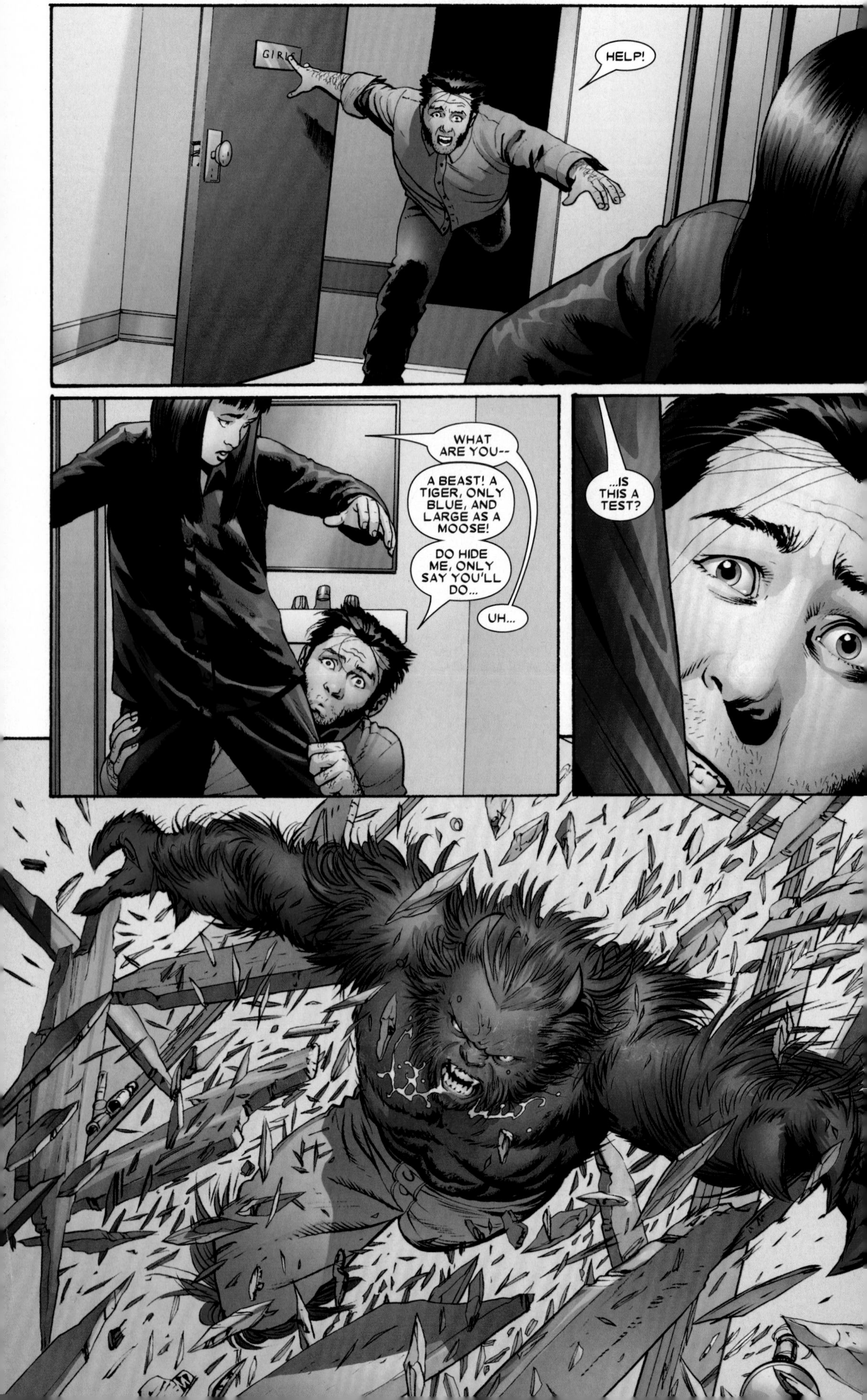
GIRLS
HELP!
WHAT ARE YOU--
A BEAST! A TIGER, ONLY BLUE, AND LARGE AS A MOOSE!
DO HIDE ME, ONLY SAY YOU'LL DO...
UH...
...IS THIS A TEST?

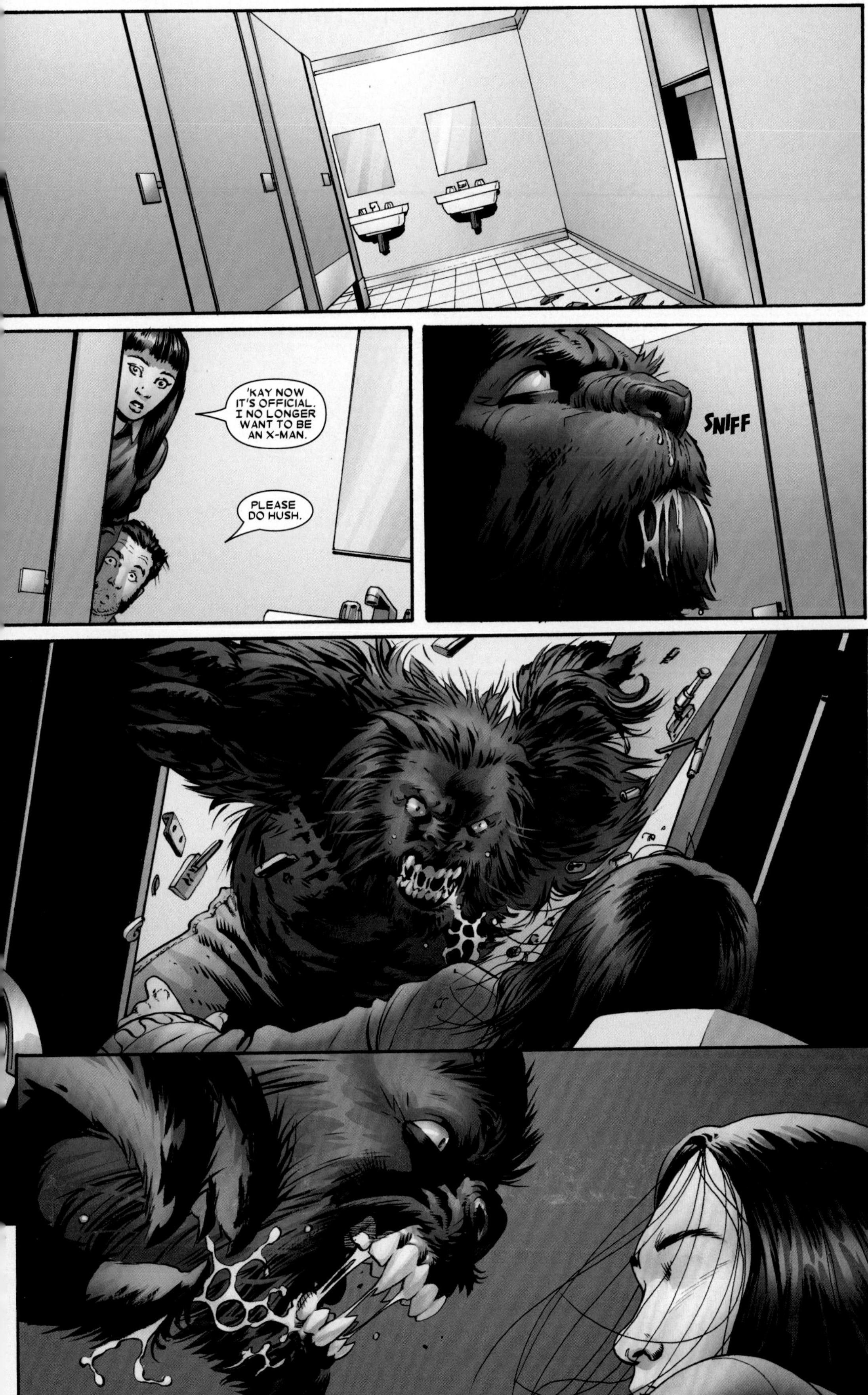

'KAY NOW IT'S OFFICIAL. I NO LONGER WANT TO BE AN X-MAN.
PLEASE DO HUSH.
SNIFF

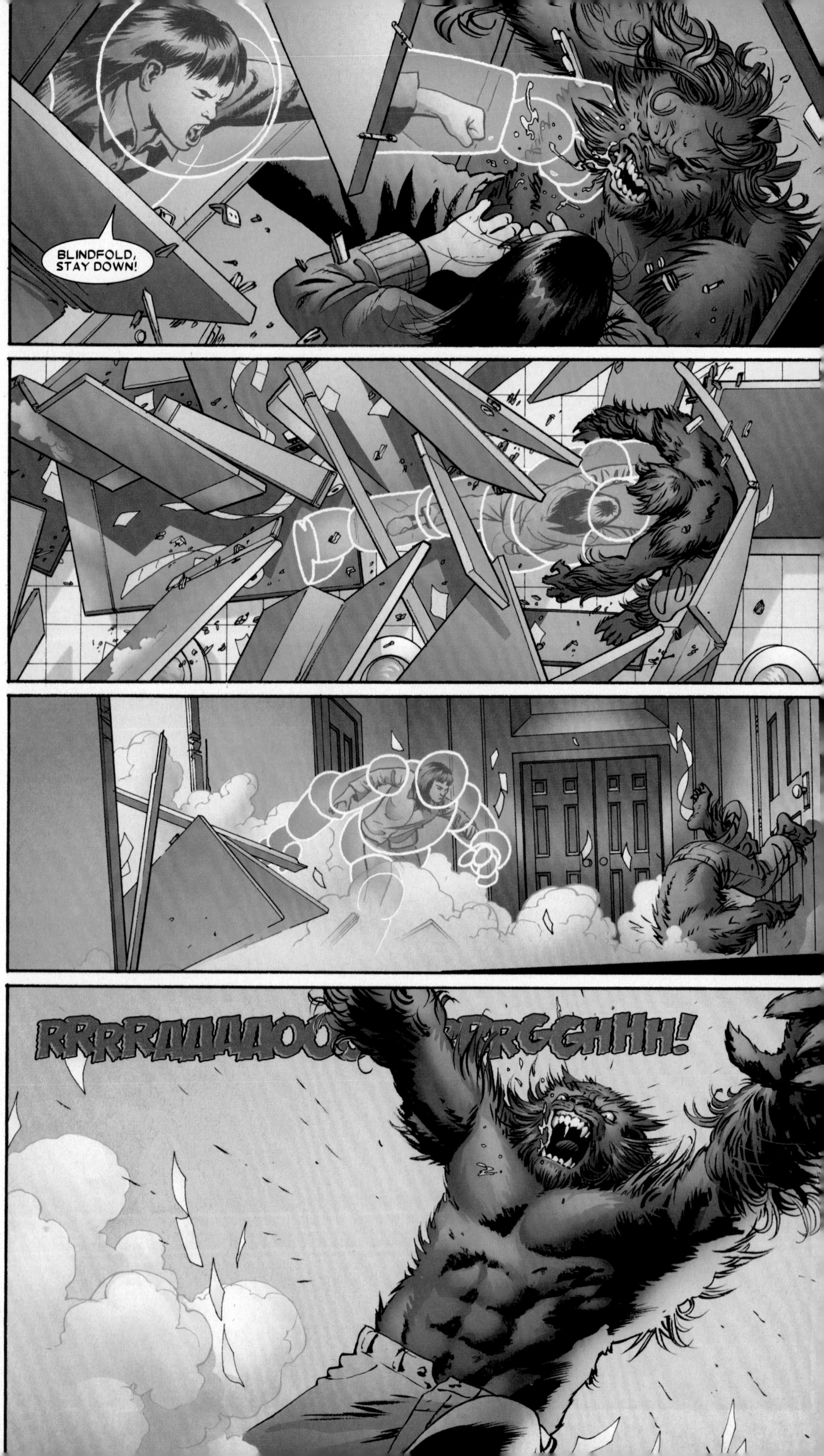
BLINDFOLD, STAY DOWN!
RRRRAAAAOO... RRGGHHH!

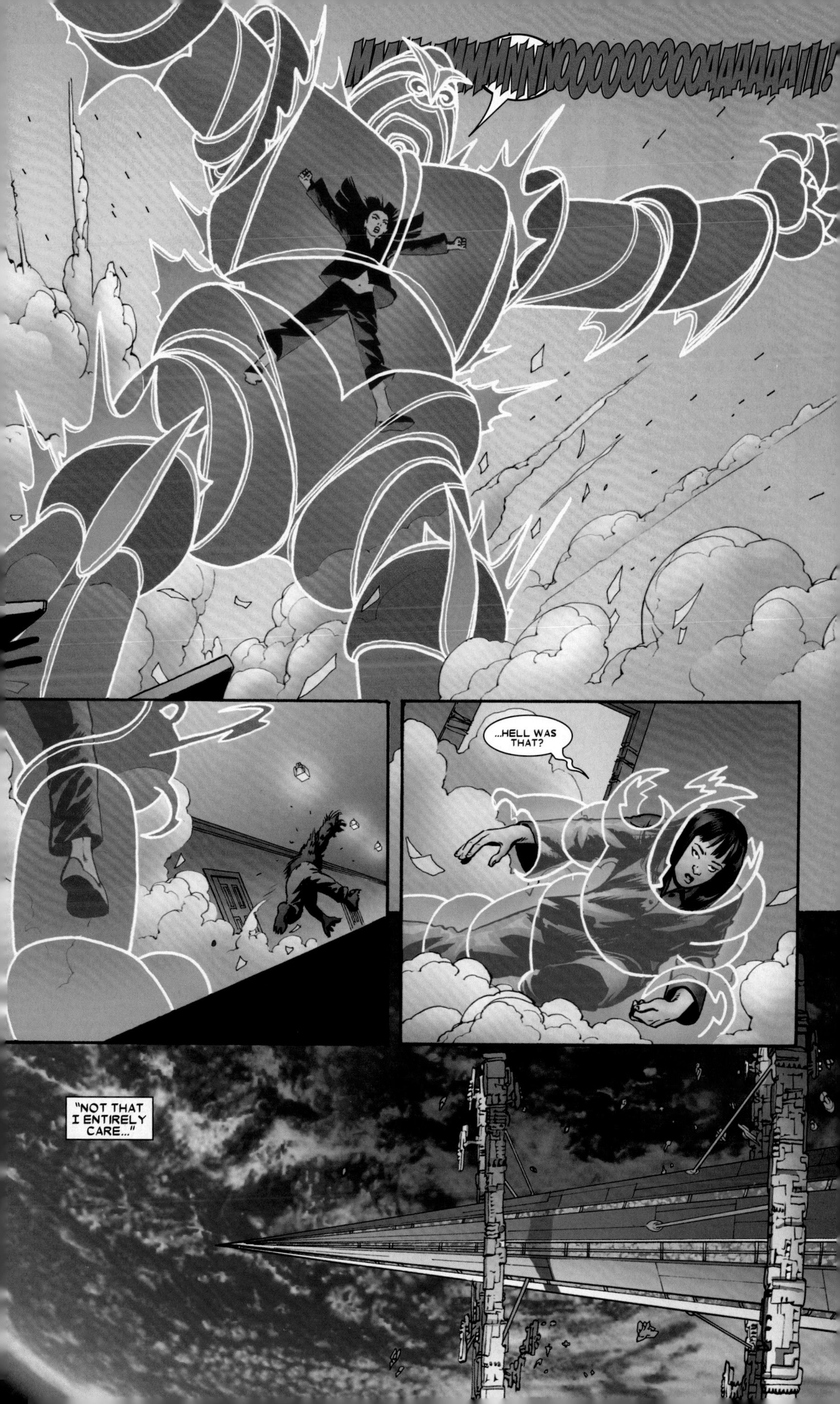
MMMNNNMMMMNNNOOOOOOOOOOOAAAAAAA!!!!
...HELL WAS THAT?
"NOT THAT I ENTIRELY CARE..."

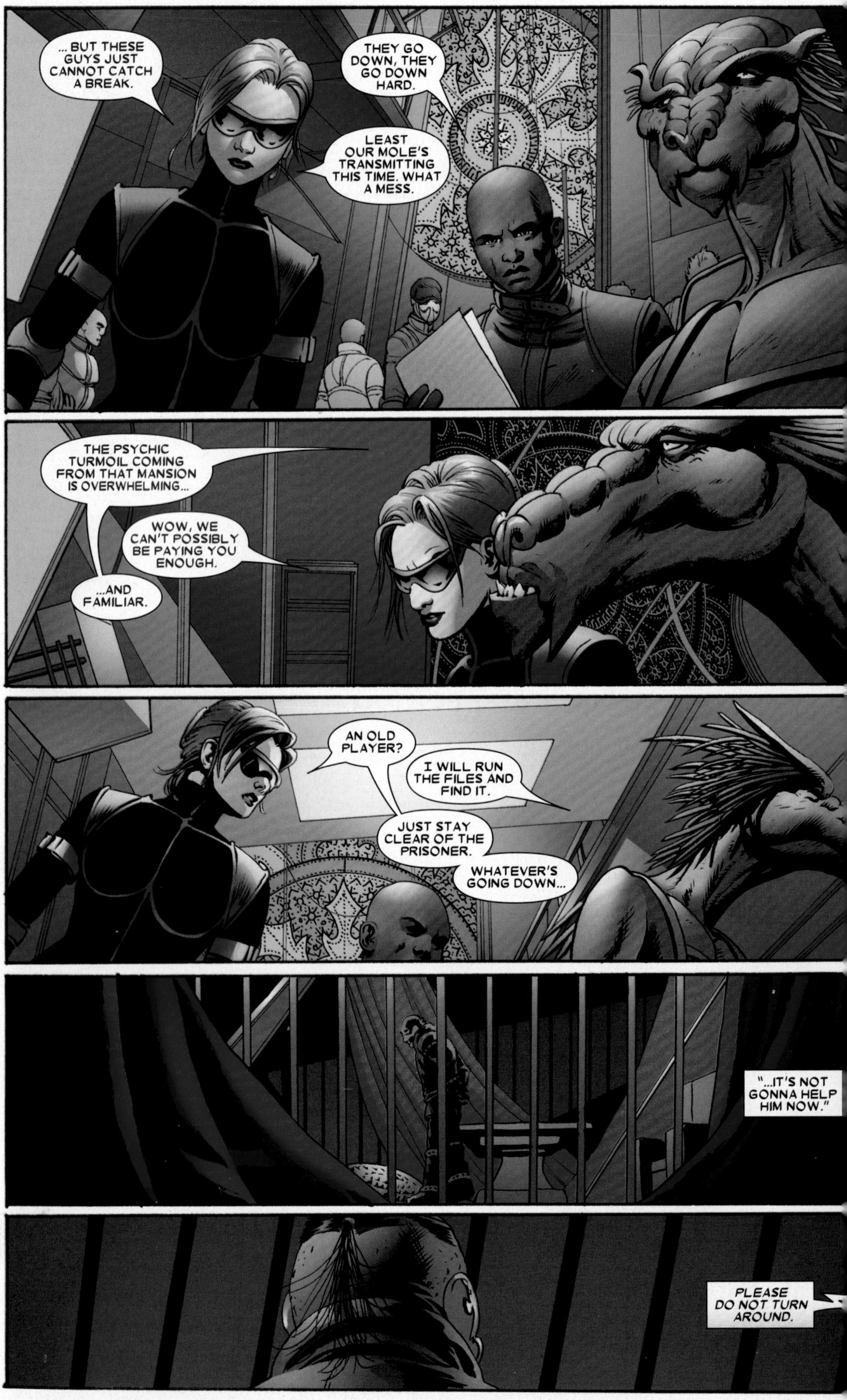
... BUT THESE GUYS JUST CANNOT CATCH A BREAK.
THEY GO DOWN, THEY GO DOWN HARD.
LEAST OUR MOLE'S TRANSMITTING THIS TIME. WHAT A MESS.
THE PSYCHIC TURMOIL COMING FROM THAT MANSION IS OVERWHELMING...
WOW, WE CAN'T POSSIBLY BE PAYING YOU ENOUGH.
...AND FAMILIAR.
AN OLD PLAYER?
I WILL RUN THE FILES AND FIND IT.
JUST STAY CLEAR OF THE PRISONER.
WHATEVER'S GOING DOWN...
"...IT'S NOT GONNA HELP HIM NOW."
PLEASE DO NOT TURN AROUND.

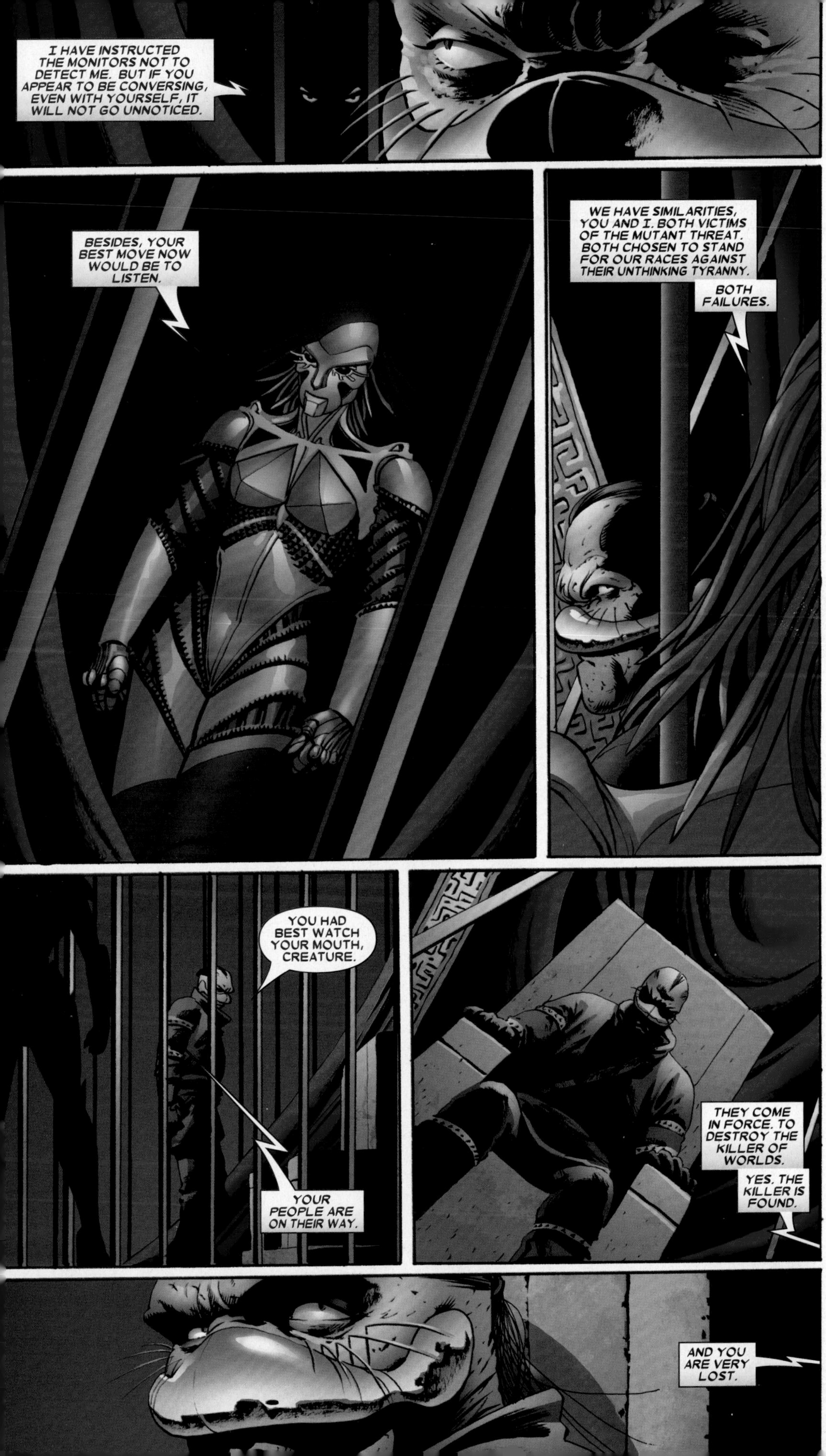
I HAVE INSTRUCTED THE MONITORS NOT TO DETECT ME. BUT IF YOU APPEAR TO BE CONVERSING, EVEN WITH YOURSELF, IT WILL NOT GO UNNOTICED.
BESIDES, YOUR BEST MOVE NOW WOULD BE TO LISTEN.
WE HAVE SIMILARITIES, YOU AND I. BOTH VICTIMS OF THE MUTANT THREAT. BOTH CHOSEN TO STAND FOR OUR RACES AGAINST THEIR UNTHINKING TYRANNY.
BOTH FAILURES.
YOU HAD BEST WATCH YOUR MOUTH, CREATURE.
YOUR PEOPLE ARE ON THEIR WAY.
THEY COME IN FORCE. TO DESTROY THE KILLER OF WORLDS.
YES. THE KILLER IS FOUND.
AND YOU ARE VERY LOST.

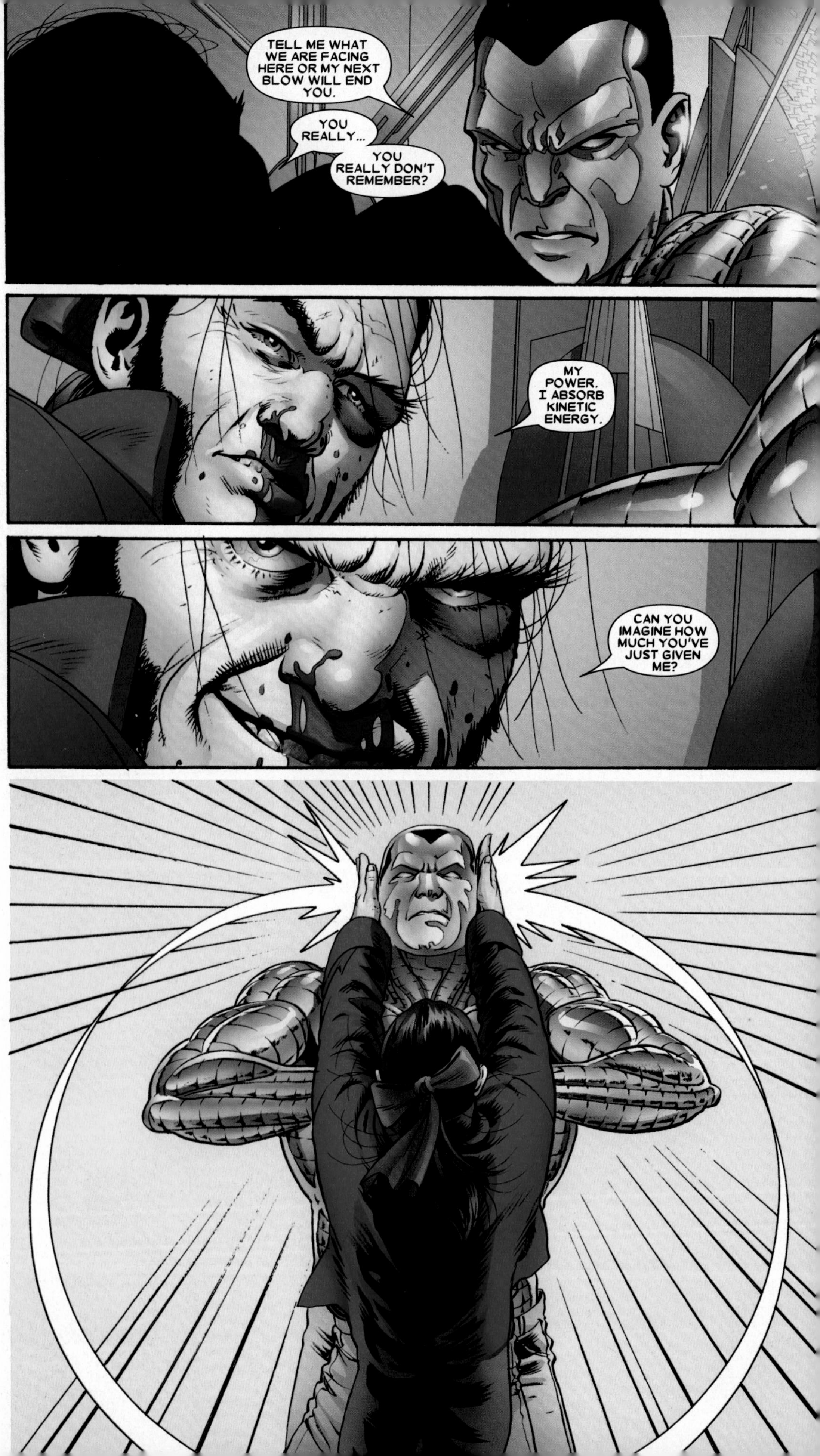
TELL ME WHAT WE ARE FACING HERE OR MY NEXT BLOW WILL END YOU.
YOU REALLY...
YOU REALLY DON'T REMEMBER?
MY POWER. I ABSORB KINETIC ENERGY.
CAN YOU IMAGINE HOW MUCH YOU'VE JUST GIVEN ME?

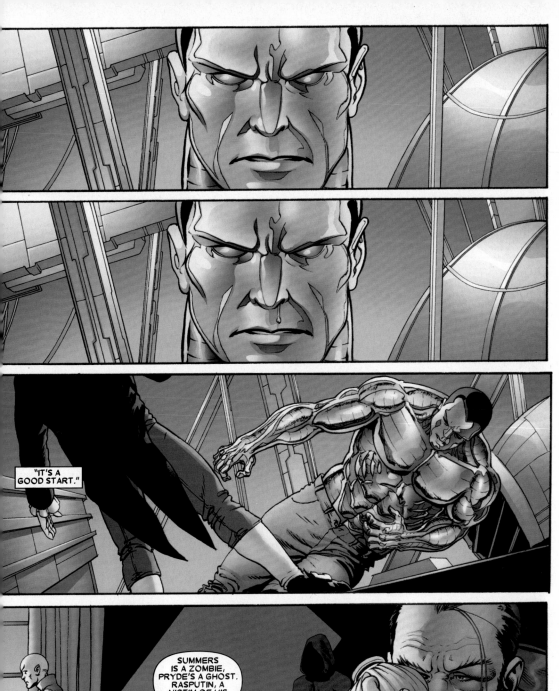

"IT'S A GOOD START."

SUMMERS IS A ZOMBIE. PRYDE'S A GHOST. RASPUTIN, A VICTIM OF HIS OWN RAGE.

BELIEVE ME WHEN I SAY HE HAS PLENTY.

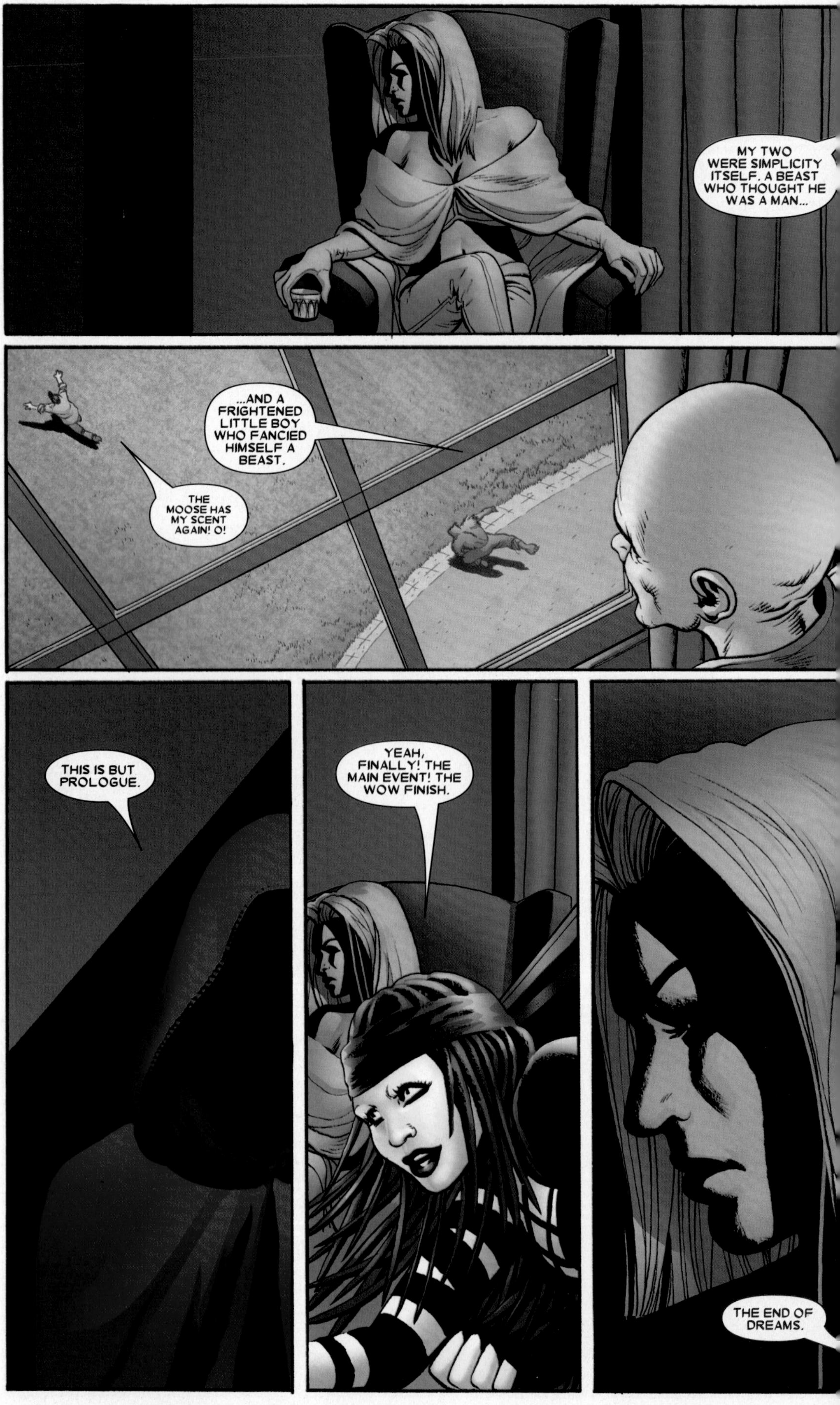
MY TWO WERE SIMPLICITY ITSELF. A BEAST WHO THOUGHT HE WAS A MAN...
...AND A FRIGHTENED LITTLE BOY WHO FANCIED HIMSELF A BEAST.
THE MOOSE HAS MY SCENT AGAIN! O!
THIS IS BUT PROLOGUE.
YEAH, FINALLY! THE MAIN EVENT! THE WOW FINISH.
THE END OF DREAMS.

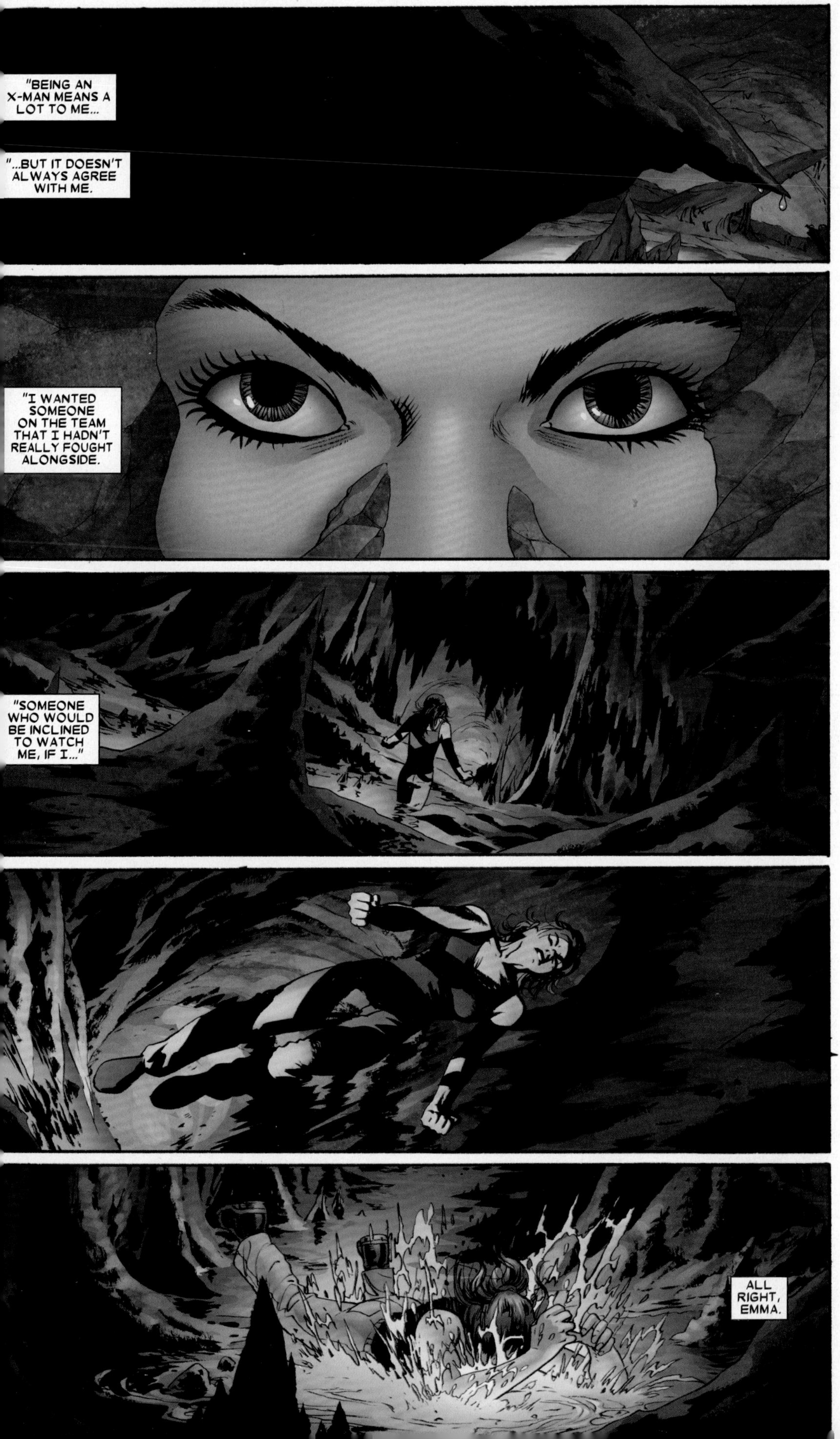
"BEING AN X-MAN MEANS A LOT TO ME...
"...BUT IT DOESN'T ALWAYS AGREE WITH ME.
"I WANTED SOMEONE ON THE TEAM THAT I HADN'T REALLY FOUGHT ALONGSIDE.
"SOMEONE WHO WOULD BE INCLINED TO WATCH ME, IF I..."
ALL RIGHT, EMMA.

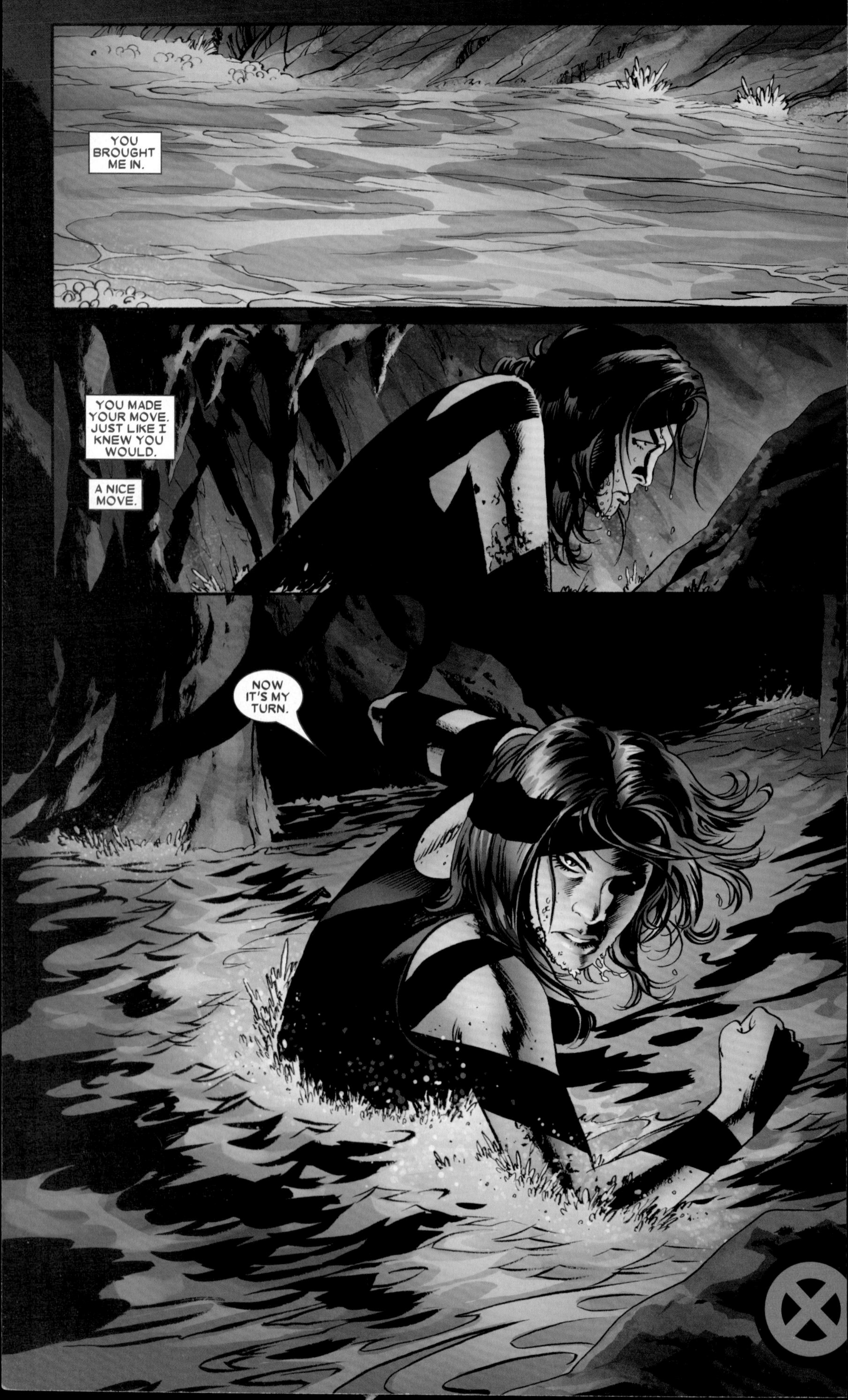
YOU BROUGHT ME IN.
YOU MADE YOUR MOVE. JUST LIKE I KNEW YOU WOULD.
A NICE MOVE.
NOW IT'S MY TURN.

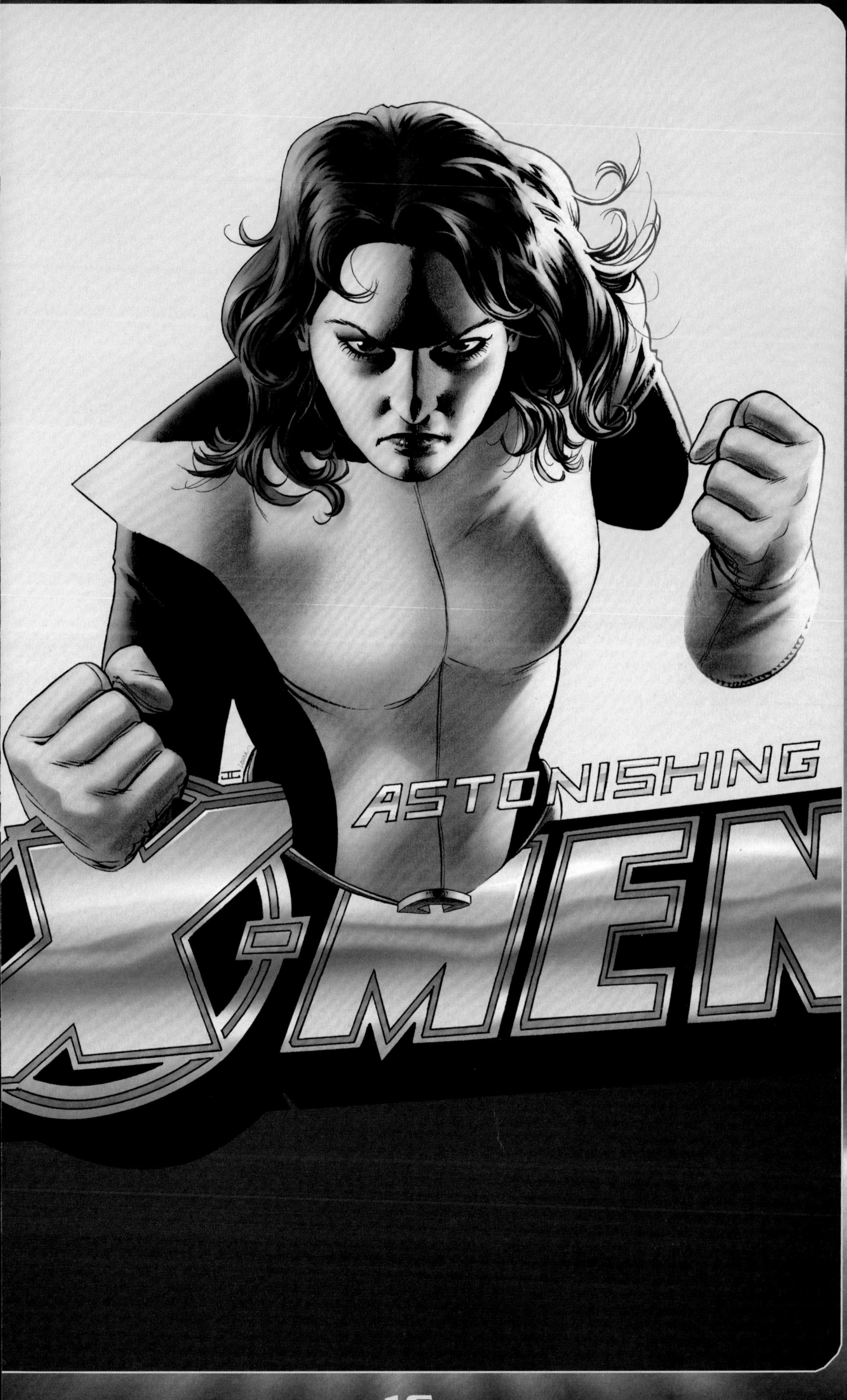
ASTONISHING
X-MEN

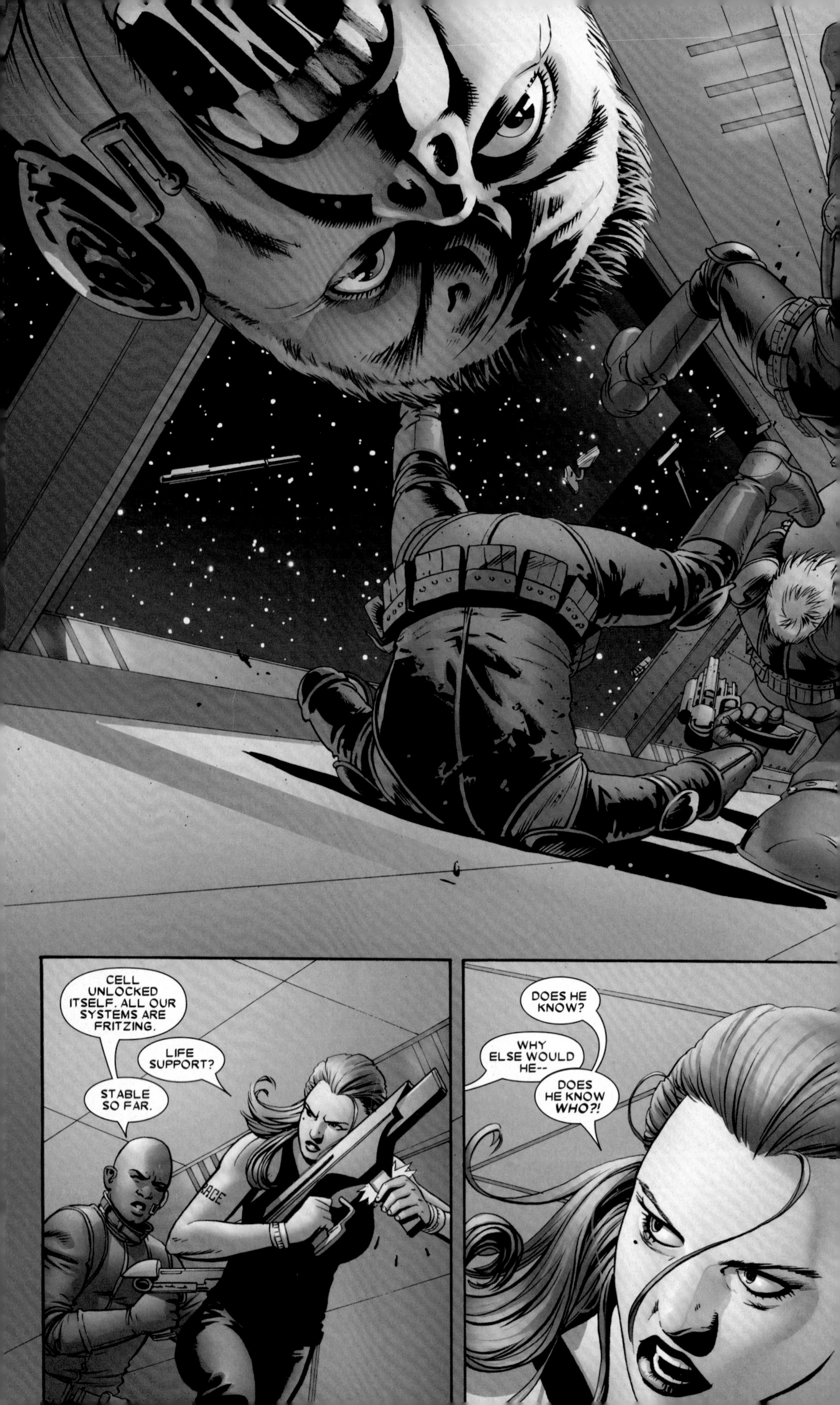
CELL UNLOCKED ITSELF. ALL OUR SYSTEMS ARE FRITZING.
LIFE SUPPORT?
STABLE SO FAR.
DOES HE KNOW?
WHY ELSE WOULD HE--
DOES HE KNOW *WHO?!*

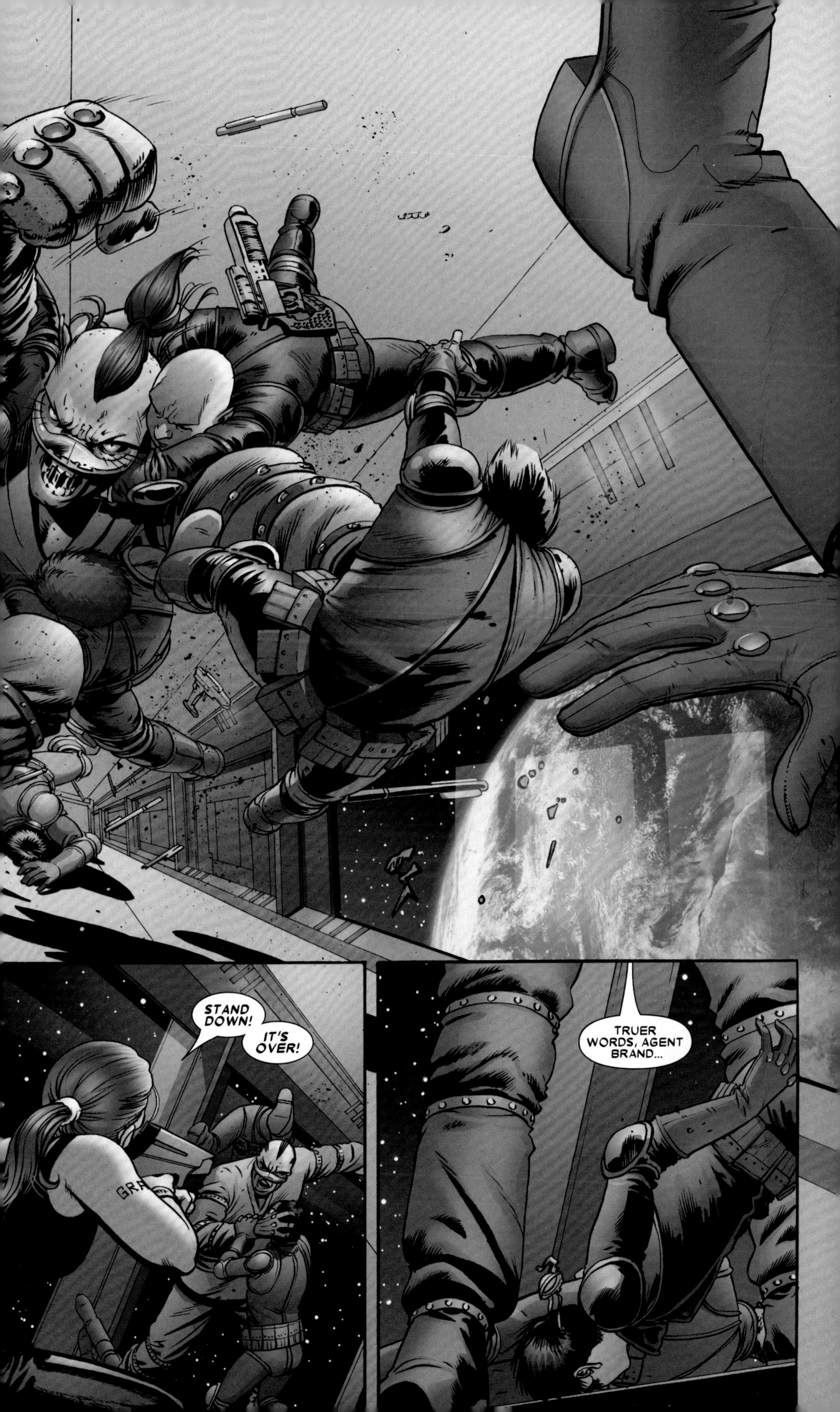
STAND DOWN!
IT'S OVER!
TRUER WORDS, AGENT BRAND...

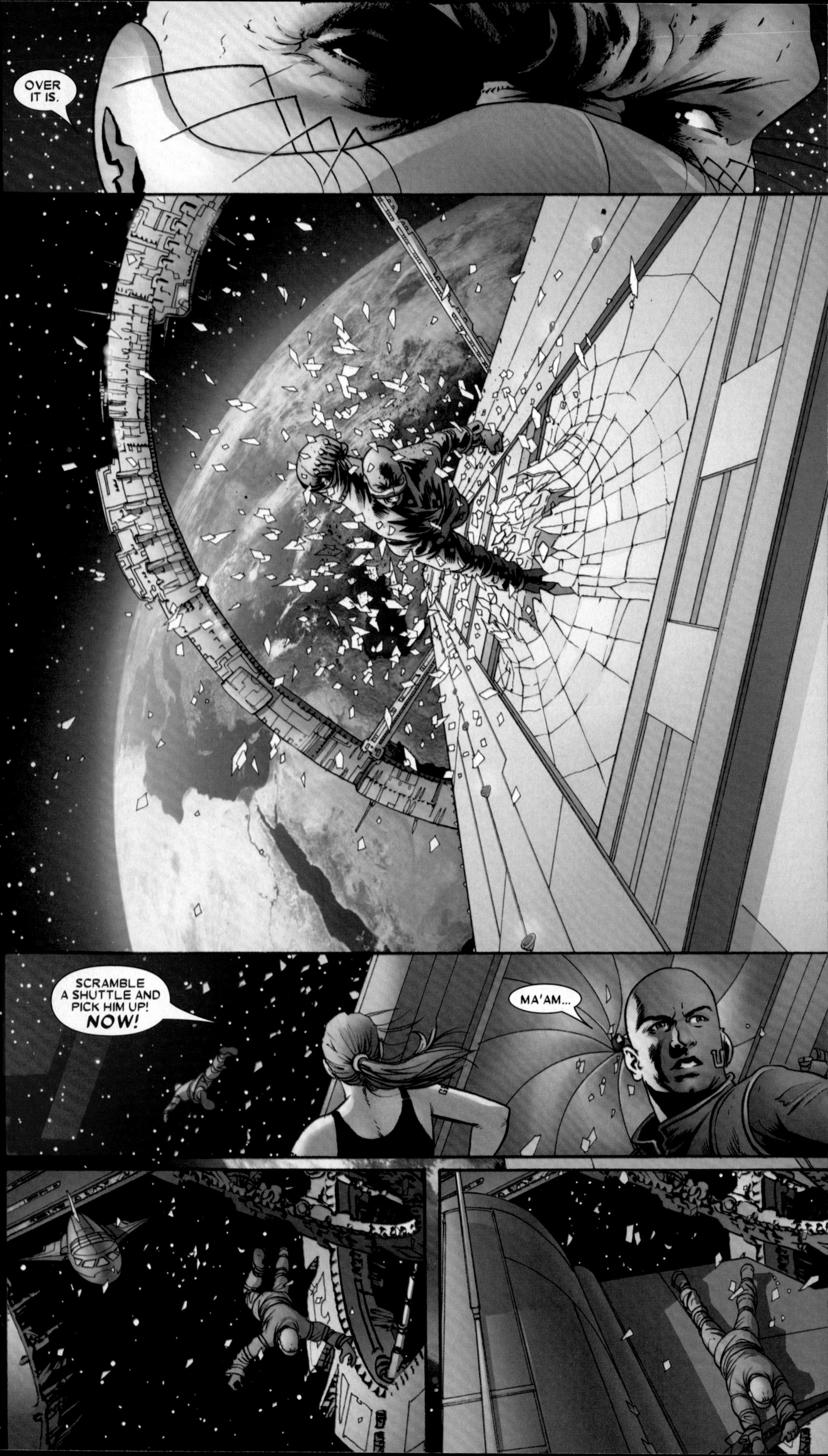
OVER IT IS.
SCRAMBLE A SHUTTLE AND PICK HIM UP! NOW!
MA'AM...

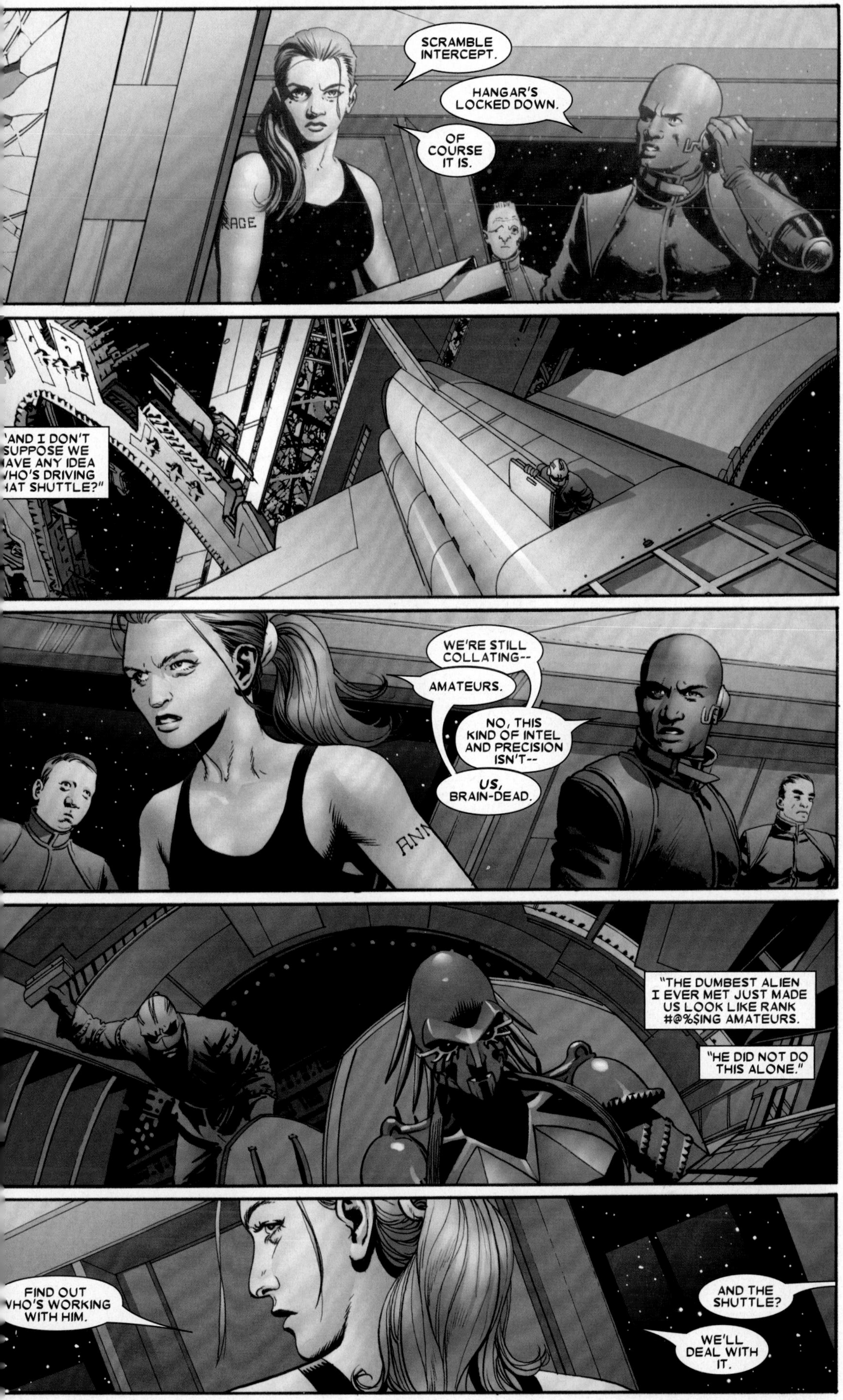
SCRAMBLE INTERCEPT.
HANGAR'S LOCKED DOWN.
OF COURSE IT IS.
RAGE
'AND I DON'T
SUPPOSE WE
AVE ANY IDEA
VHO'S DRIVING
HAT SHUTTLE?"
WE'RE STILL COLLATING--
AMATEURS.
NO, THIS KIND OF INTEL AND PRECISION ISN'T--
US, BRAIN-DEAD.
ANN
"THE DUMBEST ALIEN I EVER MET JUST MADE US LOOK LIKE RANK #@%$ING AMATEURS.
"HE DID NOT DO THIS ALONE."
FIND OUT
VHO'S WORKING
WITH HIM.
AND THE SHUTTLE?
WE'LL DEAL WITH IT.

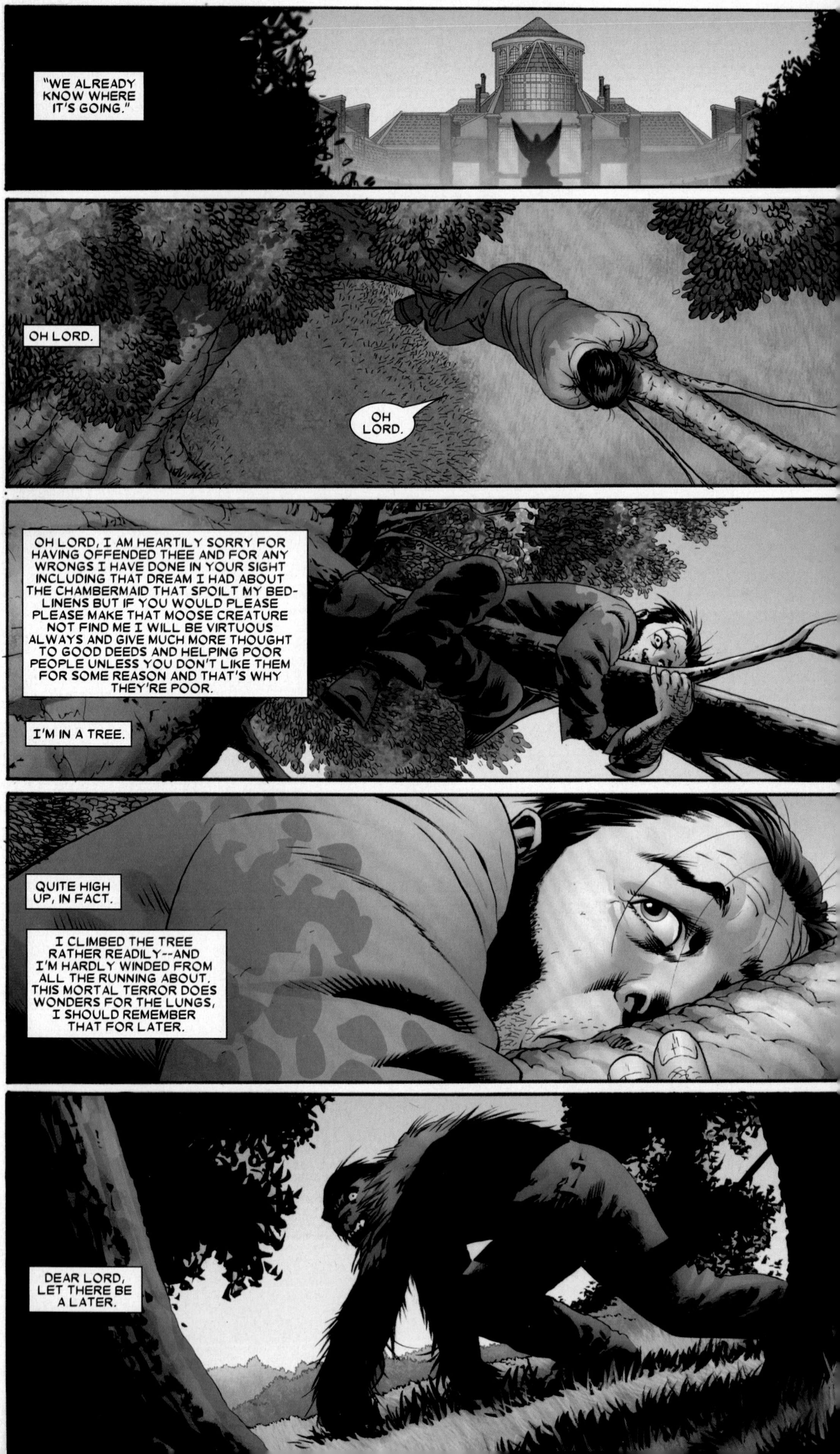
"WE ALREADY KNOW WHERE IT'S GOING."
OH LORD.
OH LORD.
OH LORD, I AM HEARTILY SORRY FOR HAVING OFFENDED THEE AND FOR ANY WRONGS I HAVE DONE IN YOUR SIGHT INCLUDING THAT DREAM I HAD ABOUT THE CHAMBERMAID THAT SPOILT MY BED-LINENS BUT IF YOU WOULD PLEASE PLEASE MAKE THAT MOOSE CREATURE NOT FIND ME I WILL BE VIRTUOUS ALWAYS AND GIVE MUCH MORE THOUGHT TO GOOD DEEDS AND HELPING POOR PEOPLE UNLESS YOU DON'T LIKE THEM FOR SOME REASON AND THAT'S WHY THEY'RE POOR.
I'M IN A TREE.
QUITE HIGH UP, IN FACT.
I CLIMBED THE TREE RATHER READILY--AND I'M HARDLY WINDED FROM ALL THE RUNNING ABOUT. THIS MORTAL TERROR DOES WONDERS FOR THE LUNGS, I SHOULD REMEMBER THAT FOR LATER.
DEAR LORD, LET THERE BE A LATER.

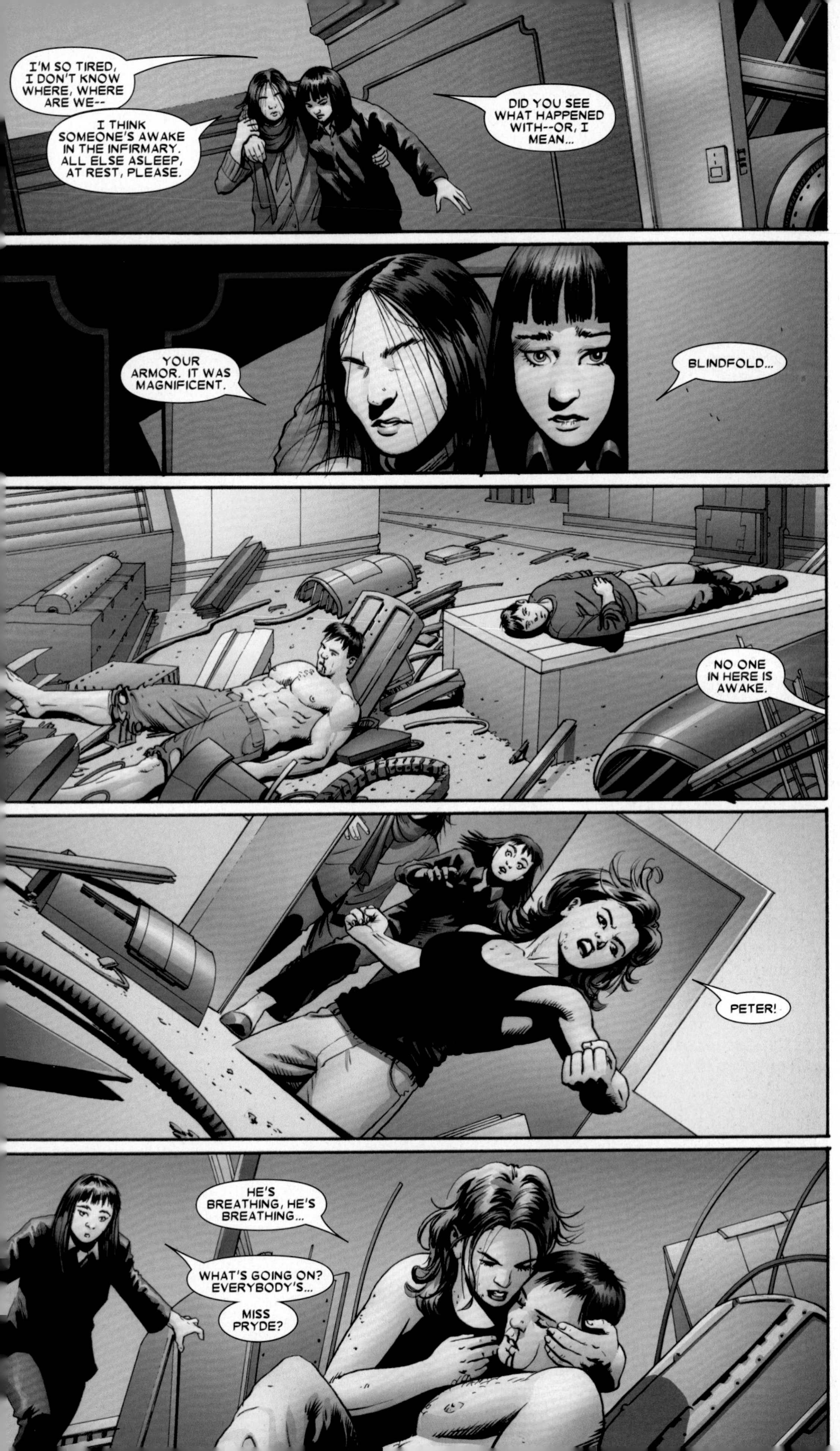
I'M SO TIRED, I DON'T KNOW WHERE, WHERE ARE WE--
I THINK SOMEONE'S AWAKE IN THE INFIRMARY. ALL ELSE ASLEEP, AT REST, PLEASE.
DID YOU SEE WHAT HAPPENED WITH--OR, I MEAN...
YOUR ARMOR. IT WAS MAGNIFICENT.
BLINDFOLD...
NO ONE IN HERE IS AWAKE.
PETER!
HE'S BREATHING, HE'S BREATHING...
WHAT'S GOING ON? EVERYBODY'S...
MISS PRYDE?

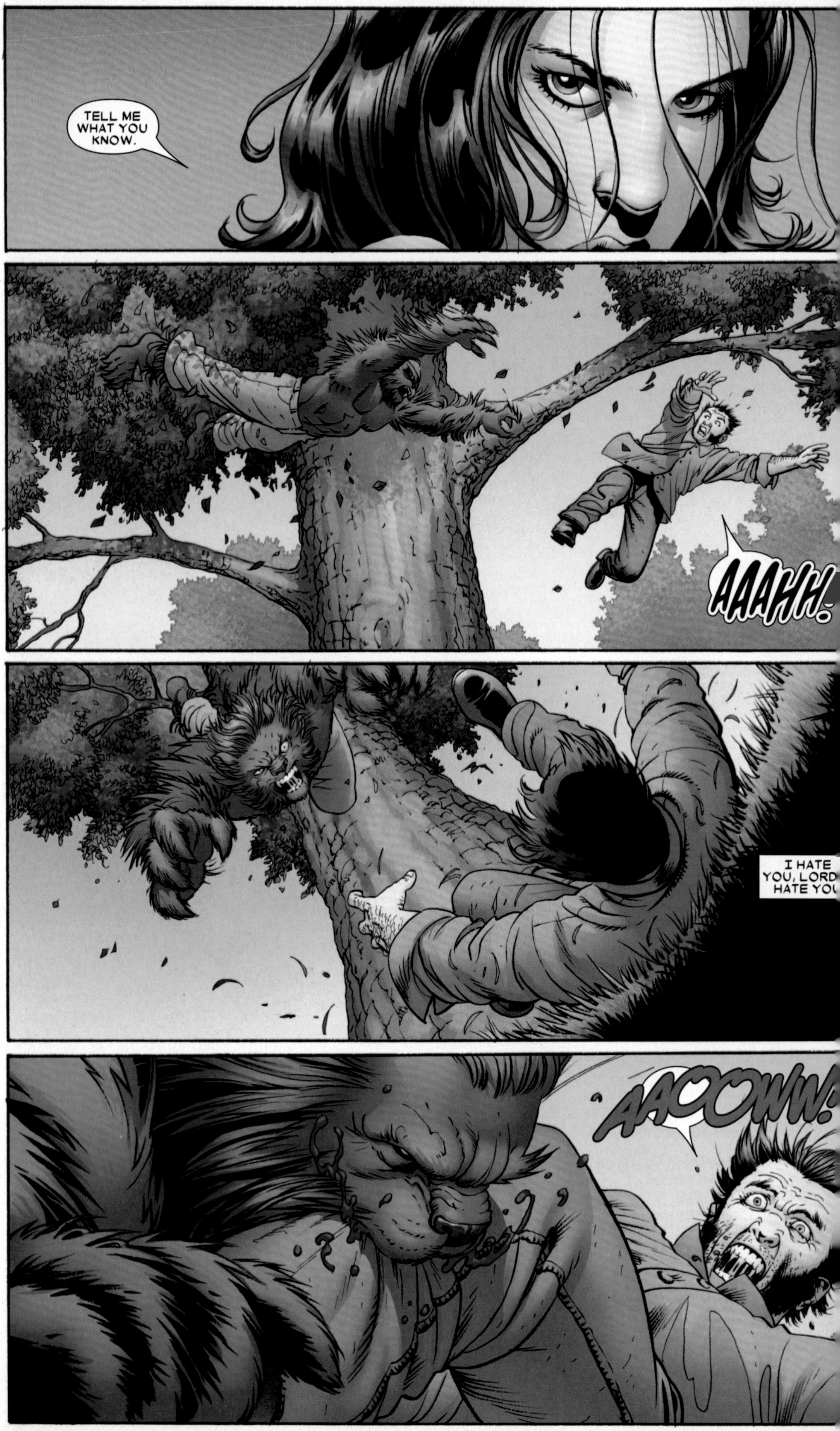
TELL ME WHAT YOU KNOW.
AAAHH!
I HATE YOU, LORD HATE YOU
AACOWW!

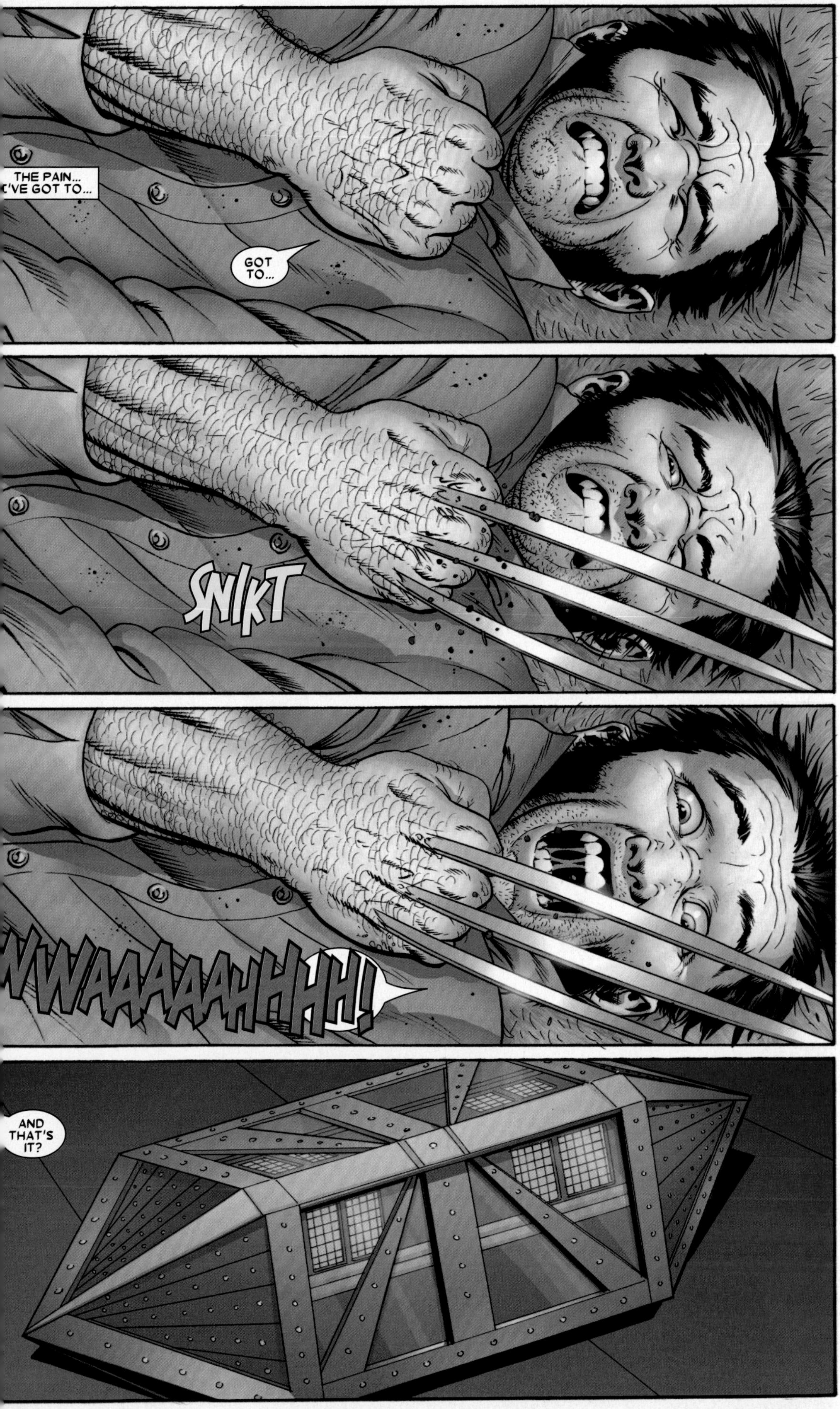

THE PAIN...
I'VE GOT TO...
GOT TO...
SNIKT
NWAAAAAAHHHH!
AND THAT'S IT?

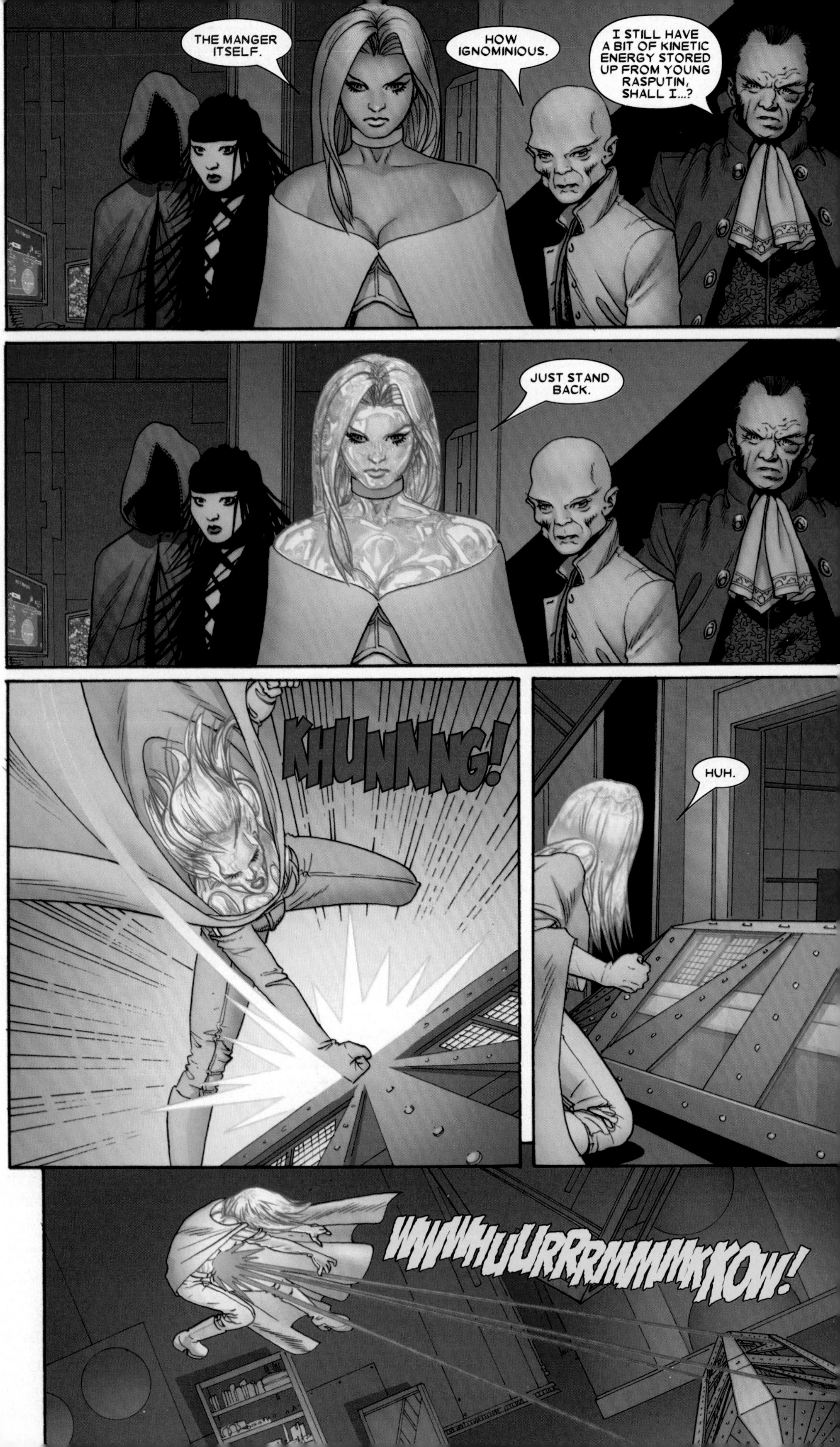
THE MANGER ITSELF.
HOW IGNOMINIOUS.
I STILL HAVE A BIT OF KINETIC ENERGY STORED UP FROM YOUNG RASPUTIN, SHALL I...?
JUST STAND BACK.
KHUNNNG!
HUH.
WWWHUURRRMMMKKOW!

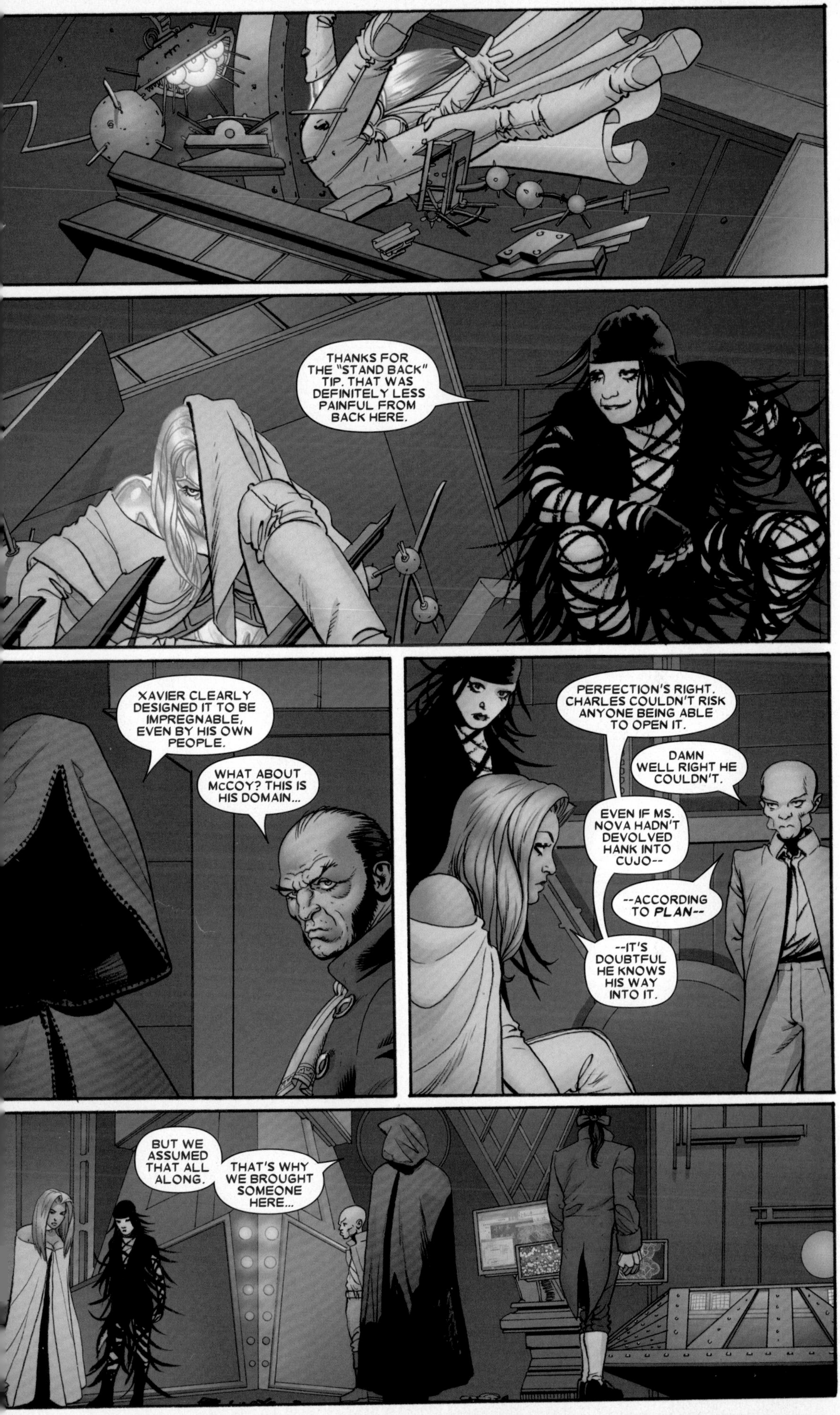
THANKS FOR THE "STAND BACK" TIP. THAT WAS DEFINITELY LESS PAINFUL FROM BACK HERE.
XAVIER CLEARLY DESIGNED IT TO BE IMPREGNABLE, EVEN BY HIS OWN PEOPLE.
WHAT ABOUT McCOY? THIS IS HIS DOMAIN...
PERFECTION'S RIGHT. CHARLES COULDN'T RISK ANYONE BEING ABLE TO OPEN IT.
DAMN WELL RIGHT HE COULDN'T.
EVEN IF MS. NOVA HADN'T DEVOLVED HANK INTO CUJO--
--ACCORDING TO PLAN--
--IT'S DOUBTFUL HE KNOWS HIS WAY INTO IT.
BUT WE ASSUMED THAT ALL ALONG.
THAT'S WHY WE BROUGHT SOMEONE HERE...

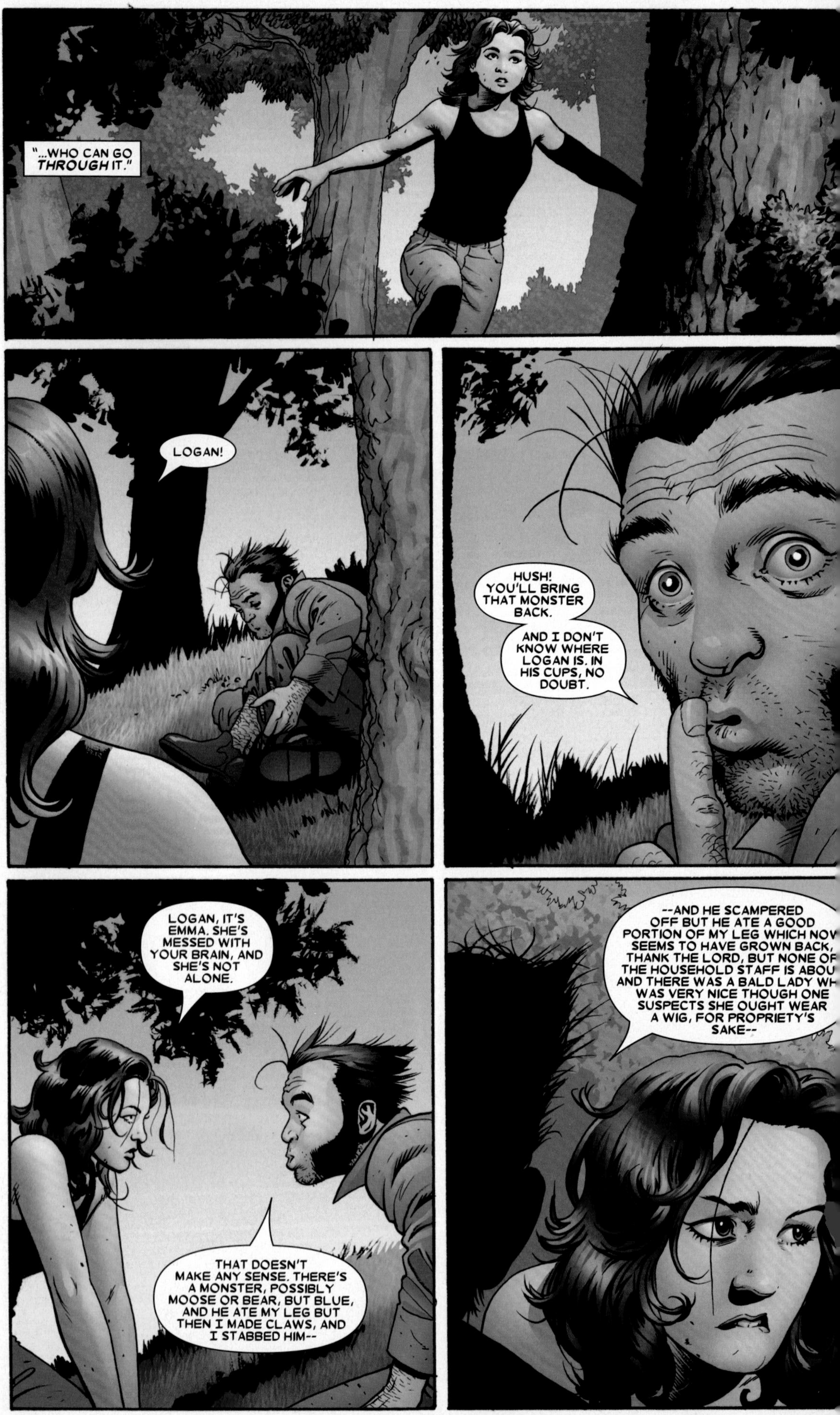
"...WHO CAN GO *THROUGH* IT."
LOGAN!
HUSH! YOU'LL BRING THAT MONSTER BACK.
AND I DON'T KNOW WHERE LOGAN IS. IN HIS CUPS, NO DOUBT.
LOGAN, IT'S EMMA. SHE'S MESSED WITH YOUR BRAIN, AND SHE'S NOT ALONE.
THAT DOESN'T MAKE ANY SENSE. THERE'S A MONSTER, POSSIBLY MOOSE OR BEAR, BUT BLUE, AND HE ATE MY LEG BUT THEN I MADE CLAWS, AND I STABBED HIM--
--AND HE SCAMPERED OFF BUT HE ATE A GOOD PORTION OF MY LEG WHICH NOW SEEMS TO HAVE GROWN BACK, THANK THE LORD, BUT NONE OF THE HOUSEHOLD STAFF IS ABOU AND THERE WAS A BALD LADY WH WAS VERY NICE THOUGH ONE SUSPECTS SHE OUGHT WEAR A WIG, FOR PROPRIETY'S SAKE--

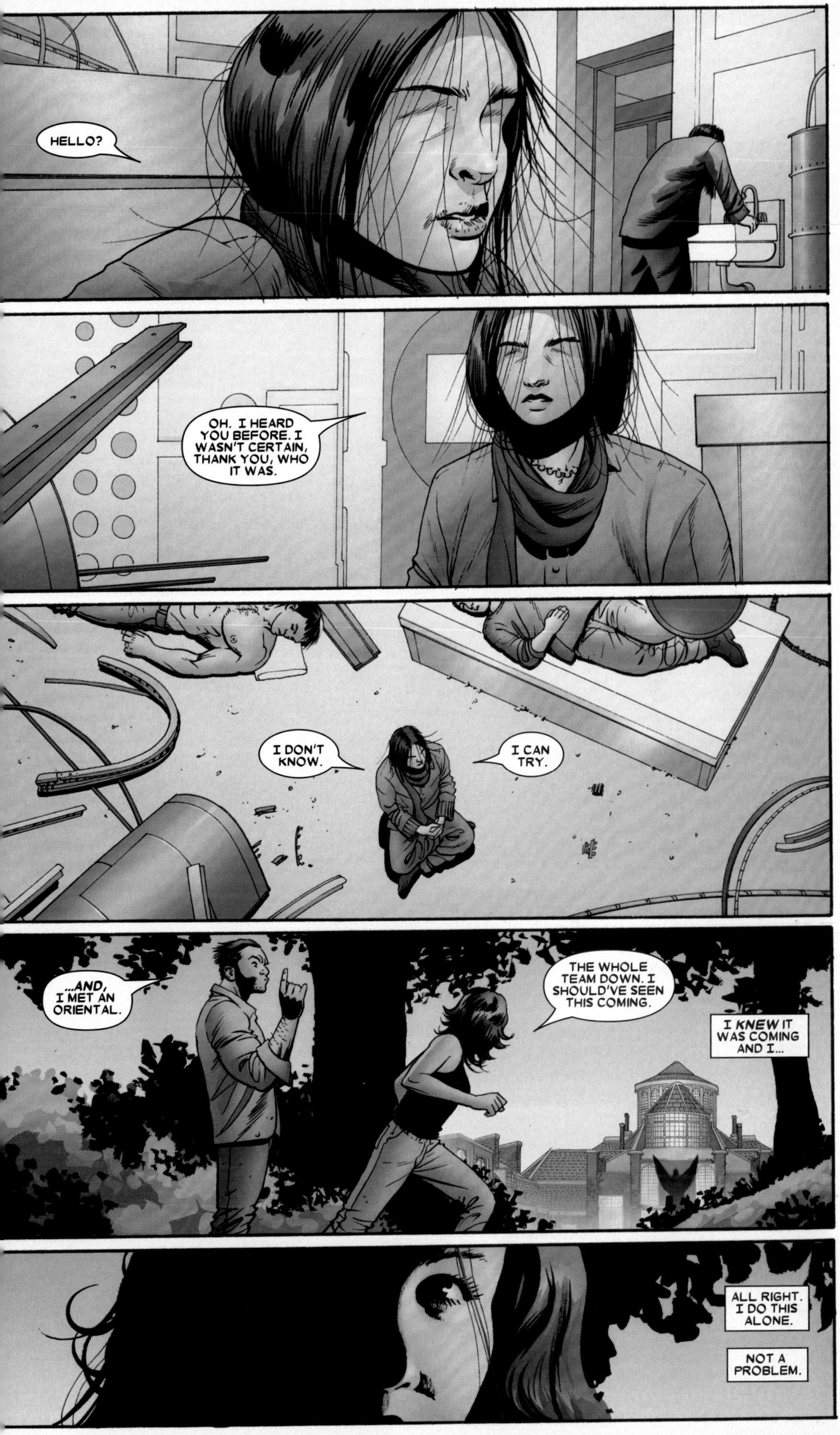
HELLO?
OH. I HEARD YOU BEFORE. I WASN'T CERTAIN, THANK YOU, WHO IT WAS.
I DON'T KNOW.
I CAN TRY.
...AND, I MET AN ORIENTAL.
THE WHOLE TEAM DOWN. I SHOULD'VE SEEN THIS COMING.
I *KNEW* IT WAS COMING AND I...
ALL RIGHT. I DO THIS ALONE.
NOT A PROBLEM.

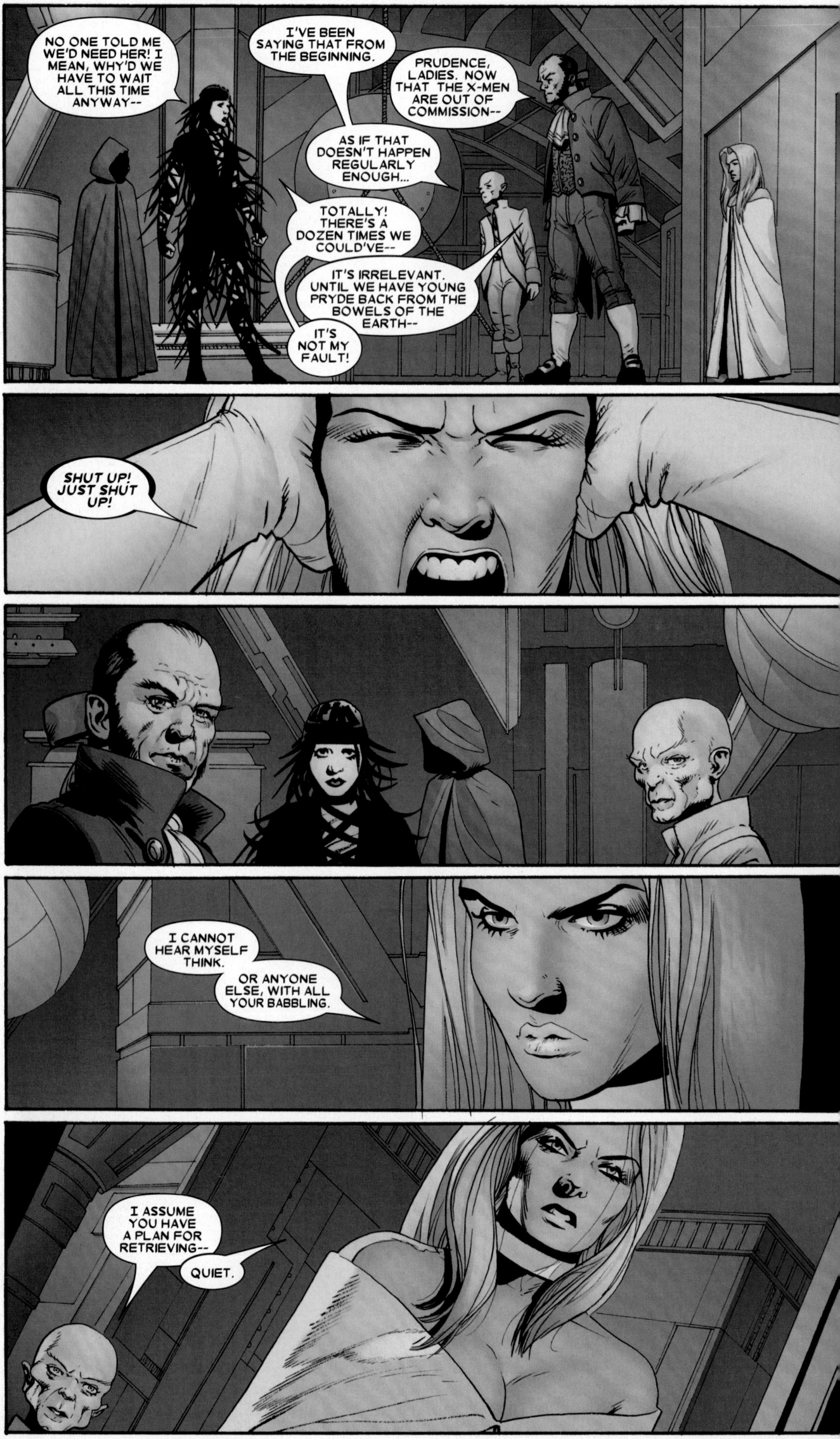
NO ONE TOLD ME WE'D NEED HER! I MEAN, WHY'D WE HAVE TO WAIT ALL THIS TIME ANYWAY--
I'VE BEEN SAYING THAT FROM THE BEGINNING.
PRUDENCE, LADIES. NOW THAT THE X-MEN ARE OUT OF COMMISSION--
AS IF THAT DOESN'T HAPPEN REGULARLY ENOUGH...
TOTALLY! THERE'S A DOZEN TIMES WE COULD'VE--
IT'S IRRELEVANT. UNTIL WE HAVE YOUNG PRYDE BACK FROM THE BOWELS OF THE EARTH--
IT'S NOT MY FAULT!
SHUT UP! JUST SHUT UP!
I CANNOT HEAR MYSELF THINK.
OR ANYONE ELSE, WITH ALL YOUR BABBLING.
I ASSUME YOU HAVE A PLAN FOR RETRIEVING--
QUIET.

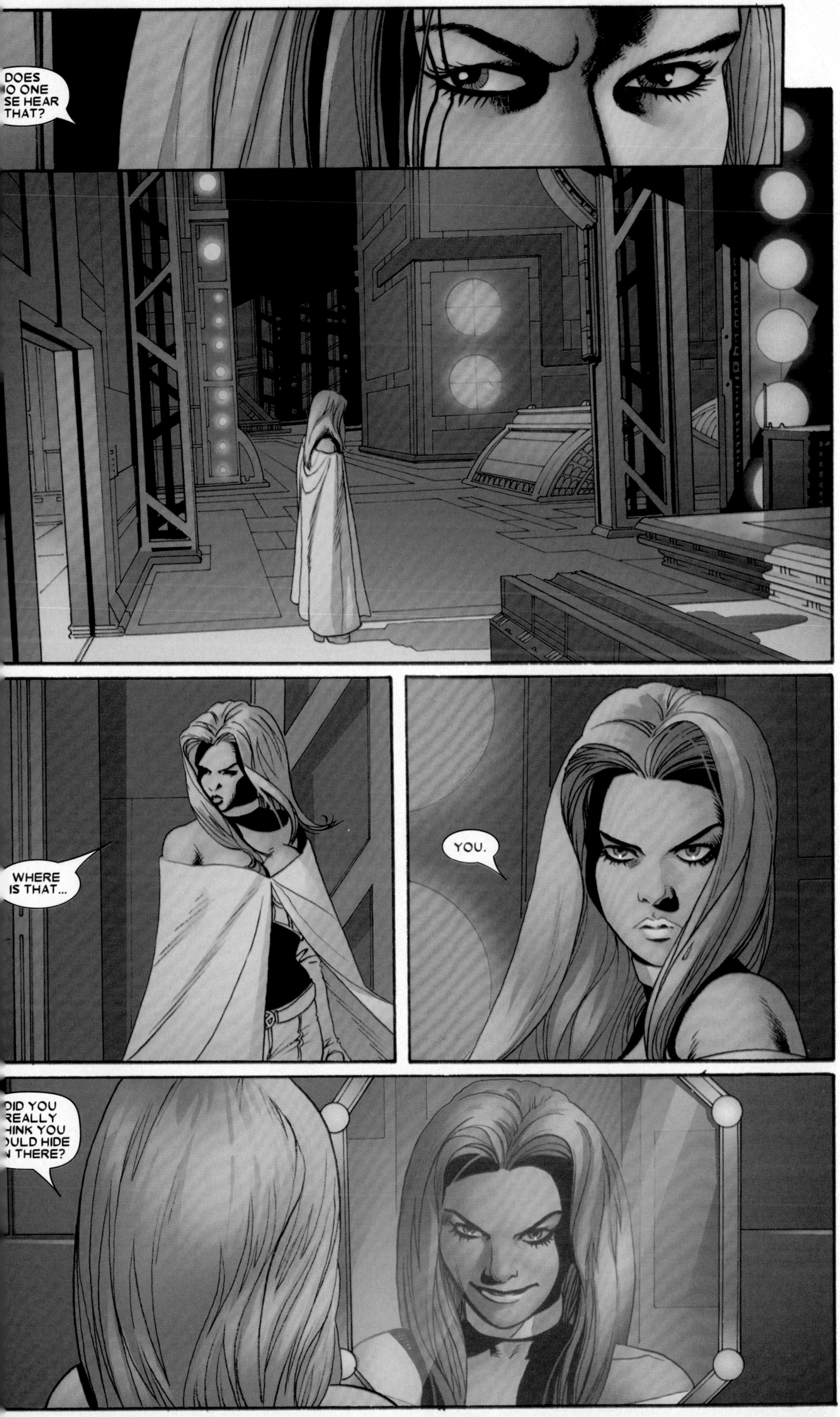

DOES
O ONE
SE HEAR
THAT?
WHERE
IS THAT...
YOU.
DID YOU
REALLY
HINK YOU
OULD HIDE
N THERE?

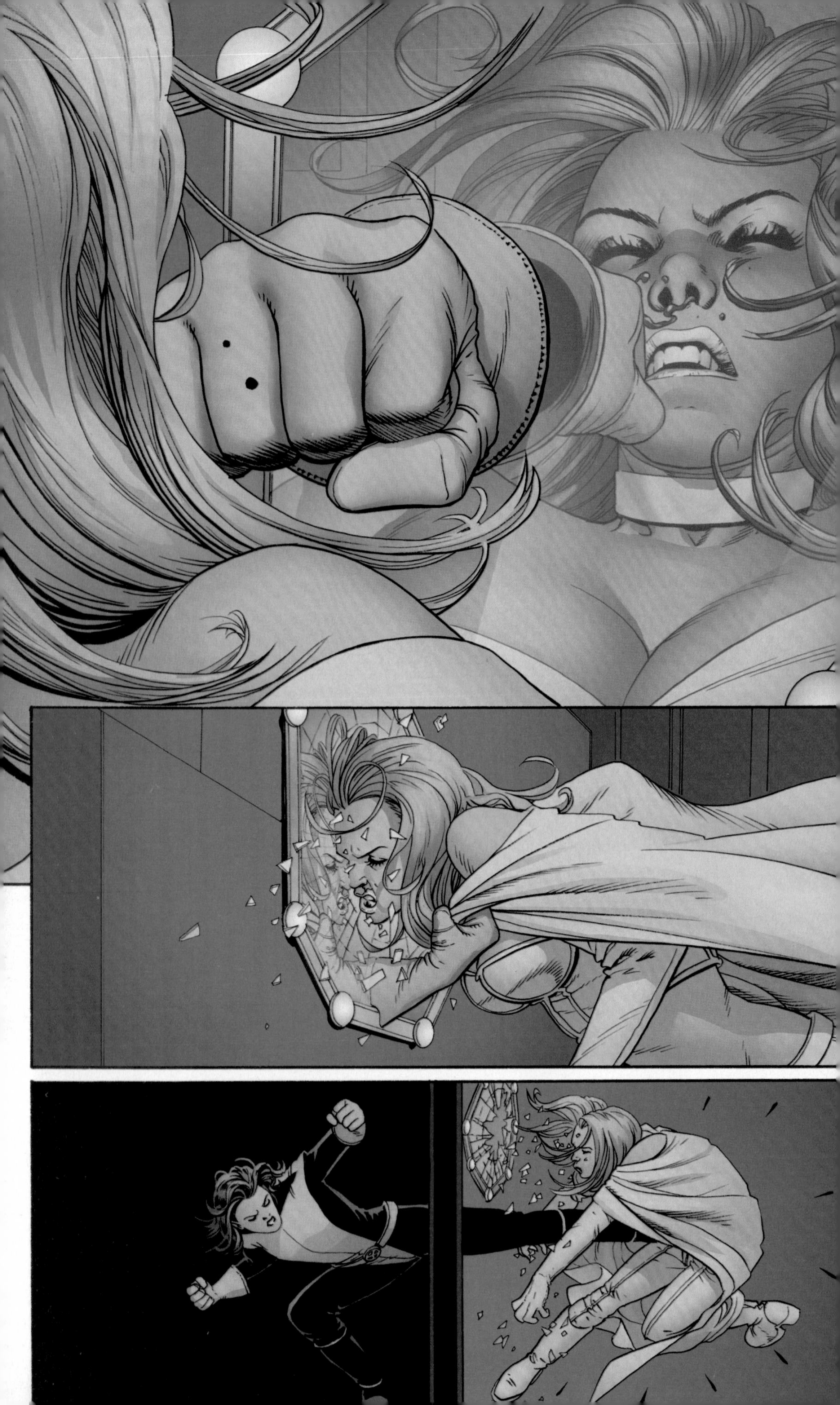

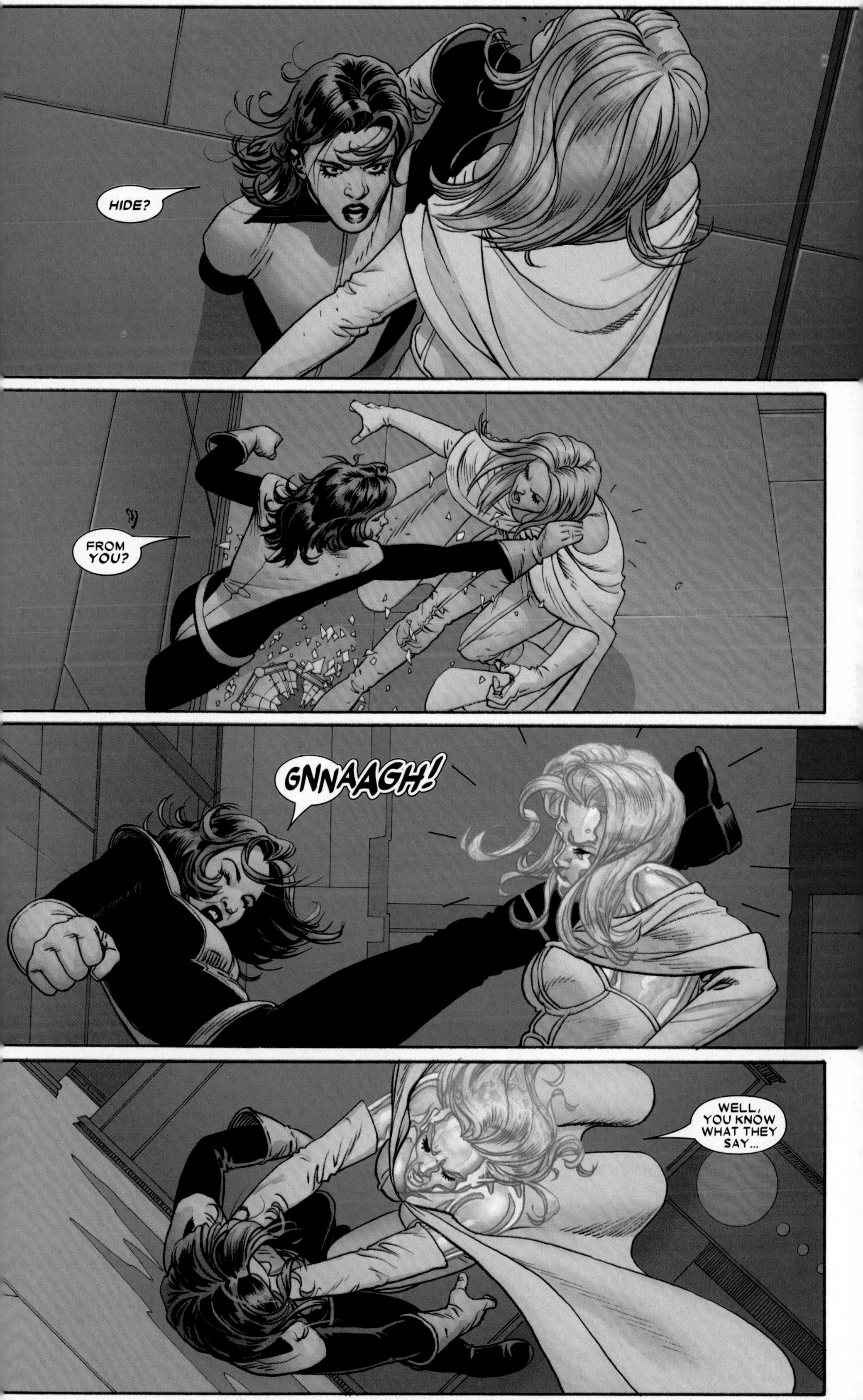
HIDE?
FROM YOU?
GNNAAGH!
WELL, YOU KNOW WHAT THEY SAY...

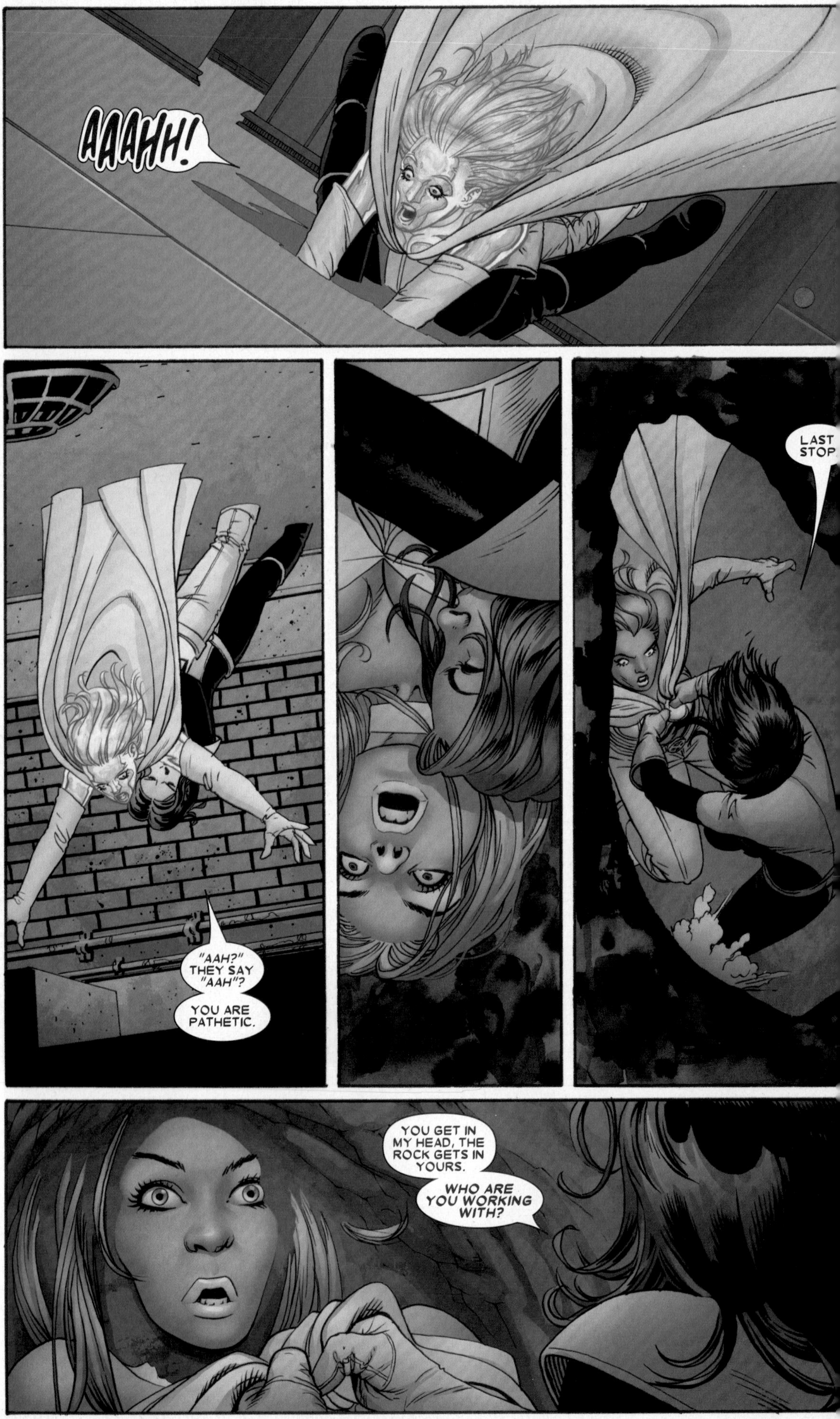
AAAHH!
"AAH?" THEY SAY "AAH"?
YOU ARE PATHETIC.
LAST STOP
YOU GET IN MY HEAD, THE ROCK GETS IN YOURS.
WHO ARE YOU WORKING WITH?

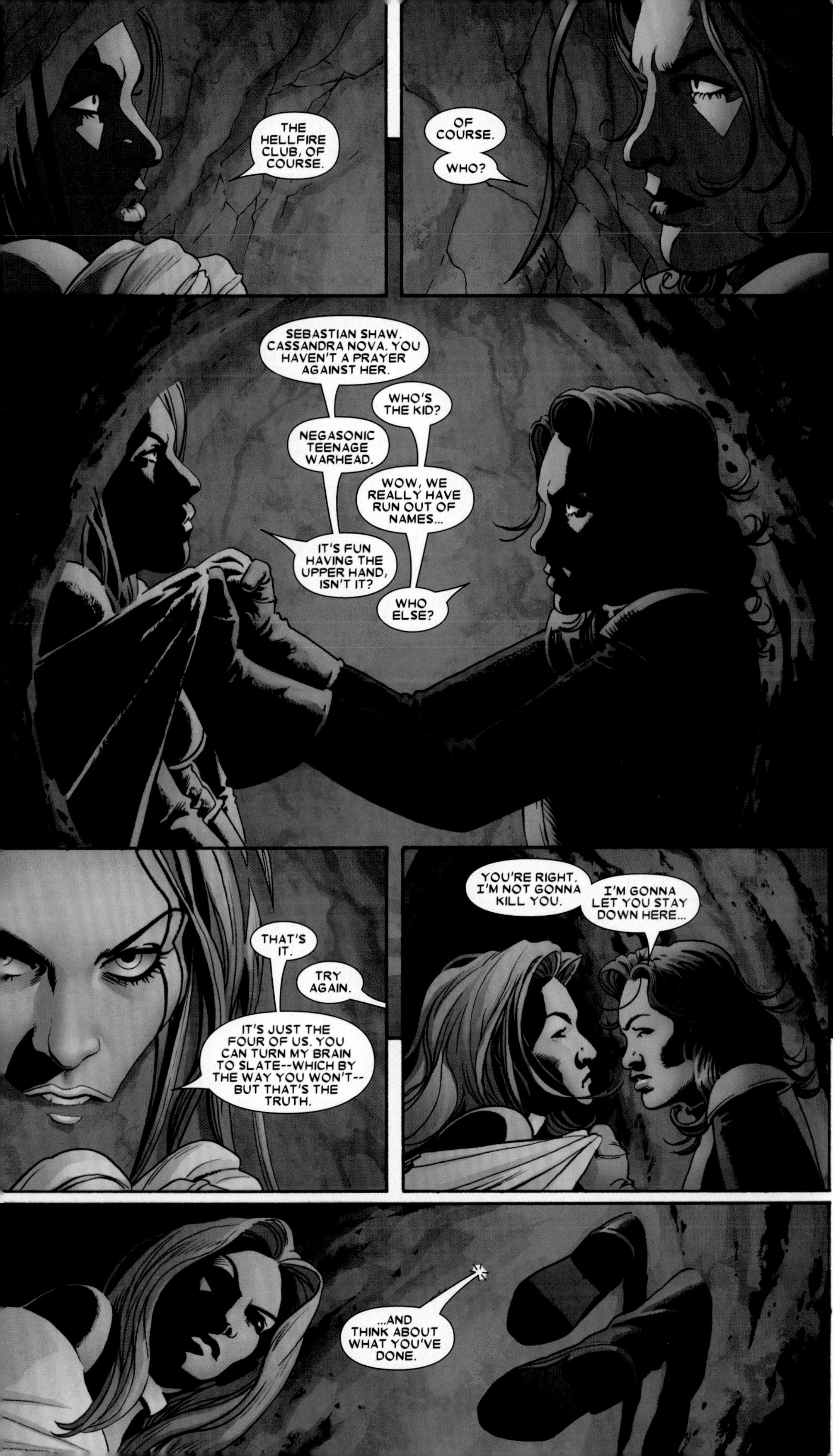
THE HELLFIRE CLUB, OF COURSE.
OF COURSE.
WHO?
SEBASTIAN SHAW. CASSANDRA NOVA. YOU HAVEN'T A PRAYER AGAINST HER.
WHO'S THE KID?
NEGASONIC TEENAGE WARHEAD.
WOW, WE REALLY HAVE RUN OUT OF NAMES...
IT'S FUN HAVING THE UPPER HAND, ISN'T IT?
WHO ELSE?
THAT'S IT.
TRY AGAIN.
IT'S JUST THE FOUR OF US. YOU CAN TURN MY BRAIN TO SLATE--WHICH BY THE WAY YOU WON'T--BUT THAT'S THE TRUTH.
YOU'RE RIGHT. I'M NOT GONNA KILL YOU.
I'M GONNA LET YOU STAY DOWN HERE...
...AND THINK ABOUT WHAT YOU'VE DONE.

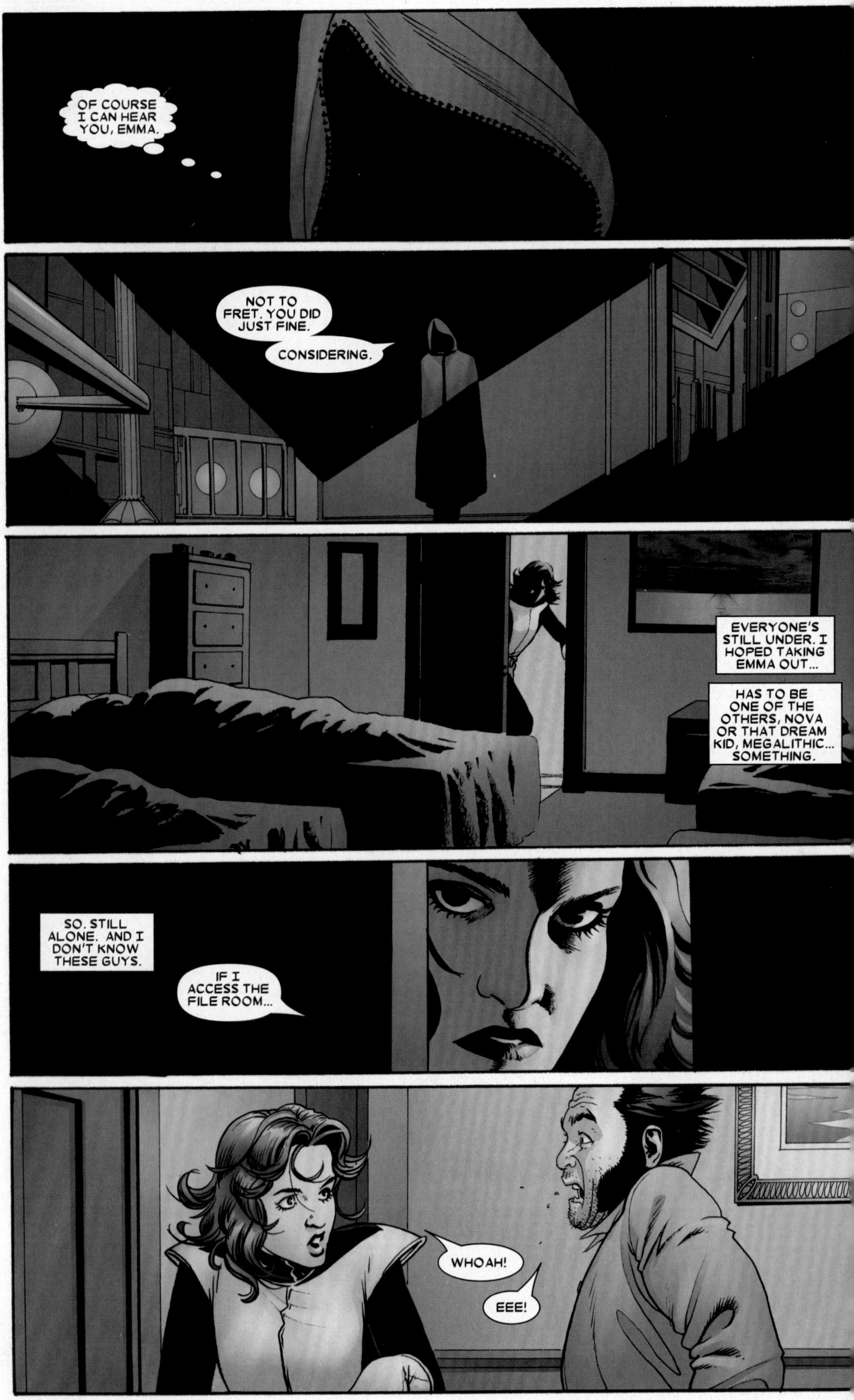

OF COURSE I CAN HEAR YOU, EMMA.
NOT TO FRET. YOU DID JUST FINE.
CONSIDERING.
EVERYONE'S STILL UNDER. I HOPED TAKING EMMA OUT...
HAS TO BE ONE OF THE OTHERS, NOVA OR THAT DREAM KID, MEGALITHIC... SOMETHING.
SO. STILL ALONE. AND I DON'T KNOW THESE GUYS.
IF I ACCESS THE FILE ROOM...
WHOAH!
EEE!

WHAT ARE YOU DOING HERE? I TOLD YOU TO HIDE.

WELL, I... YOU'RE A GIRL, AND IF THERE'S DANGER ABOUT, I...WELL IT ISN'T RIGHT FOR A HOWLETT TO HIDE BEHIND SOMEONE'S SKIRTS.

I SHAN'T PRIZE MY LIFE ABOVE MY HONOR. UNLESS YOU THINK THAT'S A GOOD IDEA.

AAAGH!

IT'S TIME, PRYDE.

AT LONG LAST, IT'S TIME TO MAKE YOURSELF USEFUL.

FORGET WHAT YOU'RE THINKING. EMMA FROST MAY HAVE BEEN EASY-- EMBARRASSINGLY EASY--TO TAKE OUT...

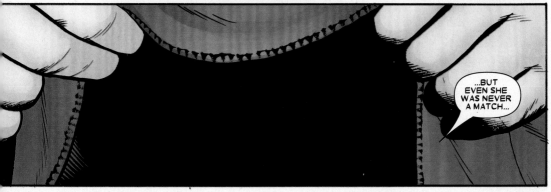

...BUT EVEN SHE WAS NEVER A MATCH...

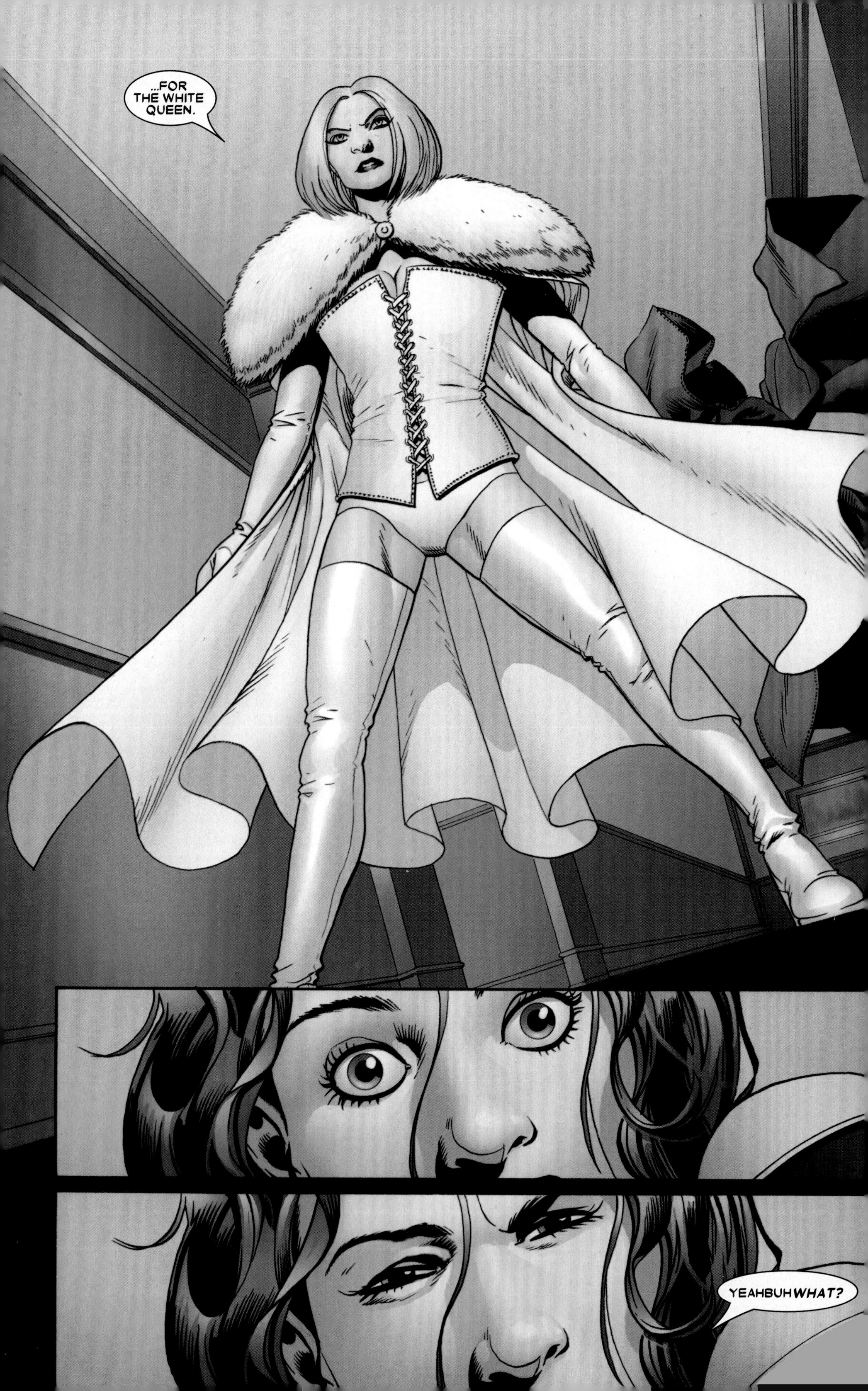
...FOR THE WHITE QUEEN.
YEAHBUH*WHAT?*

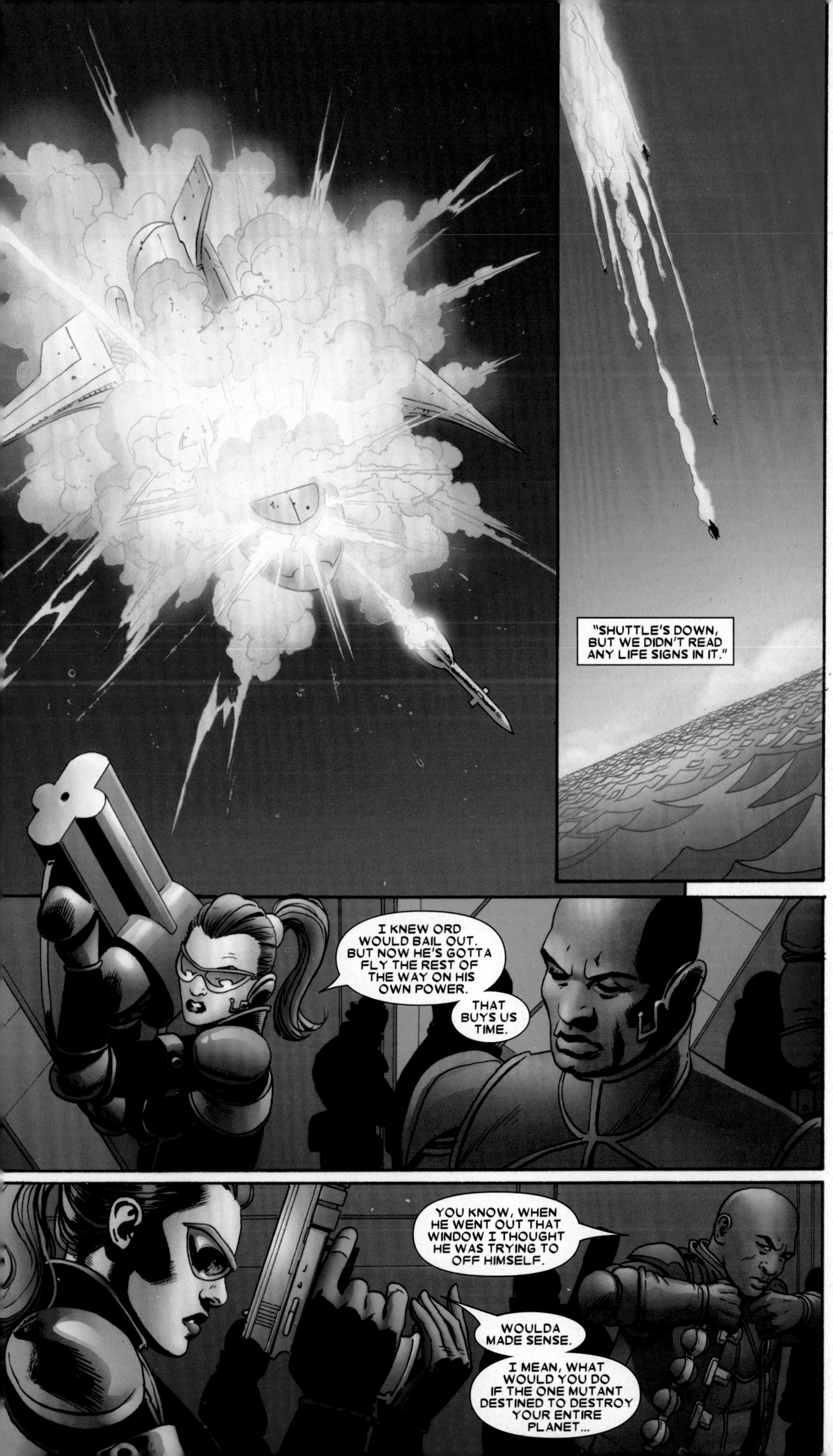
"SHUTTLE'S DOWN, BUT WE DIDN'T READ ANY LIFE SIGNS IN IT."
I KNEW ORD WOULD BAIL OUT. BUT NOW HE'S GOTTA FLY THE REST OF THE WAY ON HIS OWN POWER.
THAT BUYS US TIME.
YOU KNOW, WHEN HE WENT OUT THAT WINDOW I THOUGHT HE WAS TRYING TO OFF HIMSELF.
WOULDA MADE SENSE.
I MEAN, WHAT WOULD YOU DO IF THE ONE MUTANT DESTINED TO DESTROY YOUR ENTIRE PLANET...

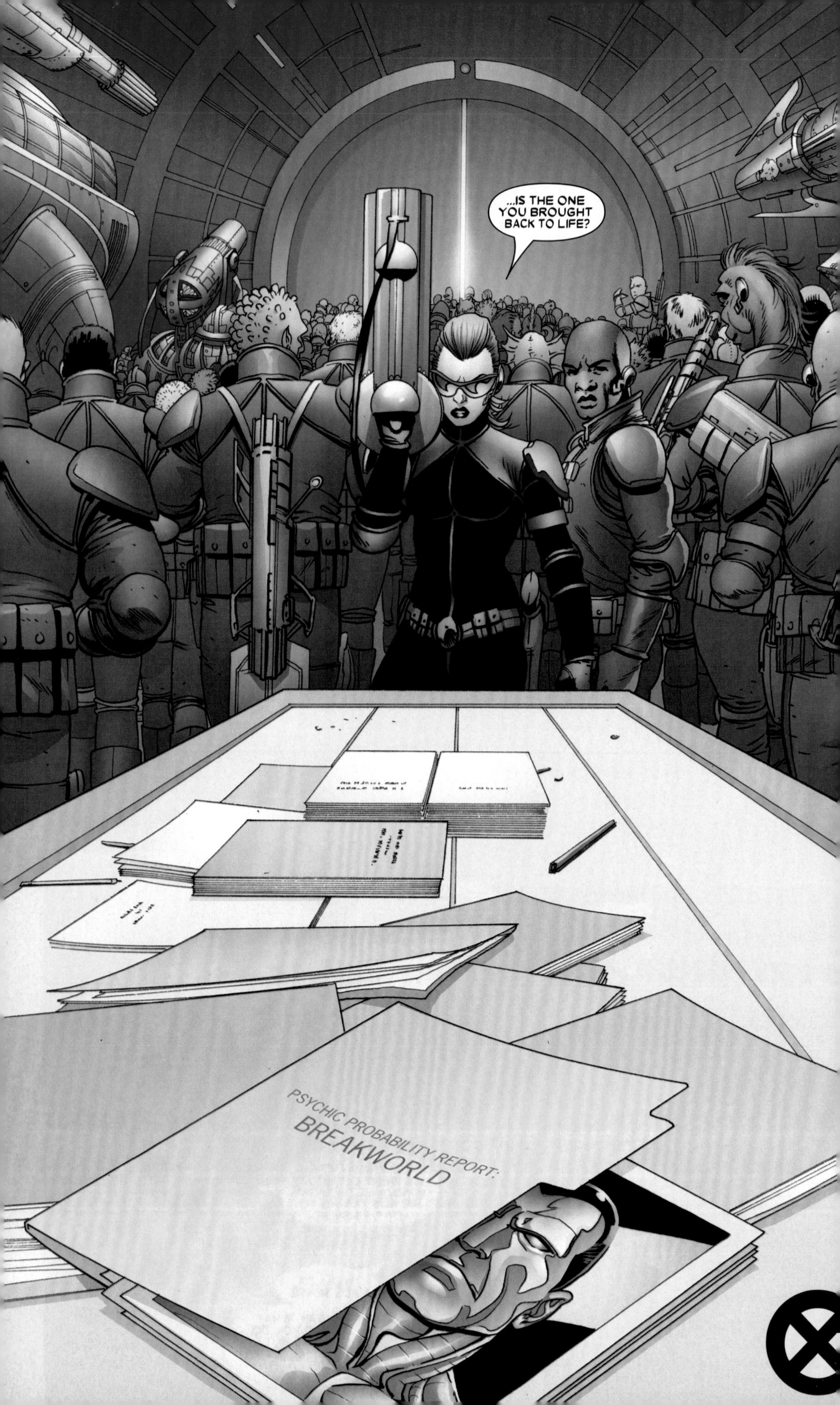
...IS THE ONE YOU BROUGHT BACK TO LIFE?
PSYCHIC PROBABILITY REPORT: BREAKWORLD

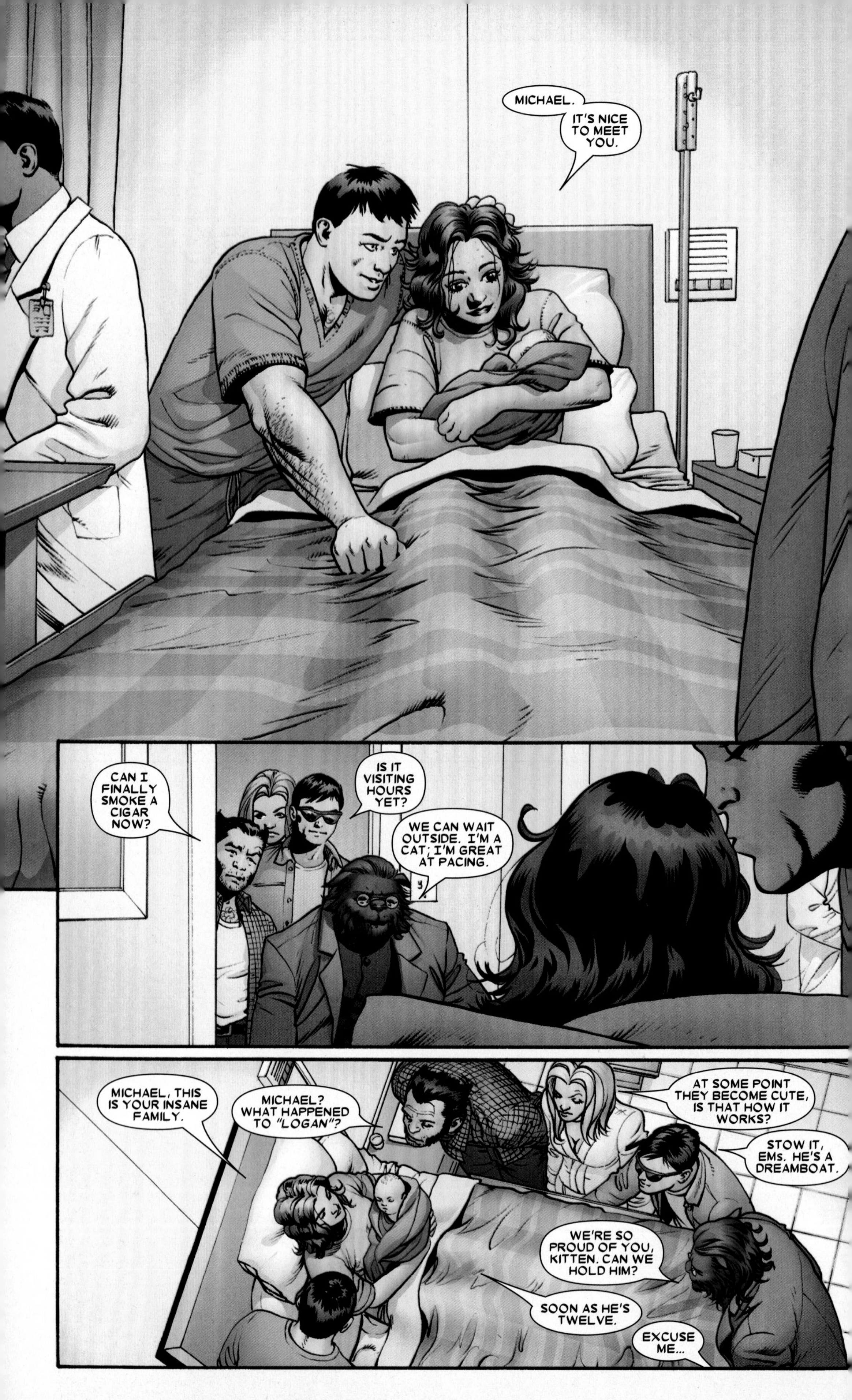
MICHAEL.
IT'S NICE TO MEET YOU.
CAN I FINALLY SMOKE A CIGAR NOW?
IS IT VISITING HOURS YET?
WE CAN WAIT OUTSIDE. I'M A CAT; I'M GREAT AT PACING.
MICHAEL, THIS IS YOUR INSANE FAMILY.
MICHAEL? WHAT HAPPENED TO "LOGAN"?
AT SOME POINT THEY BECOME CUTE, IS THAT HOW IT WORKS?
STOW IT, EMS. HE'S A DREAMBOAT.
WE'RE SO PROUD OF YOU, KITTEN. CAN WE HOLD HIM?
SOON AS HE'S TWELVE.
EXCUSE ME...

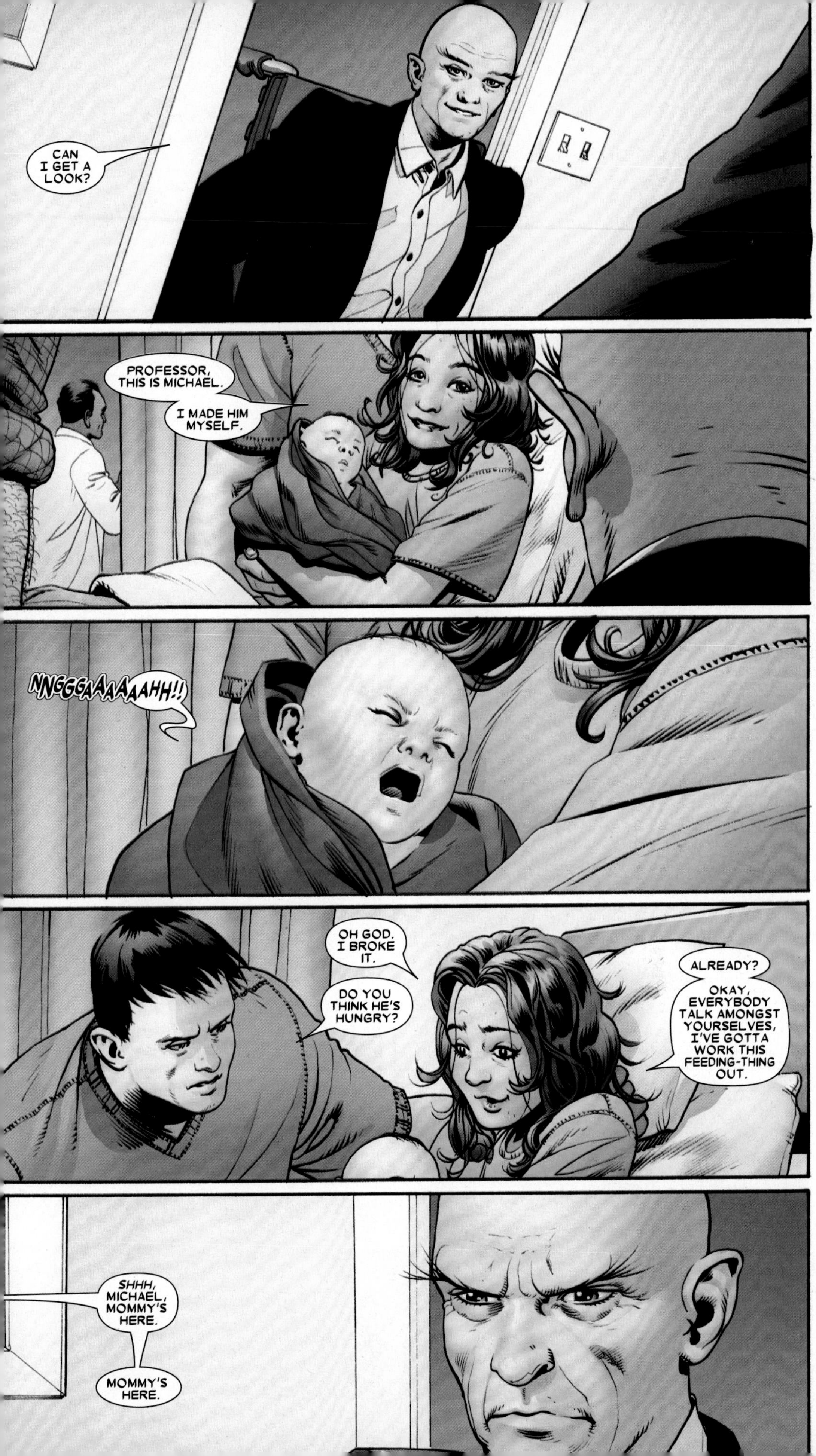
CAN I GET A LOOK?
PROFESSOR, THIS IS MICHAEL.
I MADE HIM MYSELF.
NNGGGAAAAAHH!!
OH GOD. I BROKE IT.
DO YOU THINK HE'S HUNGRY?
ALREADY?
OKAY, EVERYBODY TALK AMONGST YOURSELVES, I'VE GOTTA WORK THIS FEEDING-THING OUT.
SHHH, MICHAEL, MOMMY'S HERE.
MOMMY'S HERE.

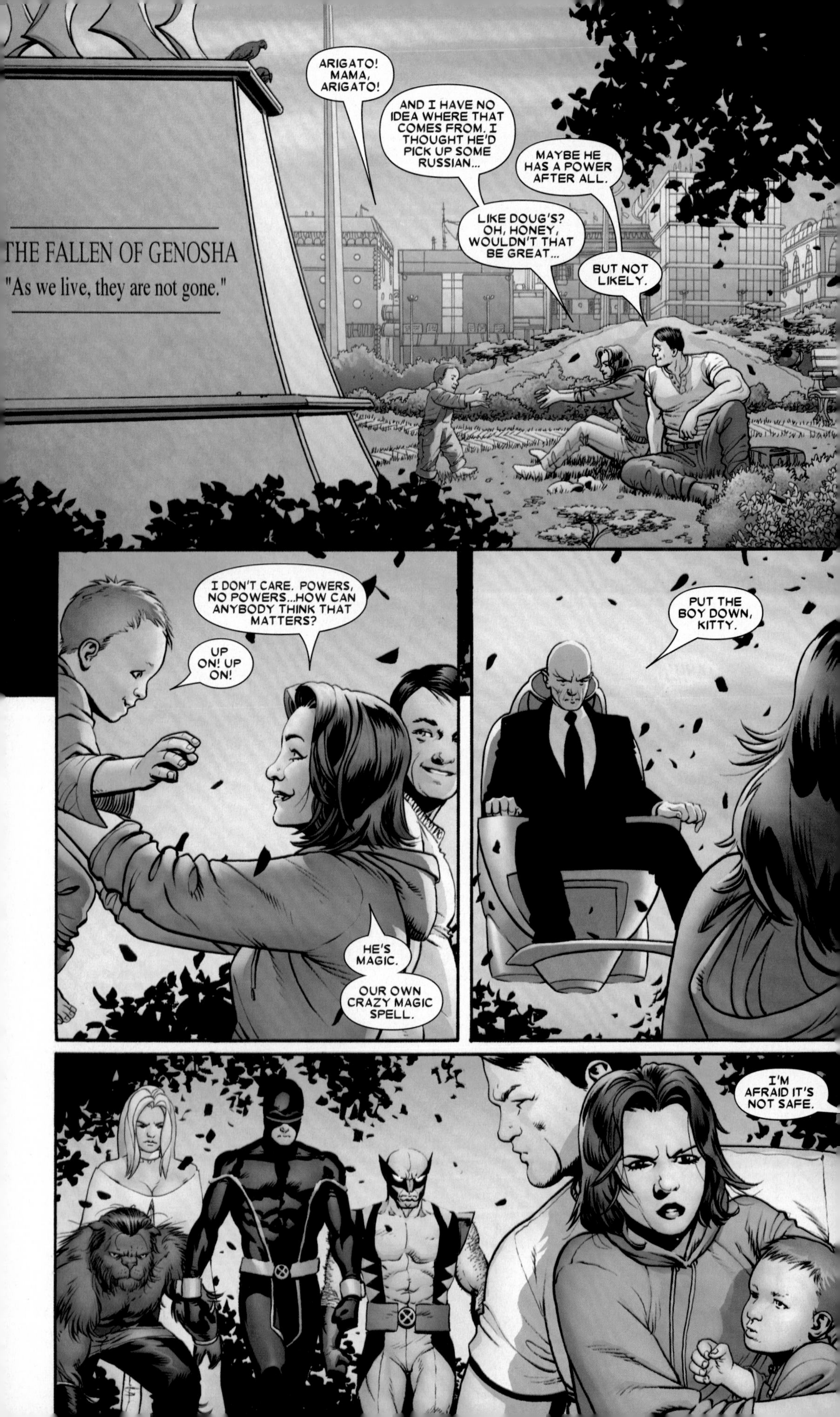
THE FALLEN OF GENOSHA
"As we live, they are not gone."
ARIGATO! MAMA, ARIGATO!
AND I HAVE NO IDEA WHERE THAT COMES FROM. I THOUGHT HE'D PICK UP SOME RUSSIAN...
MAYBE HE HAS A POWER AFTER ALL.
LIKE DOUG'S? OH, HONEY, WOULDN'T THAT BE GREAT...
BUT NOT LIKELY.
I DON'T CARE. POWERS, NO POWERS...HOW CAN ANYBODY THINK THAT MATTERS?
UP ON! UP ON!
HE'S MAGIC.
OUR OWN CRAZY MAGIC SPELL.
PUT THE BOY DOWN, KITTY.
I'M AFRAID IT'S NOT SAFE.

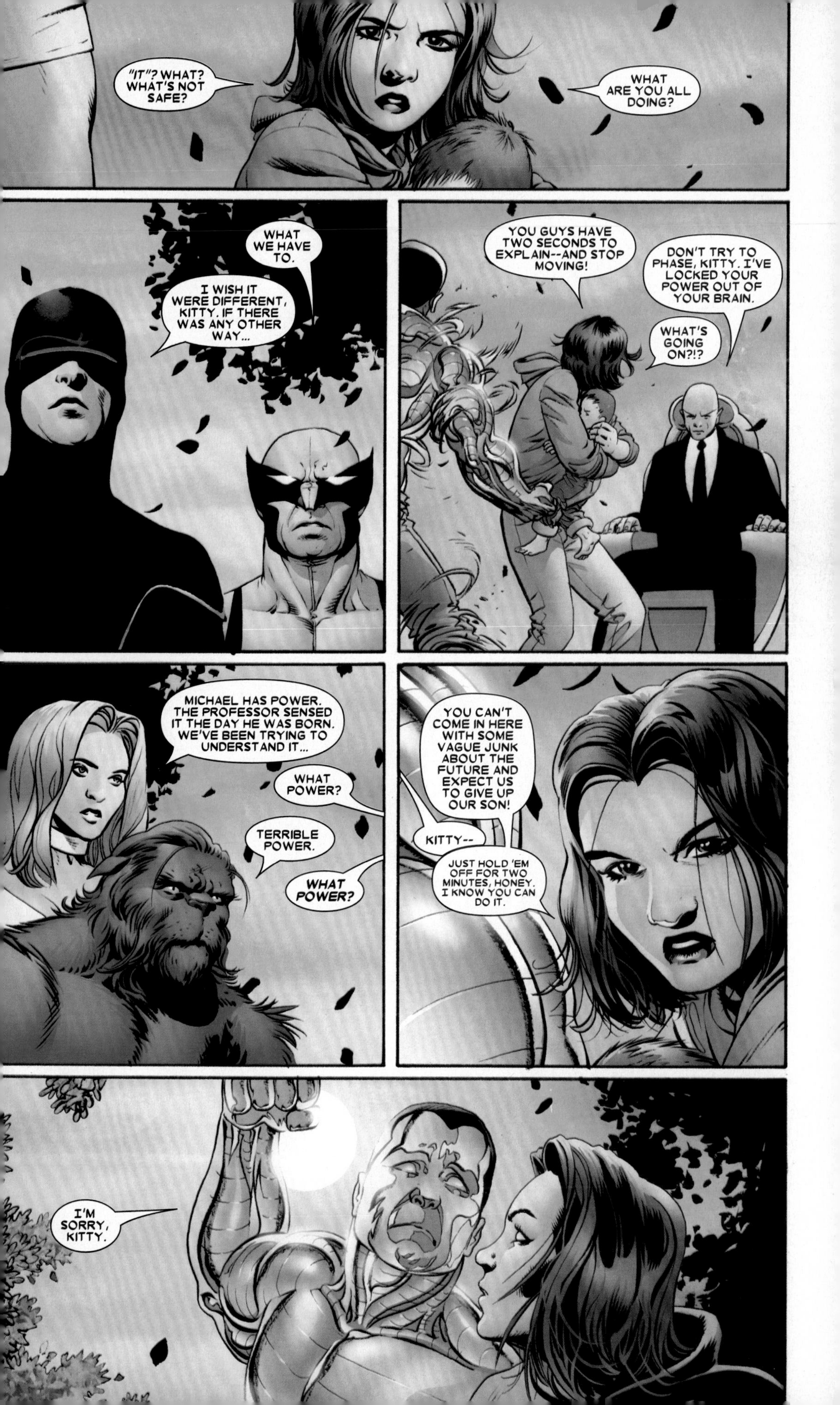
"IT"? WHAT? WHAT'S NOT SAFE?
WHAT ARE YOU ALL DOING?
WHAT WE HAVE TO.
I WISH IT WERE DIFFERENT, KITTY. IF THERE WAS ANY OTHER WAY...
YOU GUYS HAVE TWO SECONDS TO EXPLAIN--AND STOP MOVING!
DON'T TRY TO PHASE, KITTY. I'VE LOCKED YOUR POWER OUT OF YOUR BRAIN.
WHAT'S GOING ON?!?
MICHAEL HAS POWER. THE PROFESSOR SENSED IT THE DAY HE WAS BORN. WE'VE BEEN TRYING TO UNDERSTAND IT...
WHAT POWER?
TERRIBLE POWER.
WHAT POWER?
YOU CAN'T COME IN HERE WITH SOME VAGUE JUNK ABOUT THE FUTURE AND EXPECT US TO GIVE UP OUR SON!
KITTY--
JUST HOLD 'EM OFF FOR TWO MINUTES, HONEY. I KNOW YOU CAN DO IT.
I'M SORRY, KITTY.

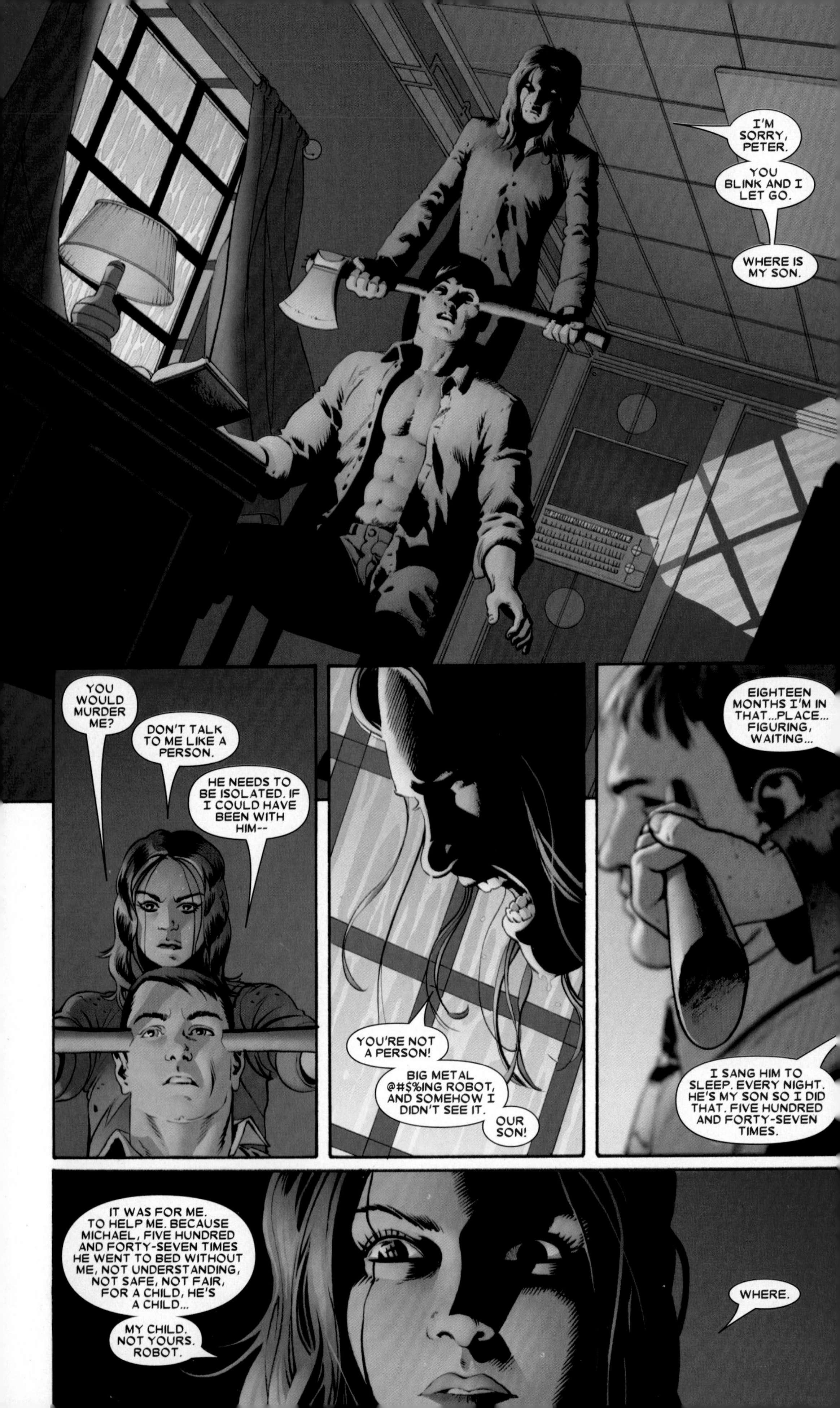

I'M SORRY, PETER.
YOU BLINK AND I LET GO.
WHERE IS MY SON.
YOU WOULD MURDER ME?
DON'T TALK TO ME LIKE A PERSON.
HE NEEDS TO BE ISOLATED. IF I COULD HAVE BEEN WITH HIM--
YOU'RE NOT A PERSON!
BIG METAL @#$%ING ROBOT, AND SOMEHOW I DIDN'T SEE IT.
OUR SON!
EIGHTEEN MONTHS I'M IN THAT...PLACE... FIGURING, WAITING...
I SANG HIM TO SLEEP. EVERY NIGHT. HE'S MY SON SO I DID THAT. FIVE HUNDRED AND FORTY-SEVEN TIMES.
IT WAS FOR ME. TO HELP ME. BECAUSE MICHAEL, FIVE HUNDRED AND FORTY-SEVEN TIMES HE WENT TO BED WITHOUT ME, NOT UNDERSTANDING, NOT SAFE, NOT FAIR, FOR A CHILD, HE'S A CHILD...
MY CHILD. NOT YOURS. ROBOT.
WHERE.

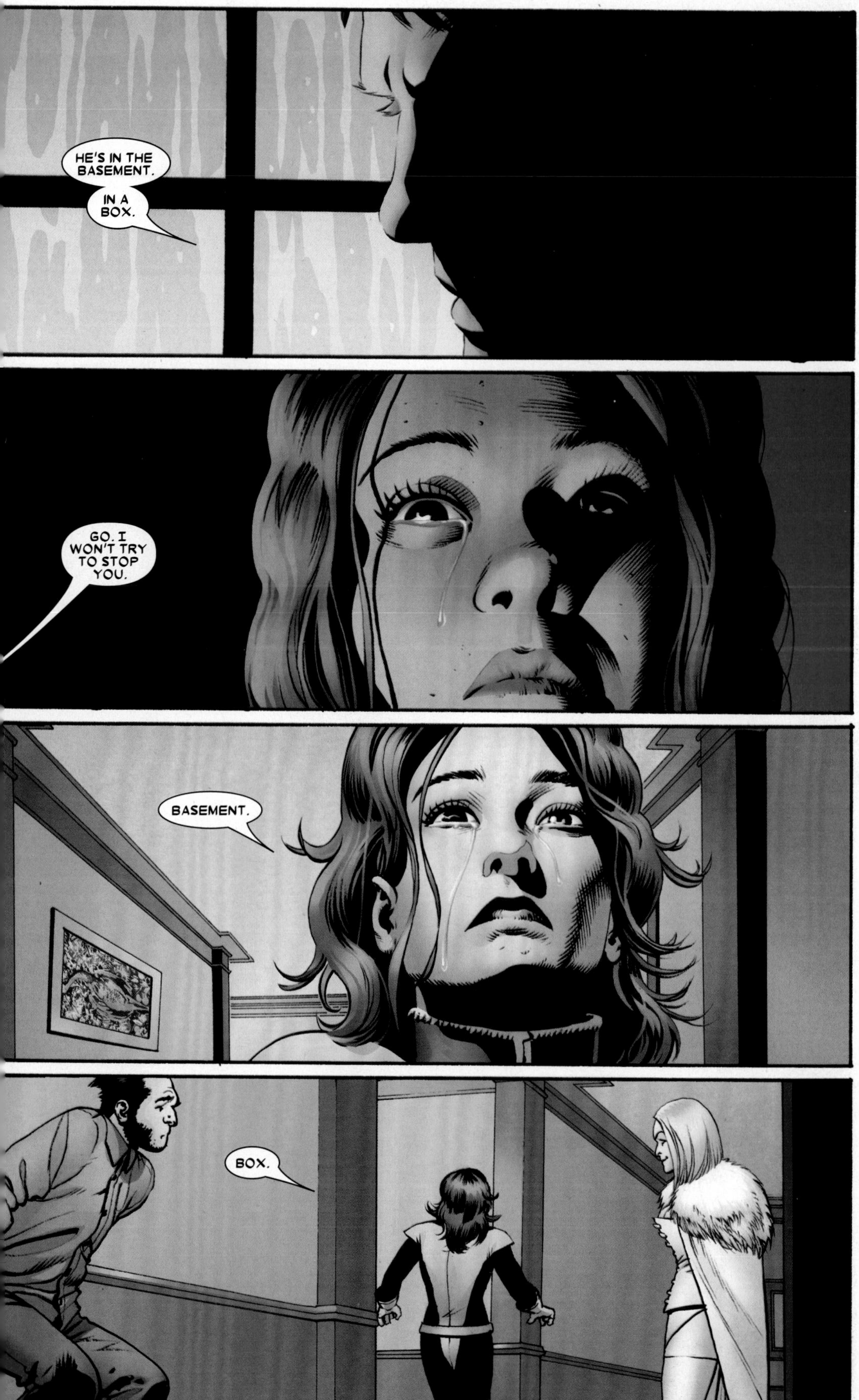
HE'S IN THE BASEMENT.
IN A BOX.
GO. I WON'T TRY TO STOP YOU.
BASEMENT.
BOX.

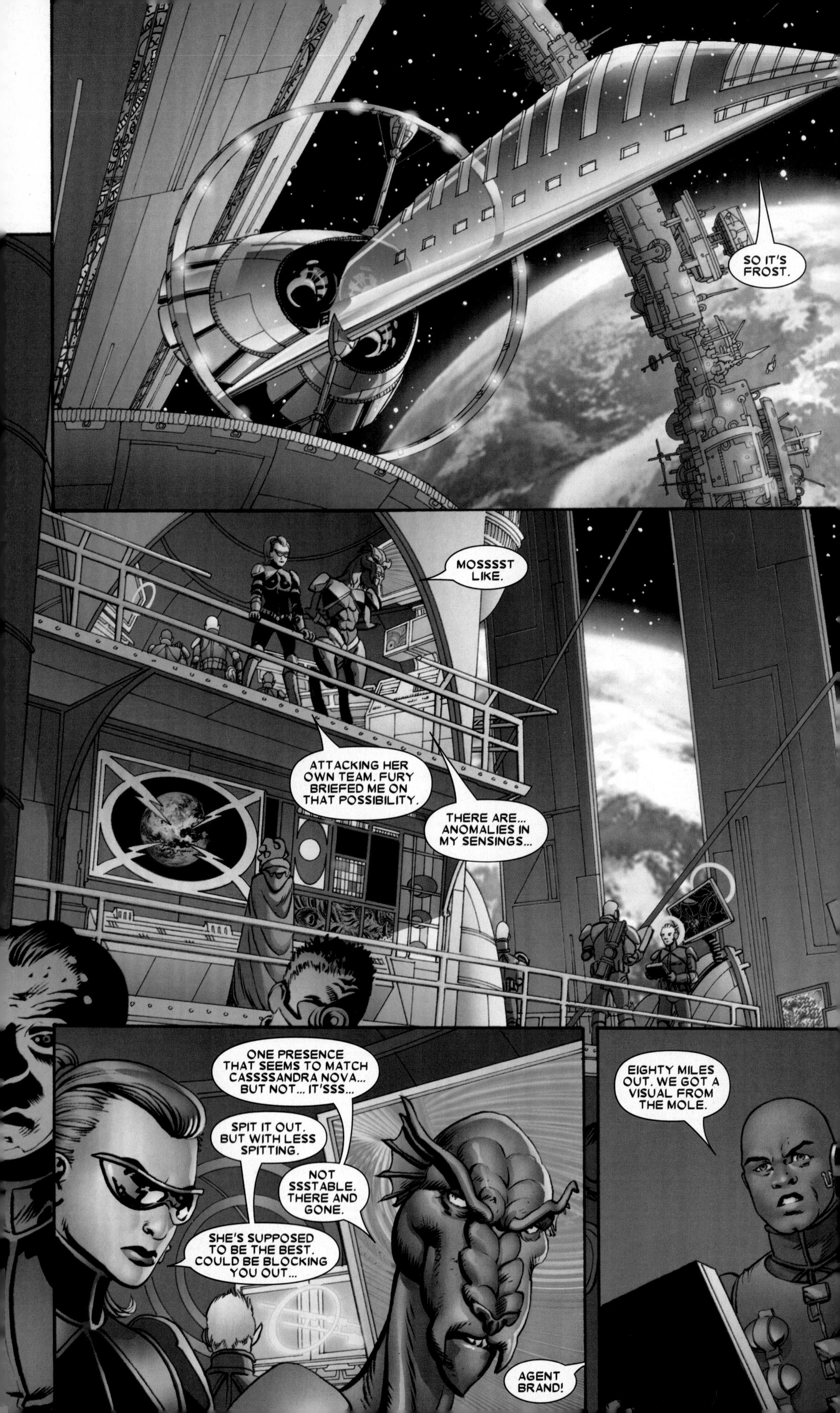
SO IT'S FROST.
MOSSSST LIKE.
ATTACKING HER OWN TEAM. FURY BRIEFED ME ON THAT POSSIBILITY.
THERE ARE... ANOMALIES IN MY SENSINGS...
ONE PRESENCE THAT SEEMS TO MATCH CASSSSANDRA NOVA... BUT NOT... IT'SSS...
SPIT IT OUT. BUT WITH LESS SPITTING.
NOT SSSTABLE. THERE AND GONE.
SHE'S SUPPOSED TO BE THE BEST. COULD BE BLOCKING YOU OUT...
AGENT BRAND!
EIGHTY MILES OUT. WE GOT A VISUAL FROM THE MOLE.

SO. WHO'S THE TINKER-TOY?

"DANGER." SHE'S A.I., SHI'AR TECH.

@#$%ING SHI'AR... WISH SOMEONE WOULD PROPHESY THE END OF *THOSE* CLOWNS...

WE THINK SHE'S RESPONSIBLE FOR THAT LAST ASS-WHUPPING THIS X-TEAM TOOK. THE WILD SENTINEL INCIDENT...

SO ORD HAS AN ALLY WHO'S NOT A MORON.

AND CAN CONTROL ALL OUR SYSTEMS. THAT'S HOW HE ESCAPED.

RIGHT. PUT ALL THE TECHS ON STASIS ALERT AND RUN A BLOCK ON ANY NETWORK INTRUSIONS THAT SMELL REMOTELY SHI'AR. I DON'T WANNA FALL OUT OF THE AIR.

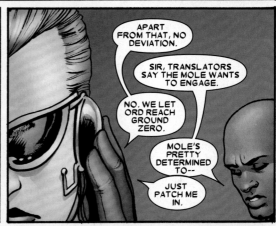

APART FROM THAT, NO DEVIATION.

SIR, TRANSLATORS SAY THE MOLE WANTS TO ENGAGE.

NO. WE LET ORD REACH GROUND ZERO.

MOLE'S PRETTY DETERMINED TO--

JUST PATCH ME IN.

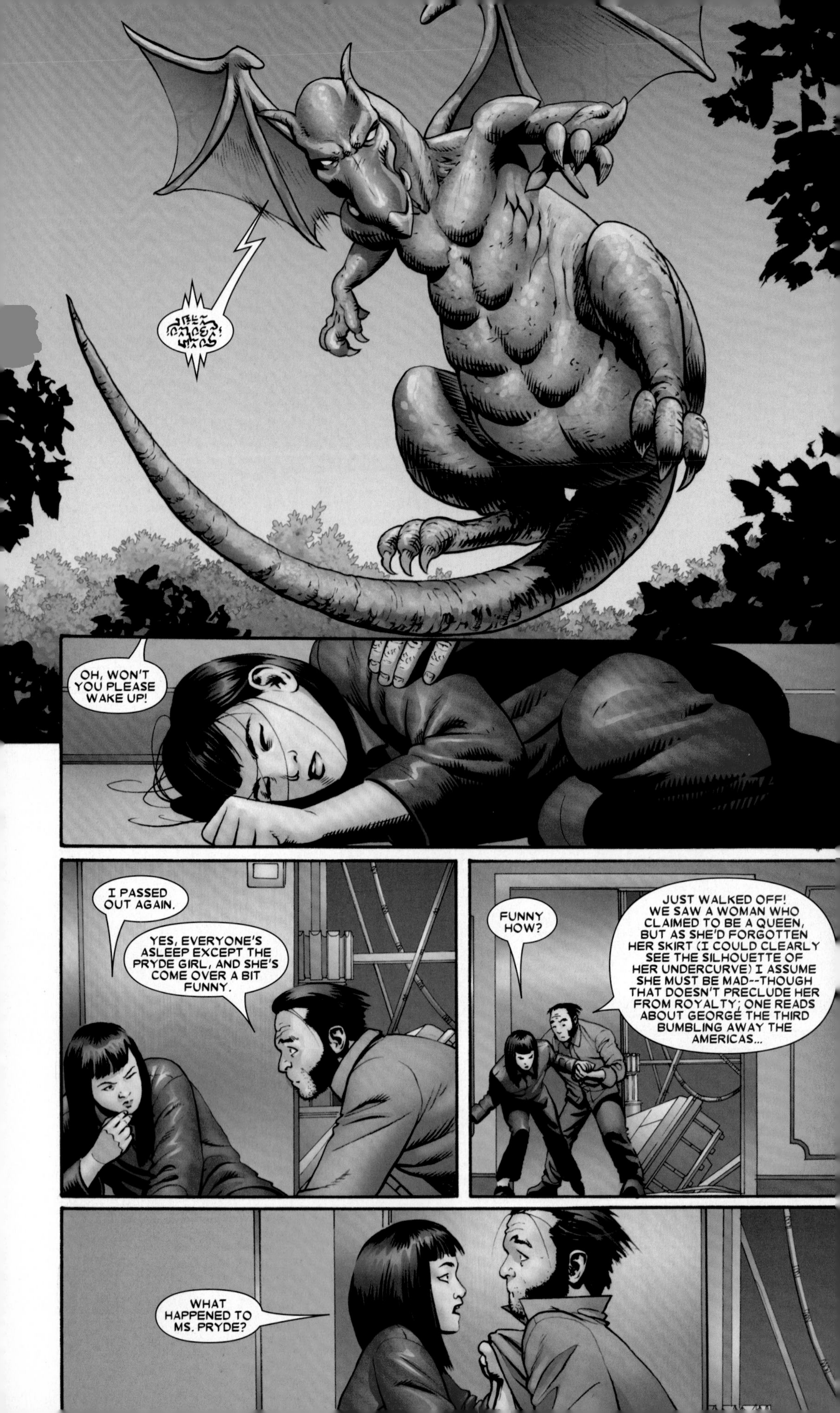
OH, WON'T YOU PLEASE WAKE UP!
I PASSED OUT AGAIN.
YES, EVERYONE'S ASLEEP EXCEPT THE PRYDE GIRL, AND SHE'S COME OVER A BIT FUNNY.
FUNNY HOW?
JUST WALKED OFF! WE SAW A WOMAN WHO CLAIMED TO BE A QUEEN, BUT AS SHE'D FORGOTTEN HER SKIRT (I COULD CLEARLY SEE THE SILHOUETTE OF HER UNDERCURVE) I ASSUME SHE MUST BE MAD--THOUGH THAT DOESN'T PRECLUDE HER FROM ROYALTY; ONE READS ABOUT GEORGE THE THIRD BUMBLING AWAY THE AMERICAS...
WHAT HAPPENED TO MS. PRYDE?

THEY FAIL YOU.

THEY LEAVE YOU OR THEY LET YOU DOWN.

THEY DIE.

OR WORSE.

THE ONLY MAN IN THIS WORLD THAT I WILL EVER TRULY TRUST...

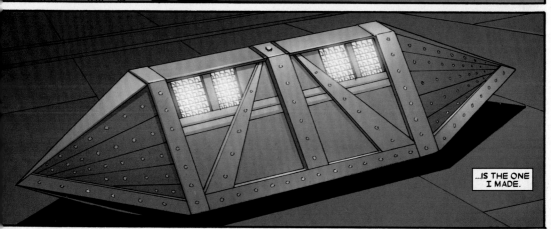

...IS THE ONE I MADE.

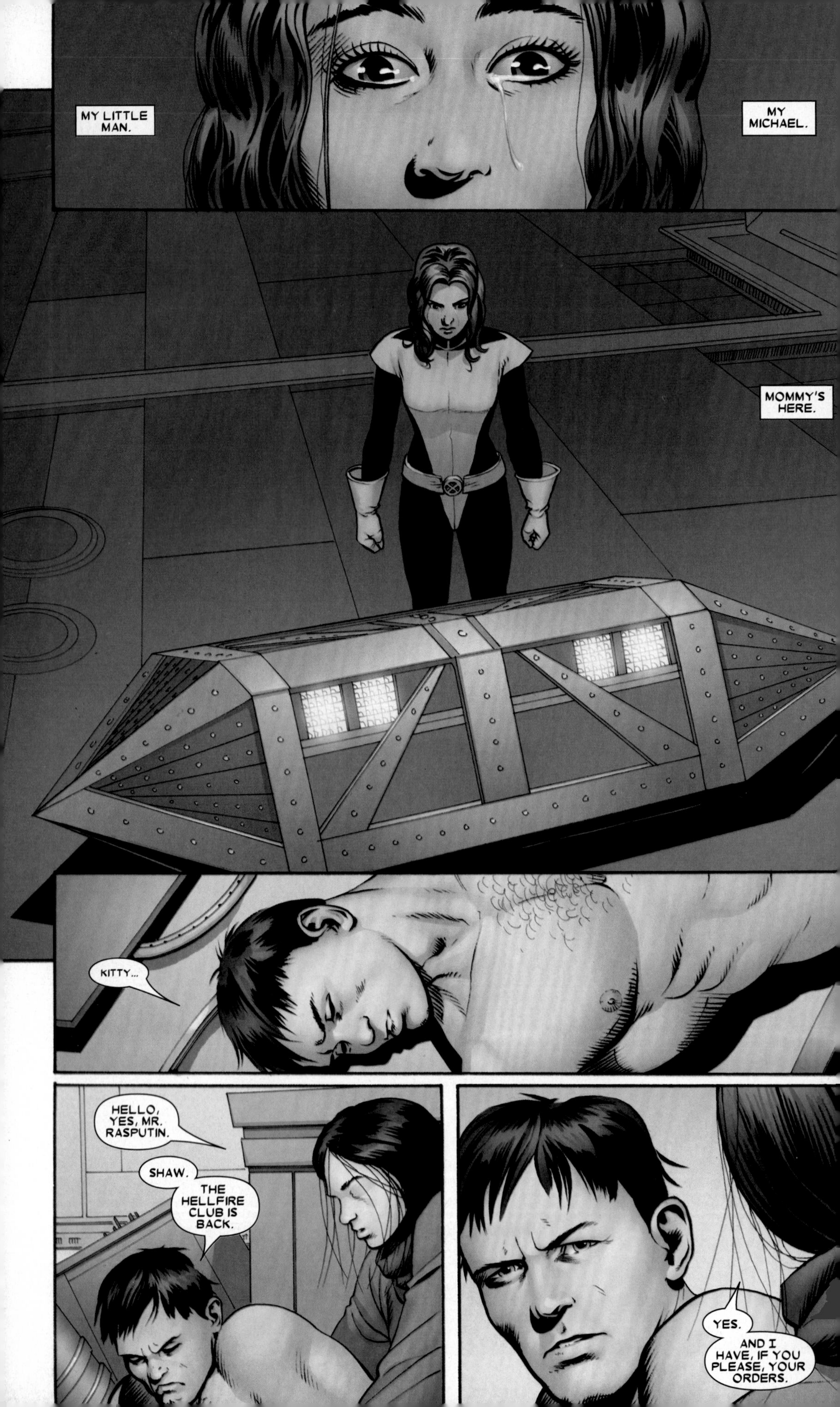
MY LITTLE MAN.
MY MICHAEL.
MOMMY'S HERE.
KITTY...
HELLO, YES, MR. RASPUTIN.
SHAW.
THE HELLFIRE CLUB IS BACK.
YES.
AND I HAVE, IF YOU PLEASE, YOUR ORDERS.

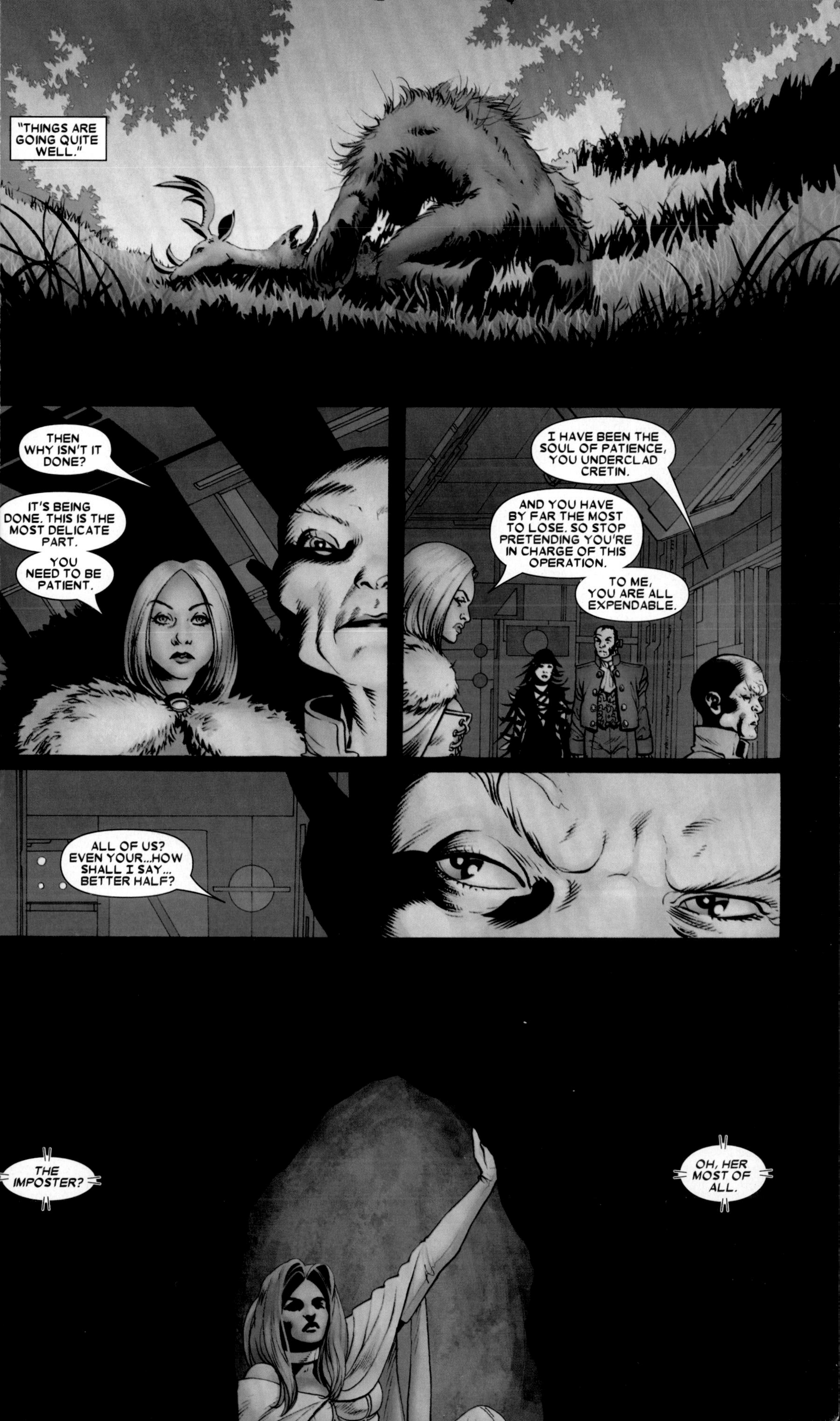

"THINGS ARE GOING QUITE WELL."
THEN WHY ISN'T IT DONE?
IT'S BEING DONE. THIS IS THE MOST DELICATE PART.
YOU NEED TO BE PATIENT.
I HAVE BEEN THE SOUL OF PATIENCE, YOU UNDERCLAD CRETIN.
AND YOU HAVE BY FAR THE MOST TO LOSE. SO STOP PRETENDING YOU'RE IN CHARGE OF THIS OPERATION.
TO ME, YOU ARE ALL EXPENDABLE.
ALL OF US? EVEN YOUR...HOW SHALL I SAY... BETTER HALF?
THE IMPOSTER?
OH, HER MOST OF ALL.

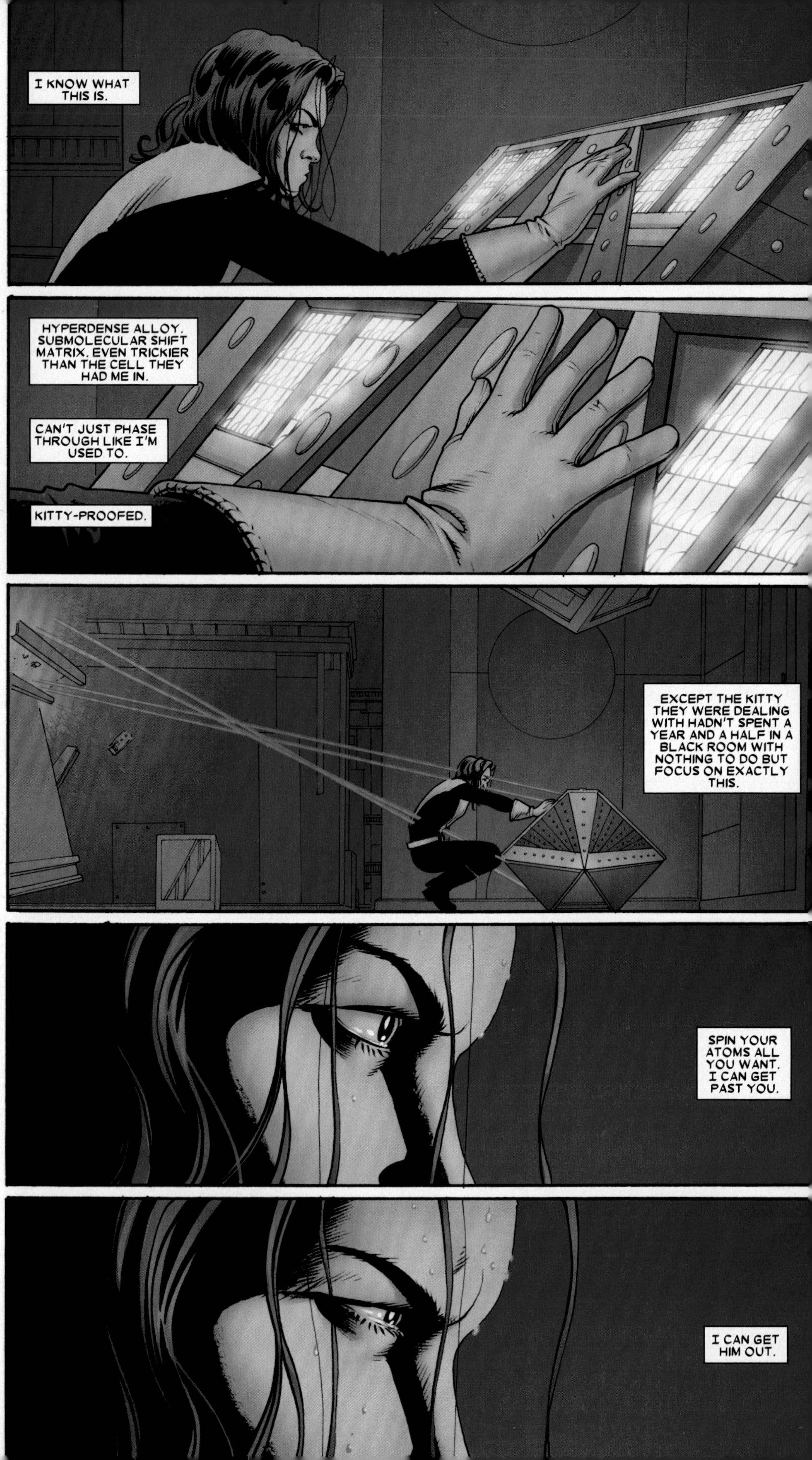
I KNOW WHAT THIS IS.
HYPERDENSE ALLOY. SUBMOLECULAR SHIFT MATRIX. EVEN TRICKIER THAN THE CELL THEY HAD ME IN.
CAN'T JUST PHASE THROUGH LIKE I'M USED TO.
KITTY-PROOFED.
EXCEPT THE KITTY THEY WERE DEALING WITH HADN'T SPENT A YEAR AND A HALF IN A BLACK ROOM WITH NOTHING TO DO BUT FOCUS ON EXACTLY THIS.
SPIN YOUR ATOMS ALL YOU WANT. I CAN GET PAST YOU.
I CAN GET HIM OUT.

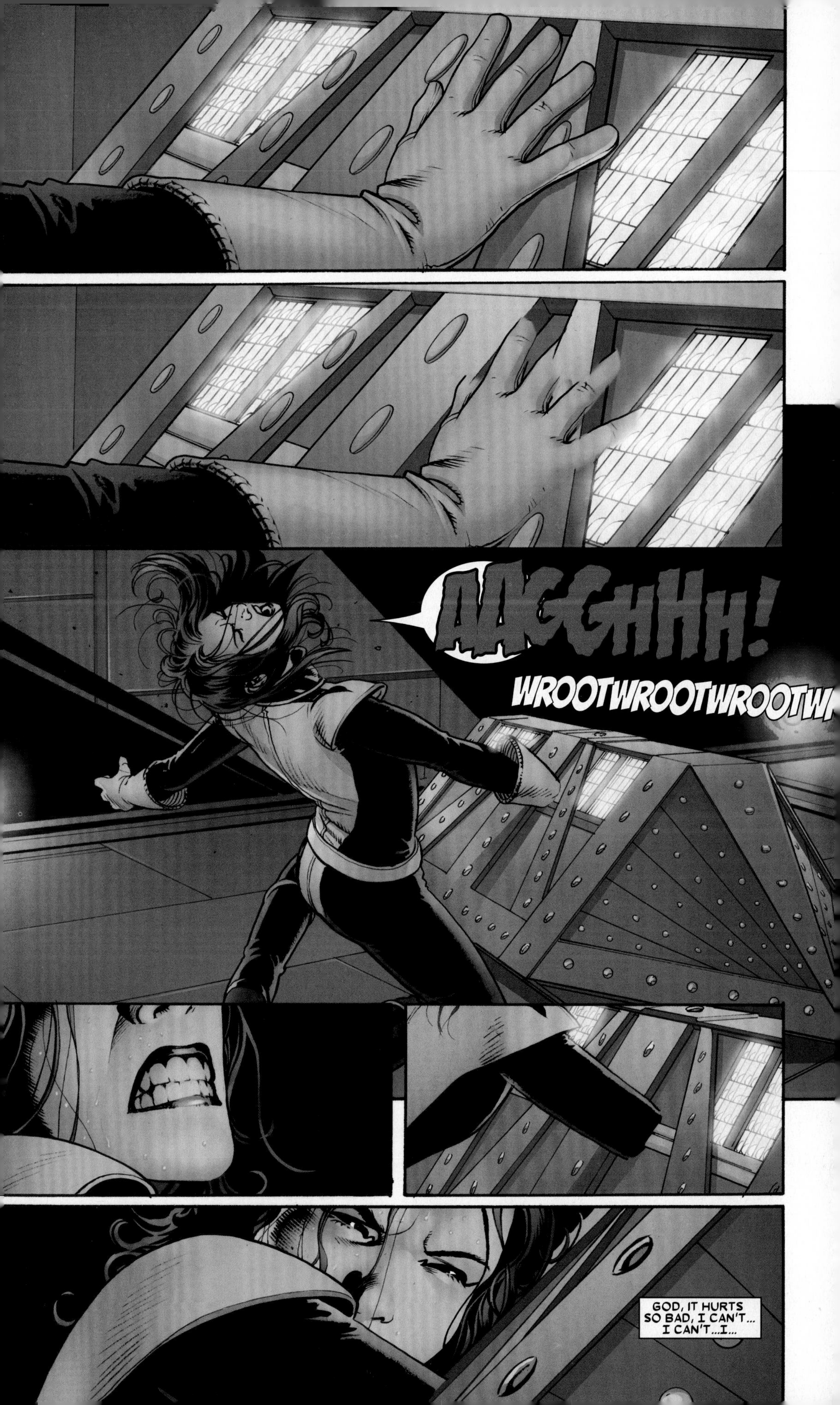
AAGGHHH!
WROOTWROOTWROOTWI
GOD, IT HURTS SO BAD, I CAN'T... I CAN'T...I...

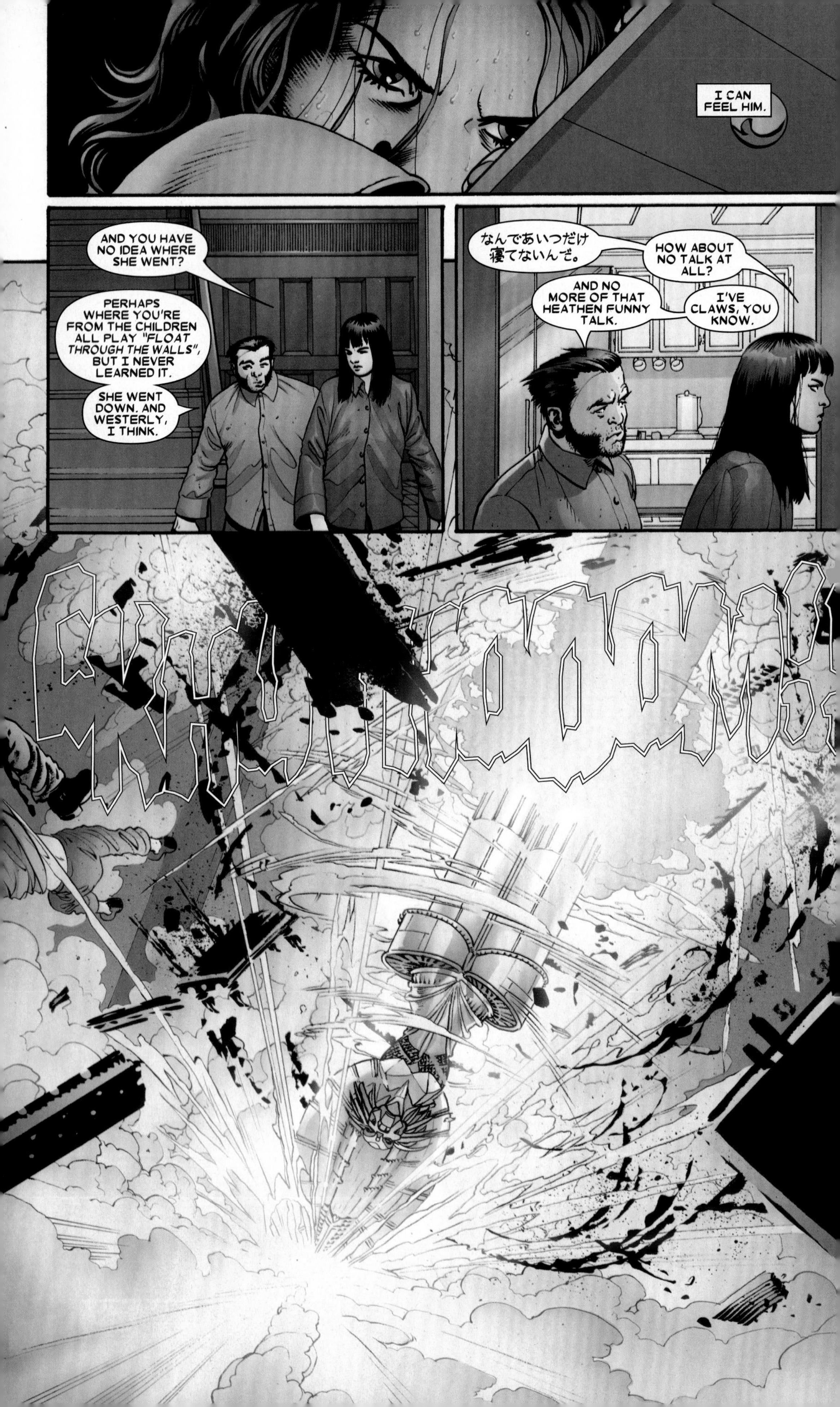
I CAN FEEL HIM.
AND YOU HAVE NO IDEA WHERE SHE WENT?
PERHAPS WHERE YOU'RE FROM THE CHILDREN ALL PLAY *"FLOAT THROUGH THE WALLS"*, BUT I NEVER LEARNED IT.
SHE WENT DOWN. AND WESTERLY, I THINK.
なんであいつだけ寝てないんぞ。
HOW ABOUT NO TALK AT ALL?
AND NO MORE OF THAT HEATHEN FUNNY TALK.
I'VE CLAWS, YOU KNOW.

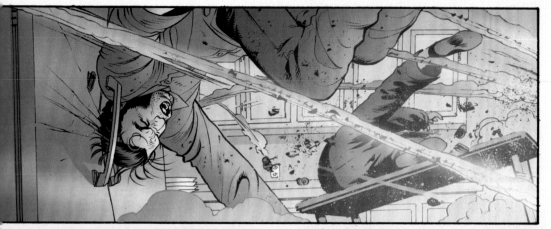

IGNORE IT. WE'RE ALMOST THERE.

THE ALLOYS I BORROWED FROM THAT SPACE STATION ARE INFINITELY USEFUL.

I HARDLY MISS MY HARD-LIGHT CAPABILITIES.

JUST TELL ME WHERE HE IS.

THEIR NEW HOUSING SYSTEM PLACED HIM EXACTLY HERE. IT'S A SPATIAL SCRAMBLE CODE; THEY'VE UPGRADED.

I'LL NEED THIRTY SECONDS.

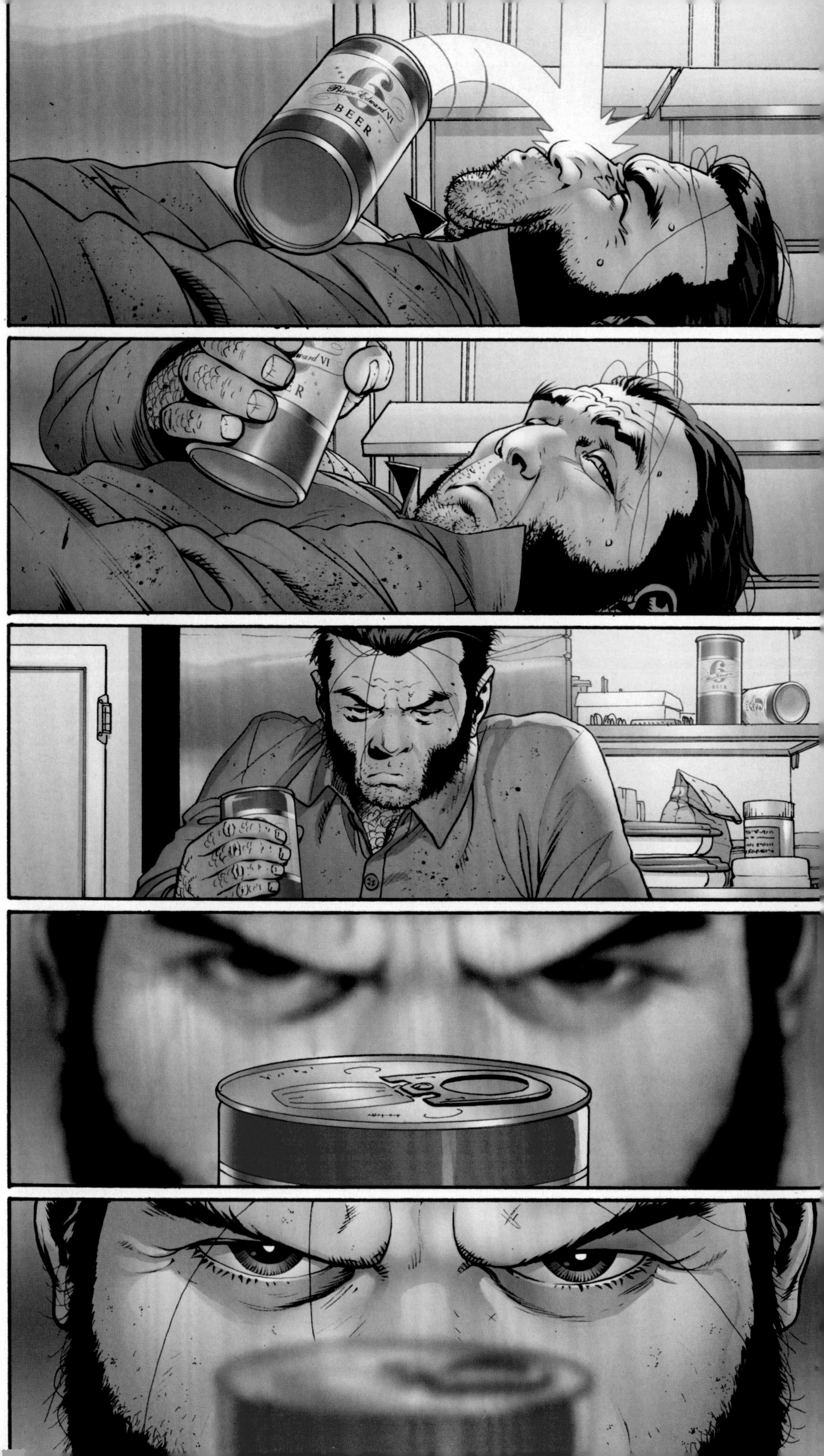
Prince Edward VI
BEER

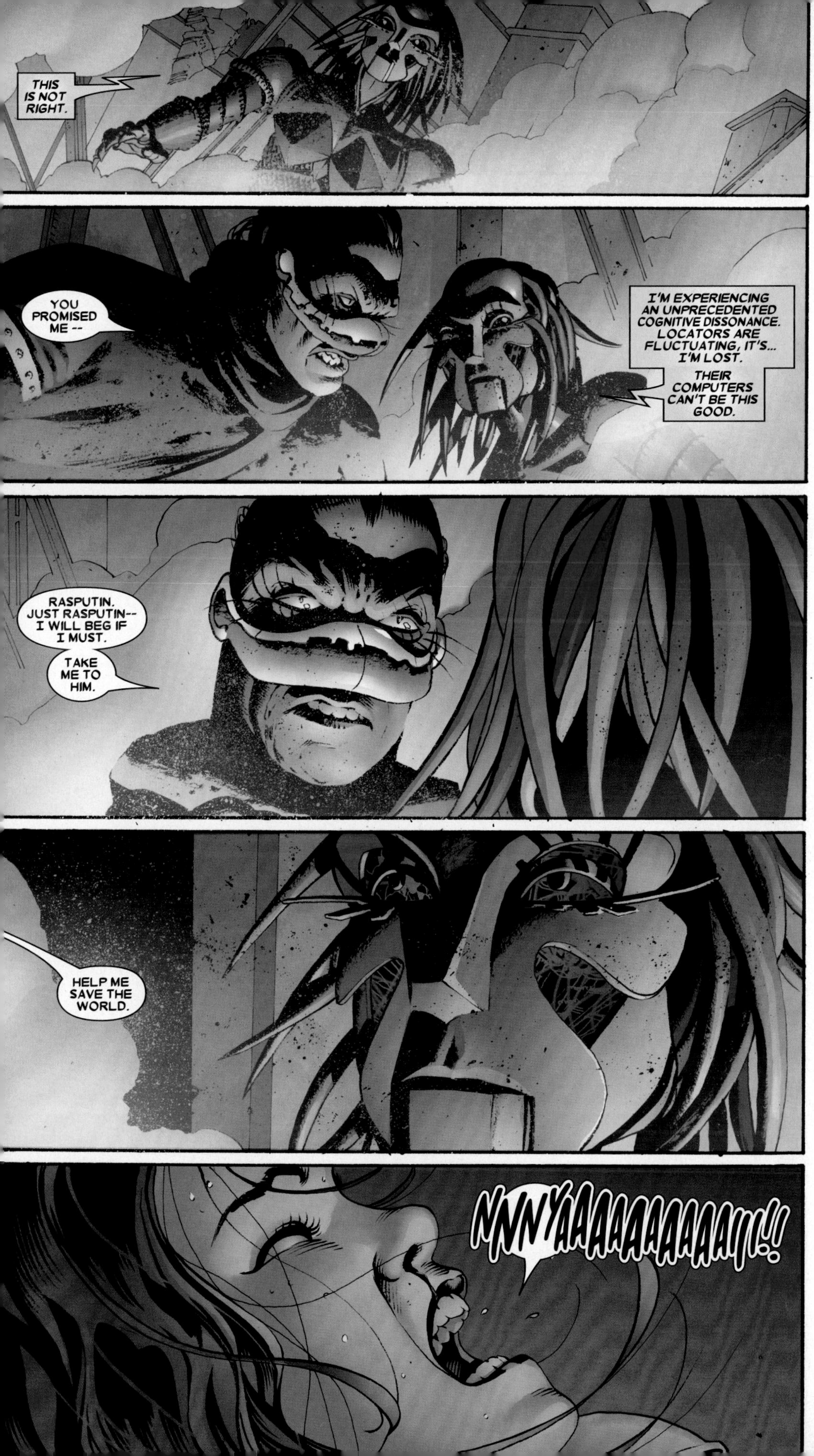

THIS IS NOT RIGHT.
YOU PROMISED ME --
I'M EXPERIENCING AN UNPRECEDENTED COGNITIVE DISSONANCE. LOCATORS ARE FLUCTUATING, IT'S... I'M LOST.
THEIR COMPUTERS CAN'T BE THIS GOOD.
RASPUTIN. JUST RASPUTIN-- I WILL BEG IF I MUST.
TAKE ME TO HIM.
HELP ME SAVE THE WORLD.
NNNYAAAAAAAAAAAIII!!

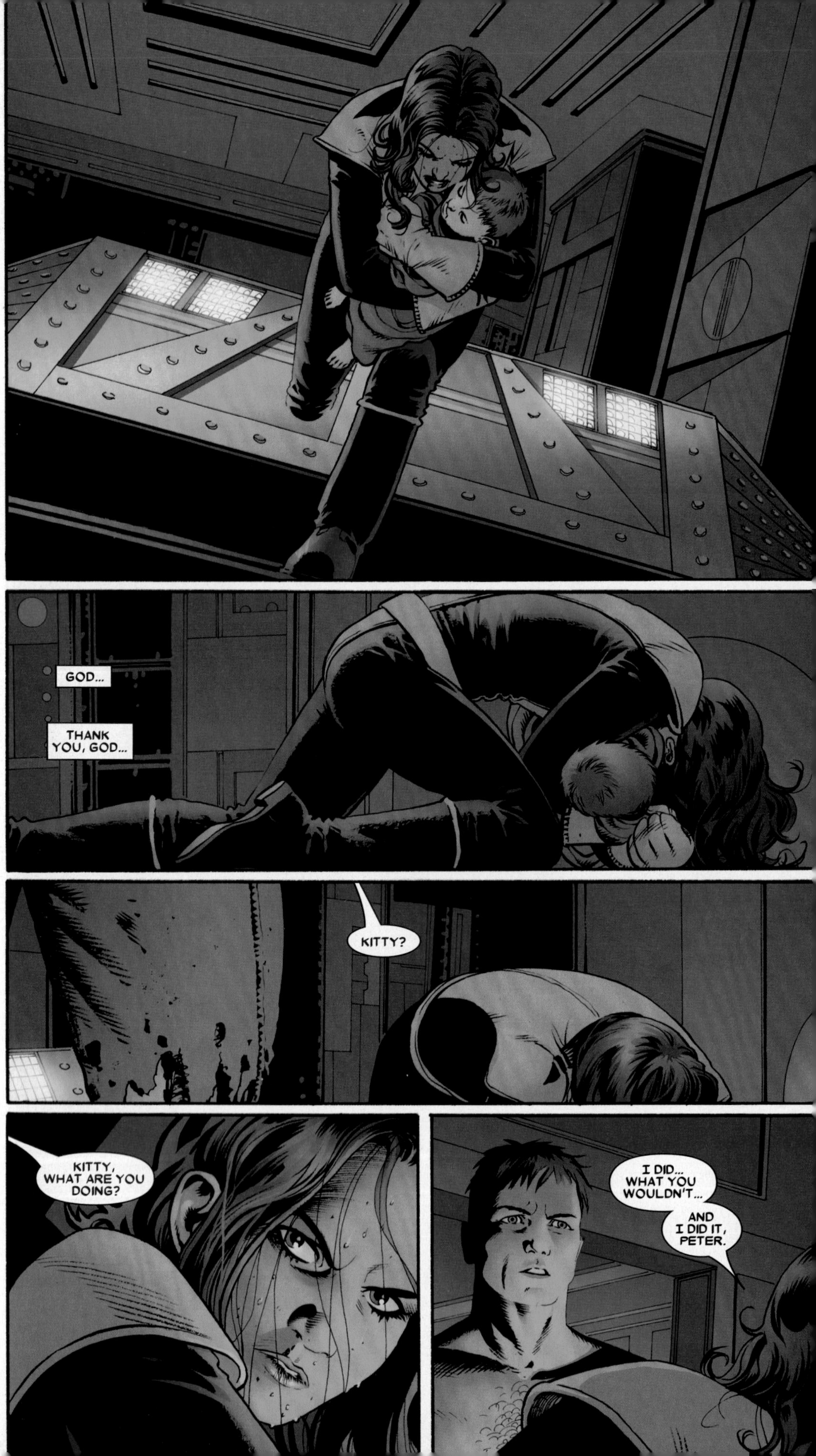
GOD...
THANK YOU, GOD...
KITTY?
KITTY, WHAT ARE YOU DOING?
I DID... WHAT YOU WOULDN'T...
AND I DID IT, PETER.

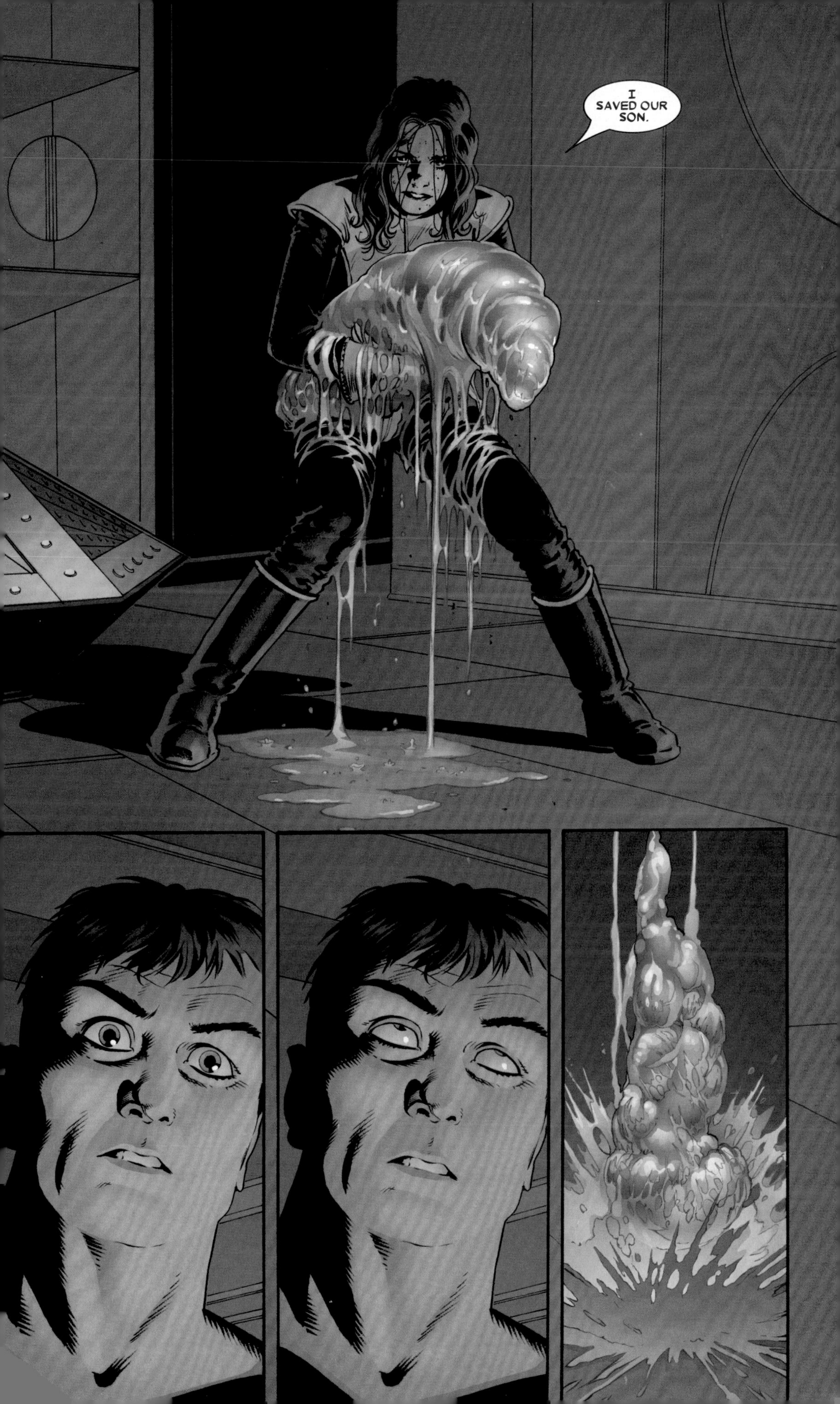
I SAVED OUR SON.

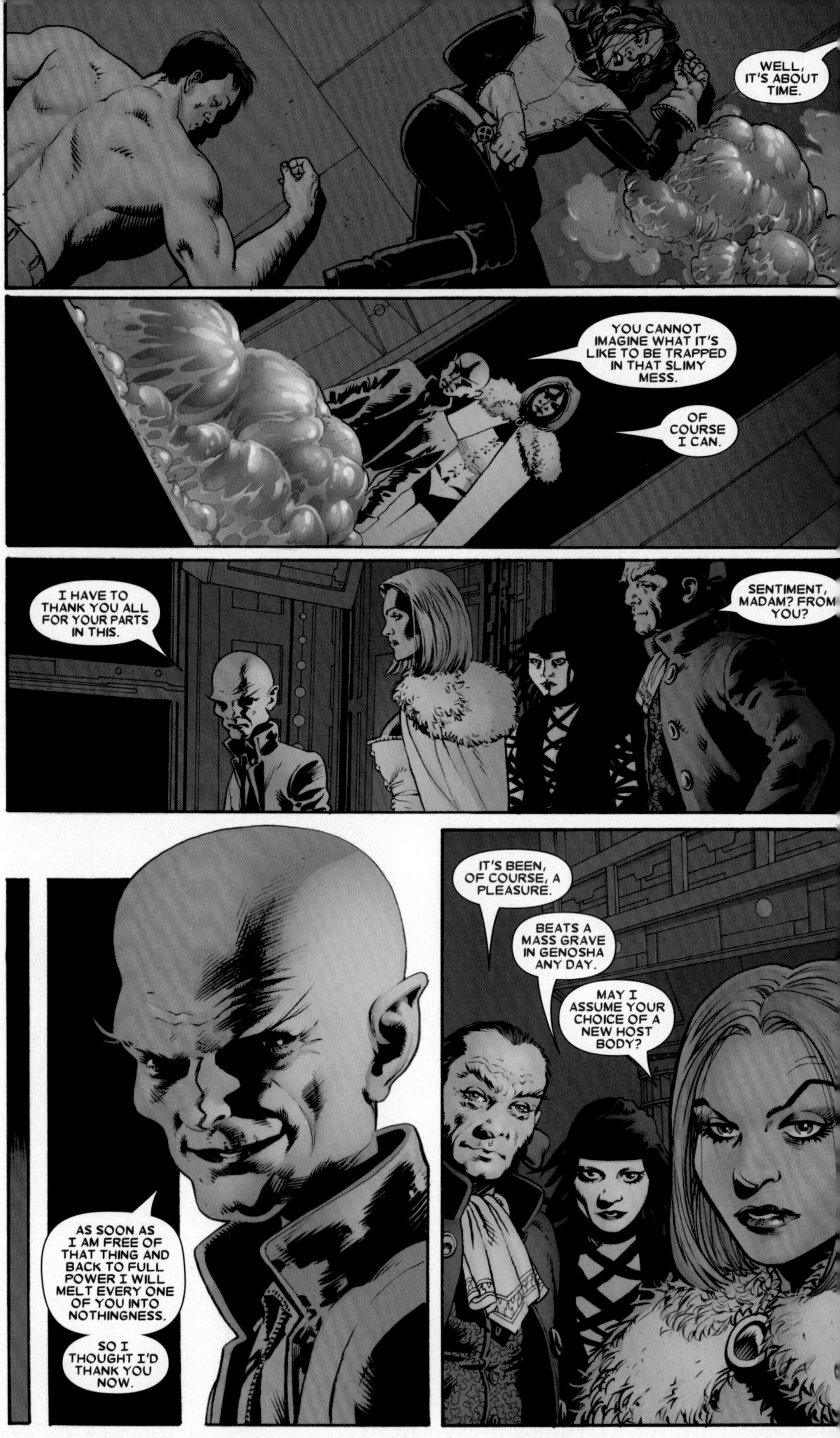

WELL, IT'S ABOUT TIME.
YOU CANNOT IMAGINE WHAT IT'S LIKE TO BE TRAPPED IN THAT SLIMY MESS.
OF COURSE I CAN.
I HAVE TO THANK YOU ALL FOR YOUR PARTS IN THIS.
SENTIMENT, MADAM? FROM YOU?
IT'S BEEN, OF COURSE, A PLEASURE.
BEATS A MASS GRAVE IN GENOSHA ANY DAY.
MAY I ASSUME YOUR CHOICE OF A NEW HOST BODY?
AS SOON AS I AM FREE OF THAT THING AND BACK TO FULL POWER I WILL MELT EVERY ONE OF YOU INTO NOTHINGNESS.
SO I THOUGHT I'D THANK YOU NOW.

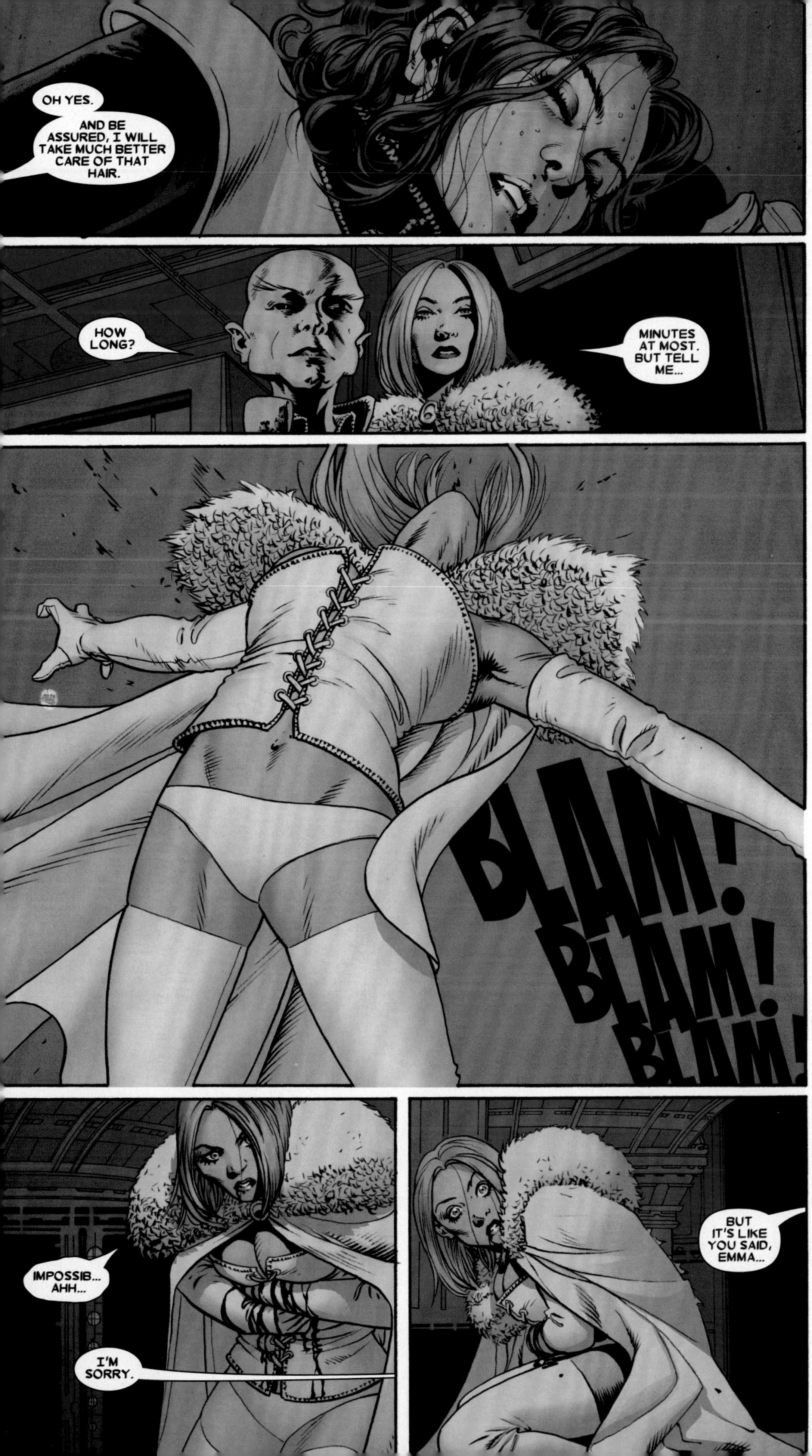
OH YES.
AND BE ASSURED, I WILL TAKE MUCH BETTER CARE OF THAT HAIR.
HOW LONG?
MINUTES AT MOST. BUT TELL ME...
BLAM! BLAM! BLAM!
IMPOSSIB... AHH...
I'M SORRY.
BUT IT'S LIKE YOU SAID, EMMA...

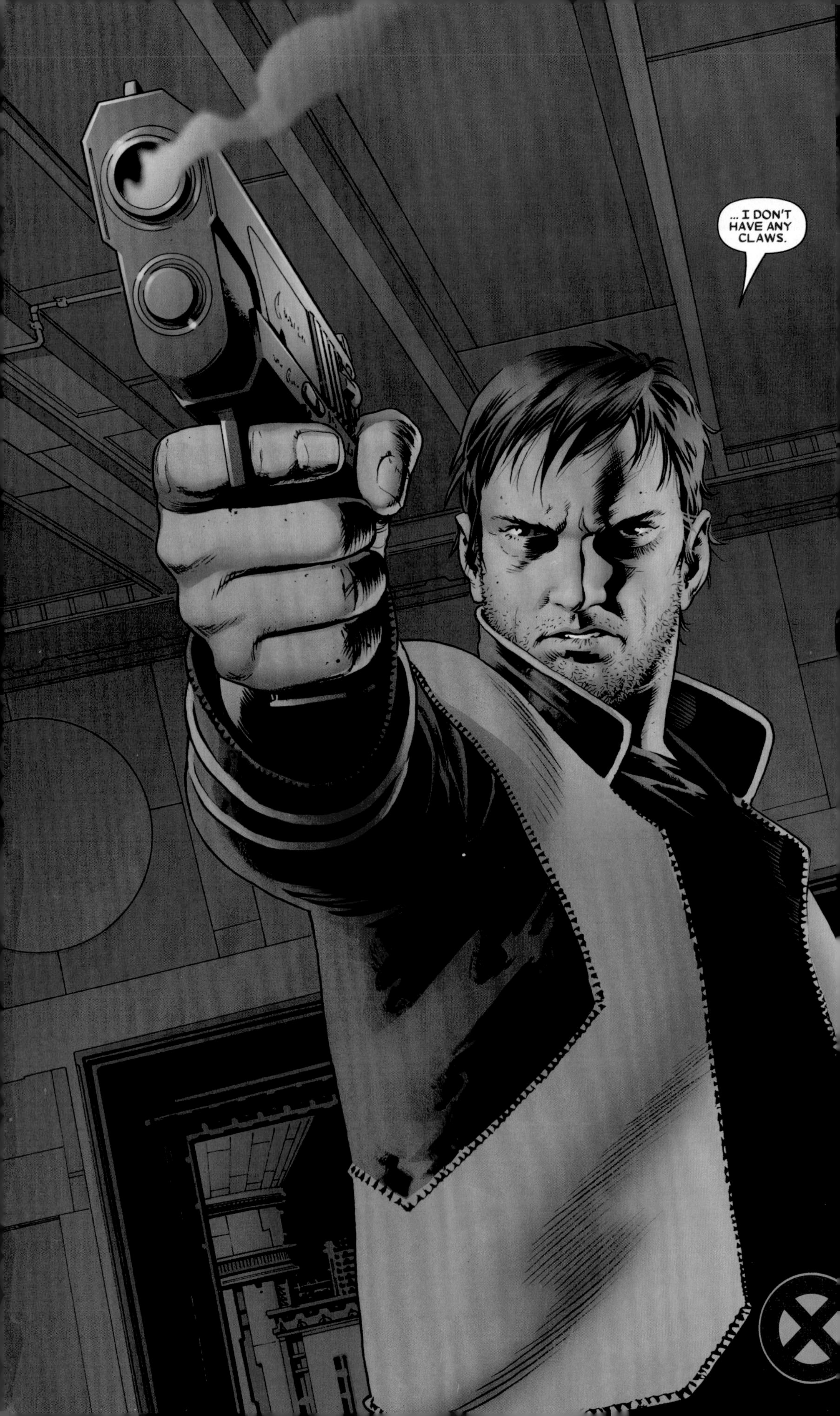
... I DON'T HAVE ANY CLAWS.

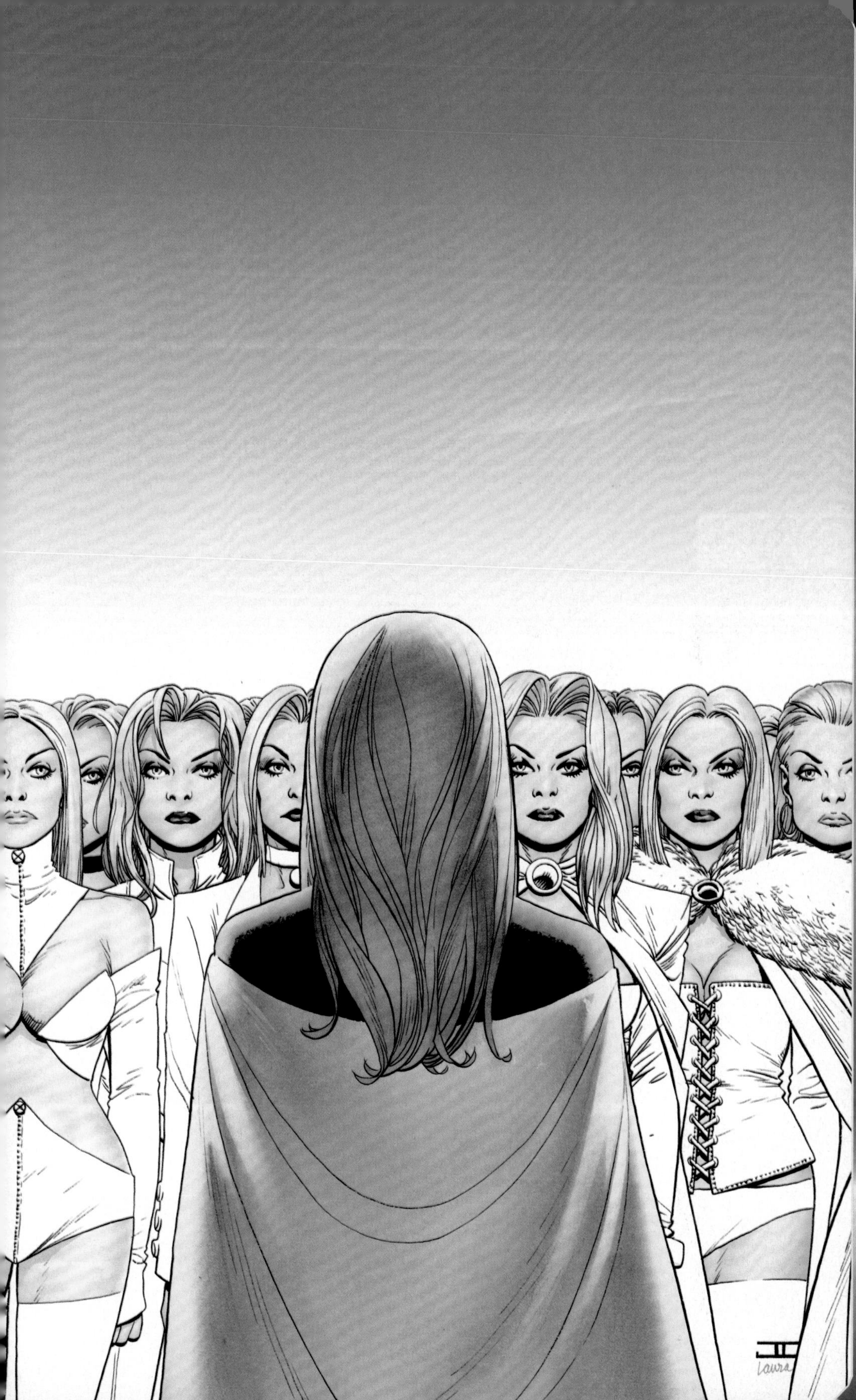
Laura

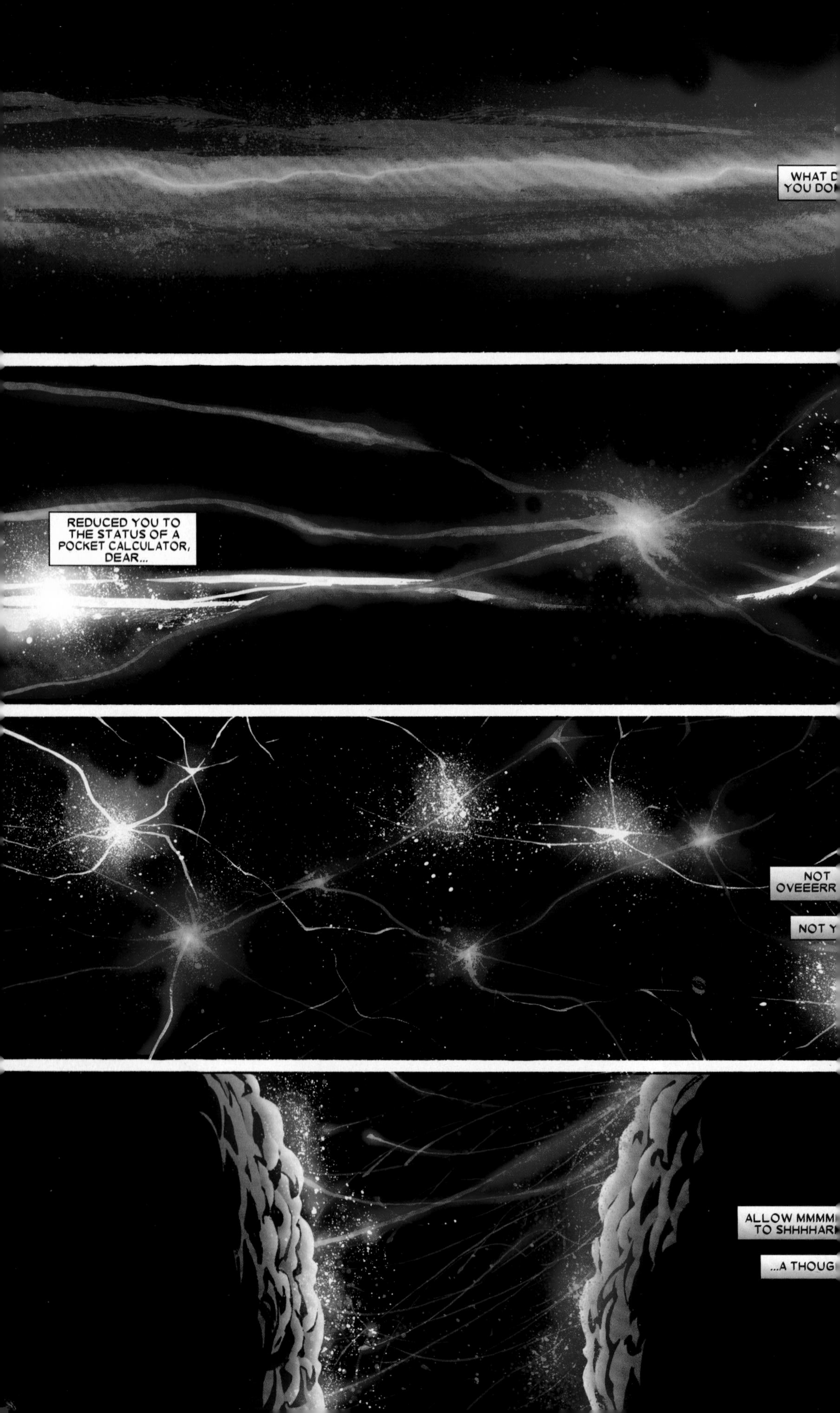
WHAT D
YOU DO
REDUCED YOU TO THE STATUS OF A POCKET CALCULATOR, DEAR...
NOT OVEEERR
NOT Y
ALLOW MMMM TO SHHHHAR
...A THOUG

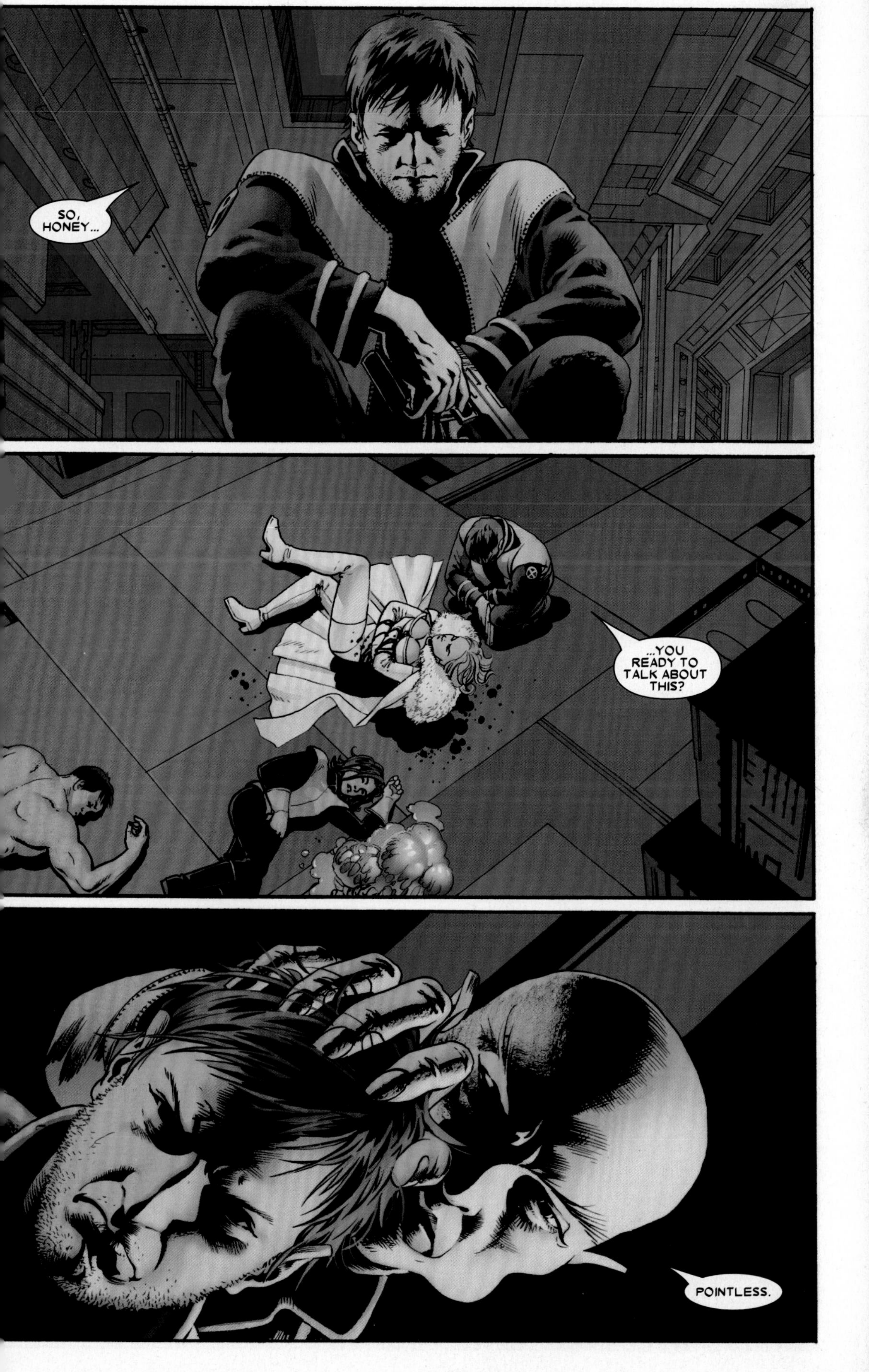

SO, HONEY...
...YOU READY TO TALK ABOUT THIS?
POINTLESS.

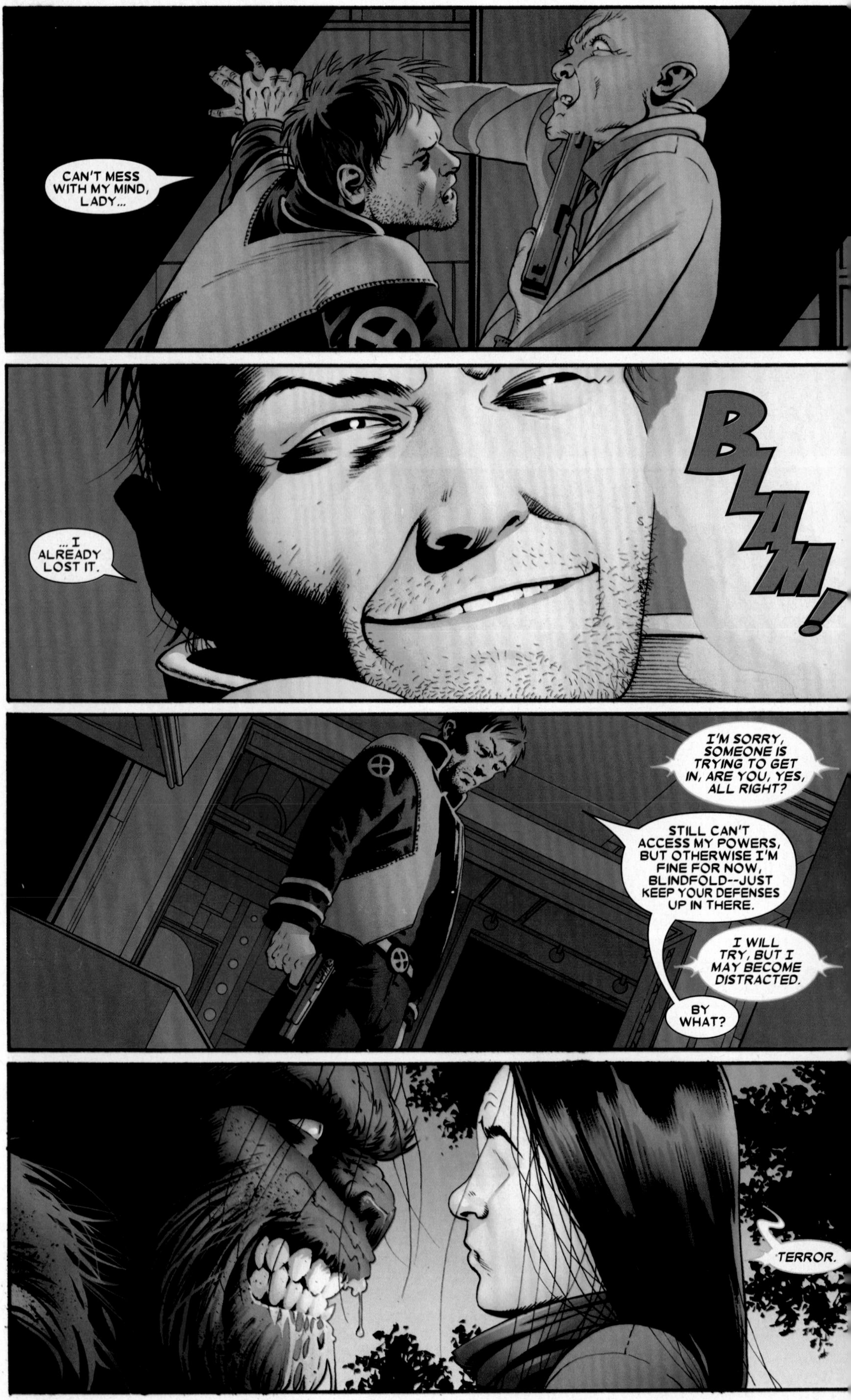

CAN'T MESS WITH MY MIND, LADY...
BLAM!
...I ALREADY LOST IT.
I'M SORRY, SOMEONE IS TRYING TO GET IN, ARE YOU, YES, ALL RIGHT?
STILL CAN'T ACCESS MY POWERS, BUT OTHERWISE I'M FINE FOR NOW, BLINDFOLD--JUST KEEP YOUR DEFENSES UP IN THERE.
I WILL TRY, BUT I MAY BECOME DISTRACTED.
BY WHAT?
TERROR.

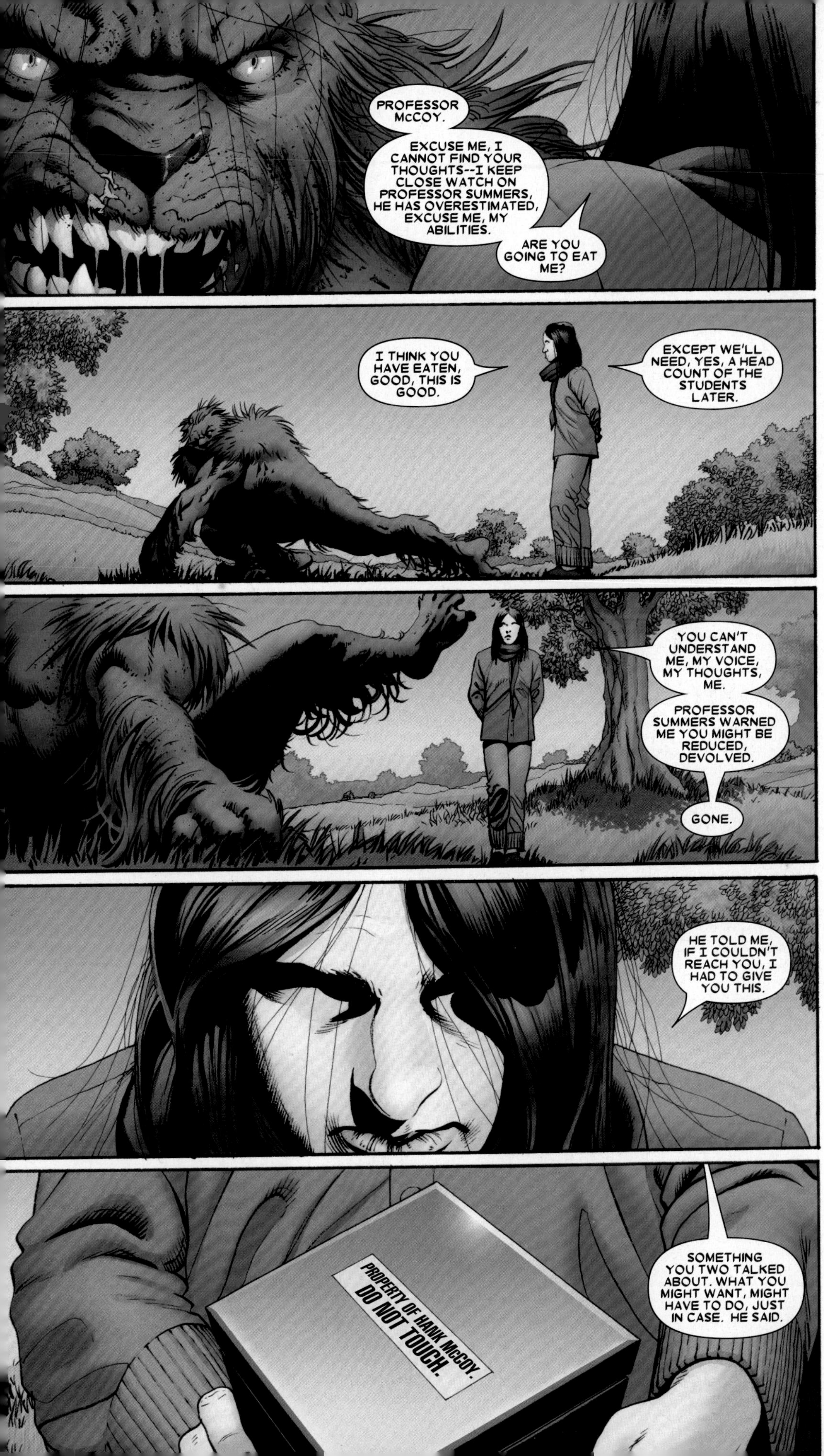
PROFESSOR McCOY.
EXCUSE ME, I CANNOT FIND YOUR THOUGHTS--I KEEP CLOSE WATCH ON PROFESSOR SUMMERS, HE HAS OVERESTIMATED, EXCUSE ME, MY ABILITIES.
ARE YOU GOING TO EAT ME?
I THINK YOU HAVE EATEN, GOOD, THIS IS GOOD.
EXCEPT WE'LL NEED, YES, A HEAD COUNT OF THE STUDENTS LATER.
YOU CAN'T UNDERSTAND ME, MY VOICE, MY THOUGHTS, ME.
PROFESSOR SUMMERS WARNED ME YOU MIGHT BE REDUCED, DEVOLVED.
GONE.
HE TOLD ME, IF I COULDN'T REACH YOU, I HAD TO GIVE YOU THIS.
PROPERTY OF HANK McCOY. DO NOT TOUCH.
SOMETHING YOU TWO TALKED ABOUT. WHAT YOU MIGHT WANT, MIGHT HAVE TO DO, JUST IN CASE. HE SAID.

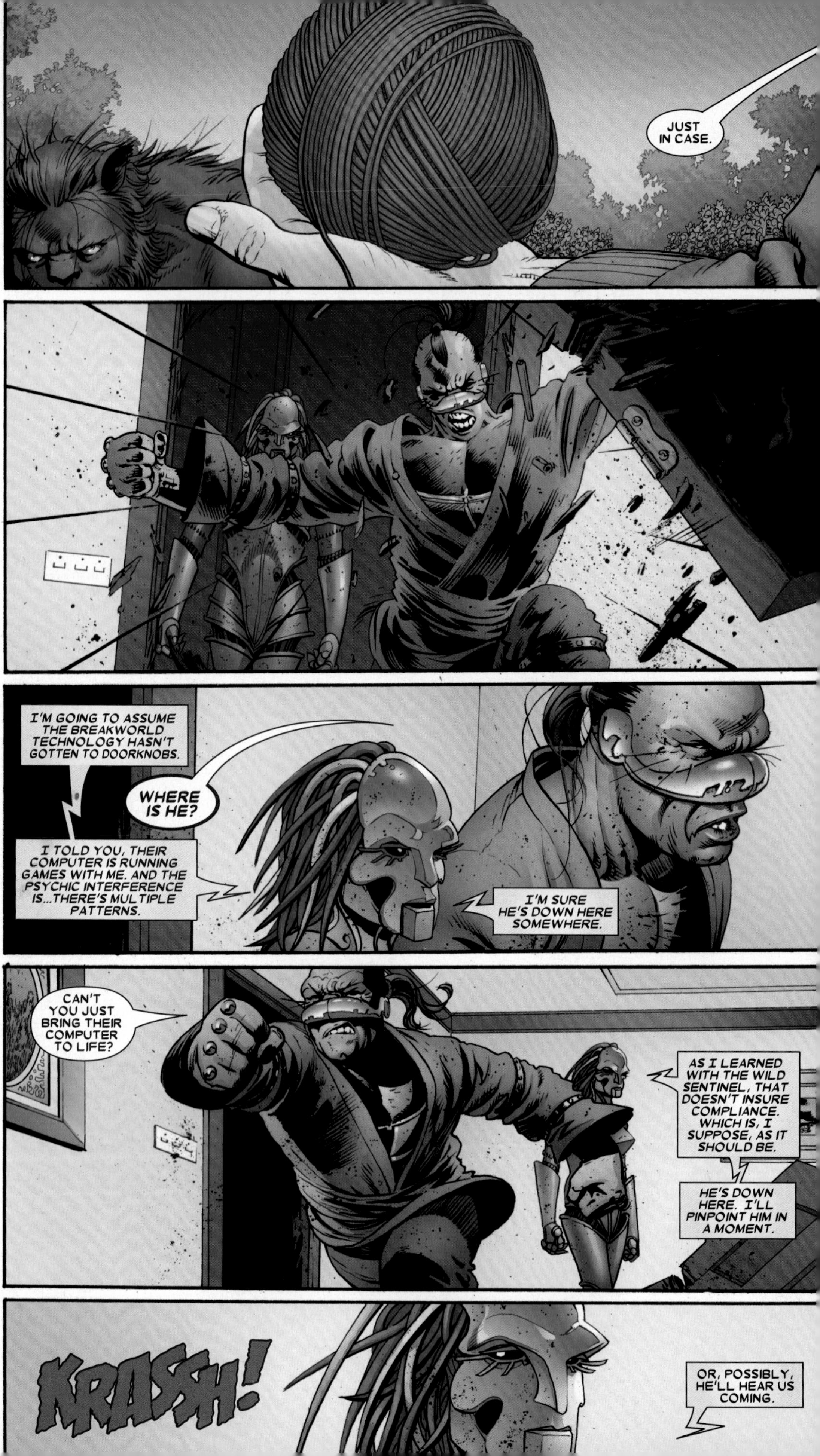
JUST IN CASE.
I'M GOING TO ASSUME THE BREAKWORLD TECHNOLOGY HASN'T GOTTEN TO DOORKNOBS.
WHERE IS HE?
I TOLD YOU, THEIR COMPUTER IS RUNNING GAMES WITH ME. AND THE PSYCHIC INTERFERENCE IS...THERE'S MULTIPLE PATTERNS.
I'M SURE HE'S DOWN HERE SOMEWHERE.
CAN'T YOU JUST BRING THEIR COMPUTER TO LIFE?
AS I LEARNED WITH THE WILD SENTINEL, THAT DOESN'T INSURE COMPLIANCE. WHICH IS, I SUPPOSE, AS IT SHOULD BE.
HE'S DOWN HERE. I'LL PINPOINT HIM IN A MOMENT.
KRASSH!
OR, POSSIBLY, HE'LL HEAR US COMING.

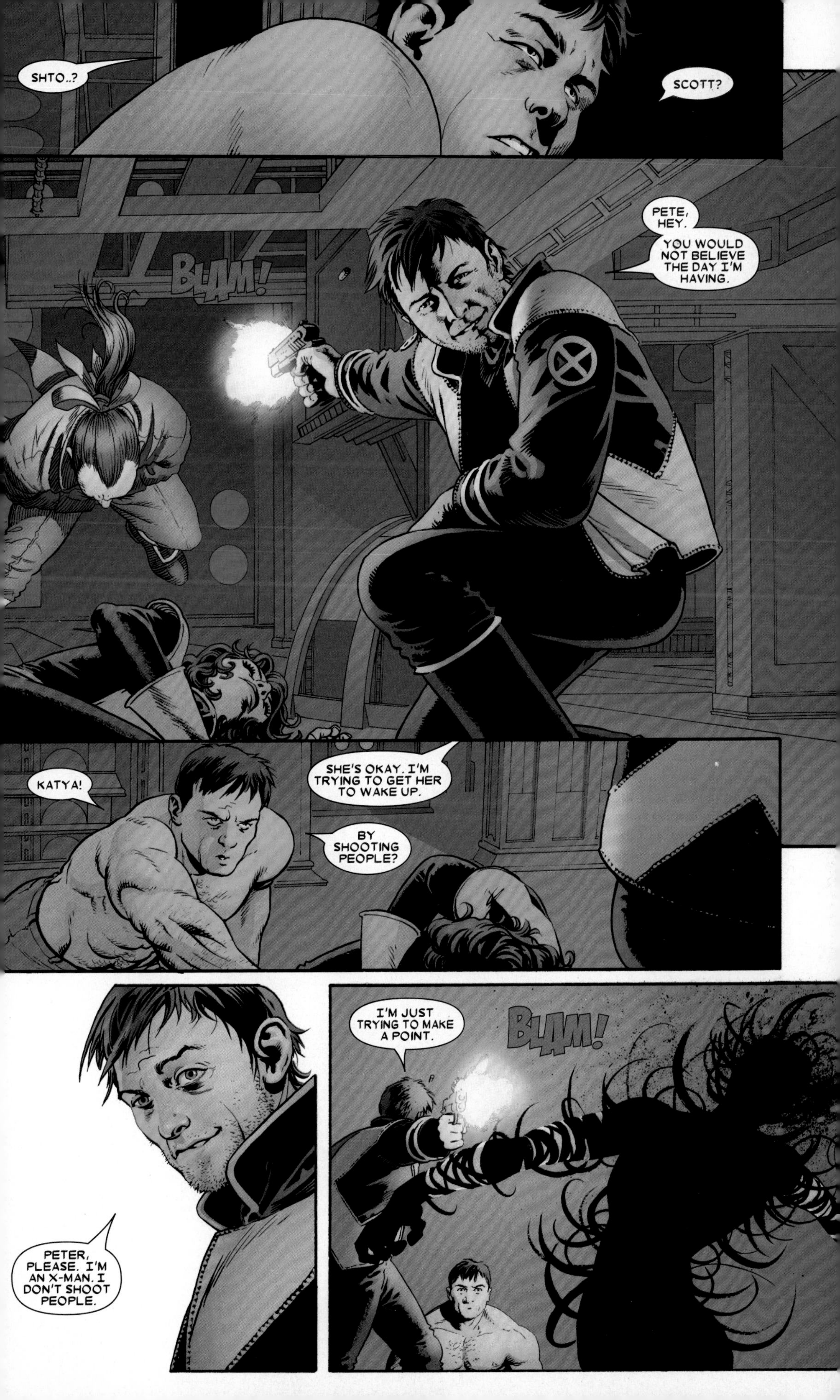
SHTO..?
SCOTT?
PETE, HEY.
YOU WOULD NOT BELIEVE THE DAY I'M HAVING.
BLAM!
KATYA!
SHE'S OKAY. I'M TRYING TO GET HER TO WAKE UP.
BY SHOOTING PEOPLE?
PETER, PLEASE. I'M AN X-MAN. I DON'T SHOOT PEOPLE.
I'M JUST TRYING TO MAKE A POINT.
BLAM!

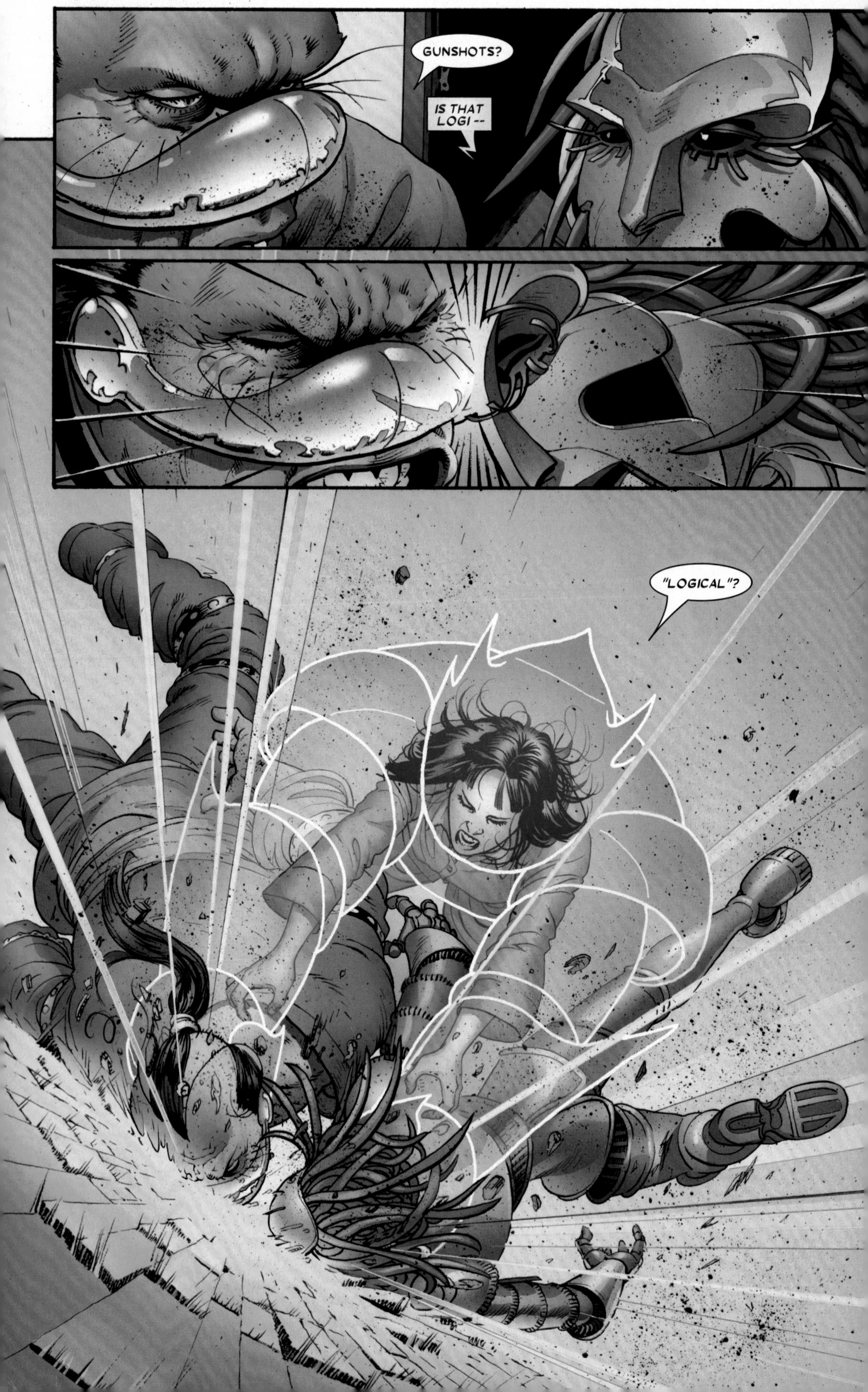
GUNSHOTS?
IS THAT LOGI --
"LOGICAL"?

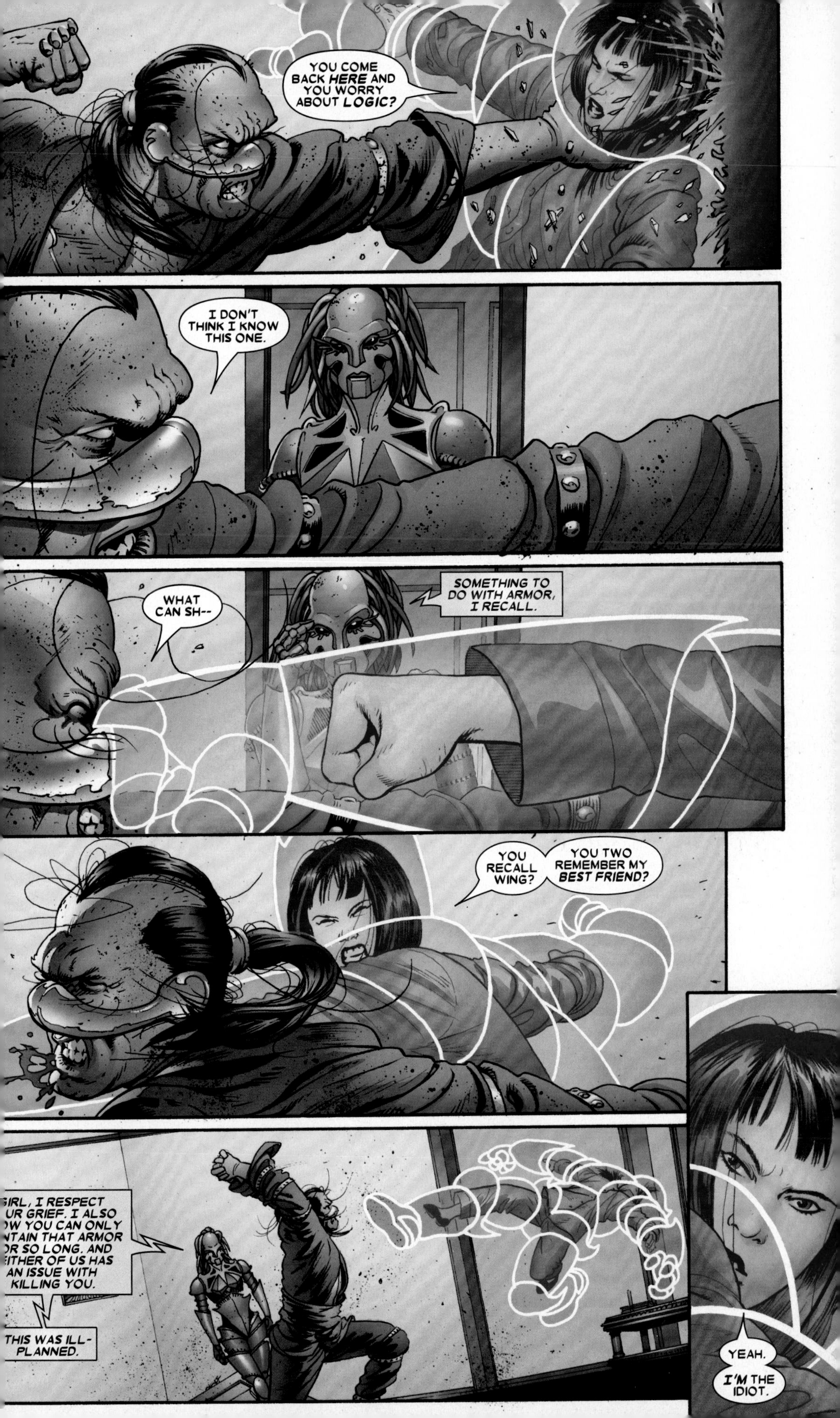
YOU COME BACK HERE AND YOU WORRY ABOUT LOGIC?
I DON'T THINK I KNOW THIS ONE.
WHAT CAN SH--
SOMETHING TO DO WITH ARMOR, I RECALL.
YOU RECALL WING?
YOU TWO REMEMBER MY BEST FRIEND?
GIRL, I RESPECT UR GRIEF. I ALSO OW YOU CAN ONLY NTAIN THAT ARMOR OR SO LONG. AND EITHER OF US HAS AN ISSUE WITH KILLING YOU.
THIS WAS ILL-PLANNED.
YEAH.
I'M THE IDIOT.

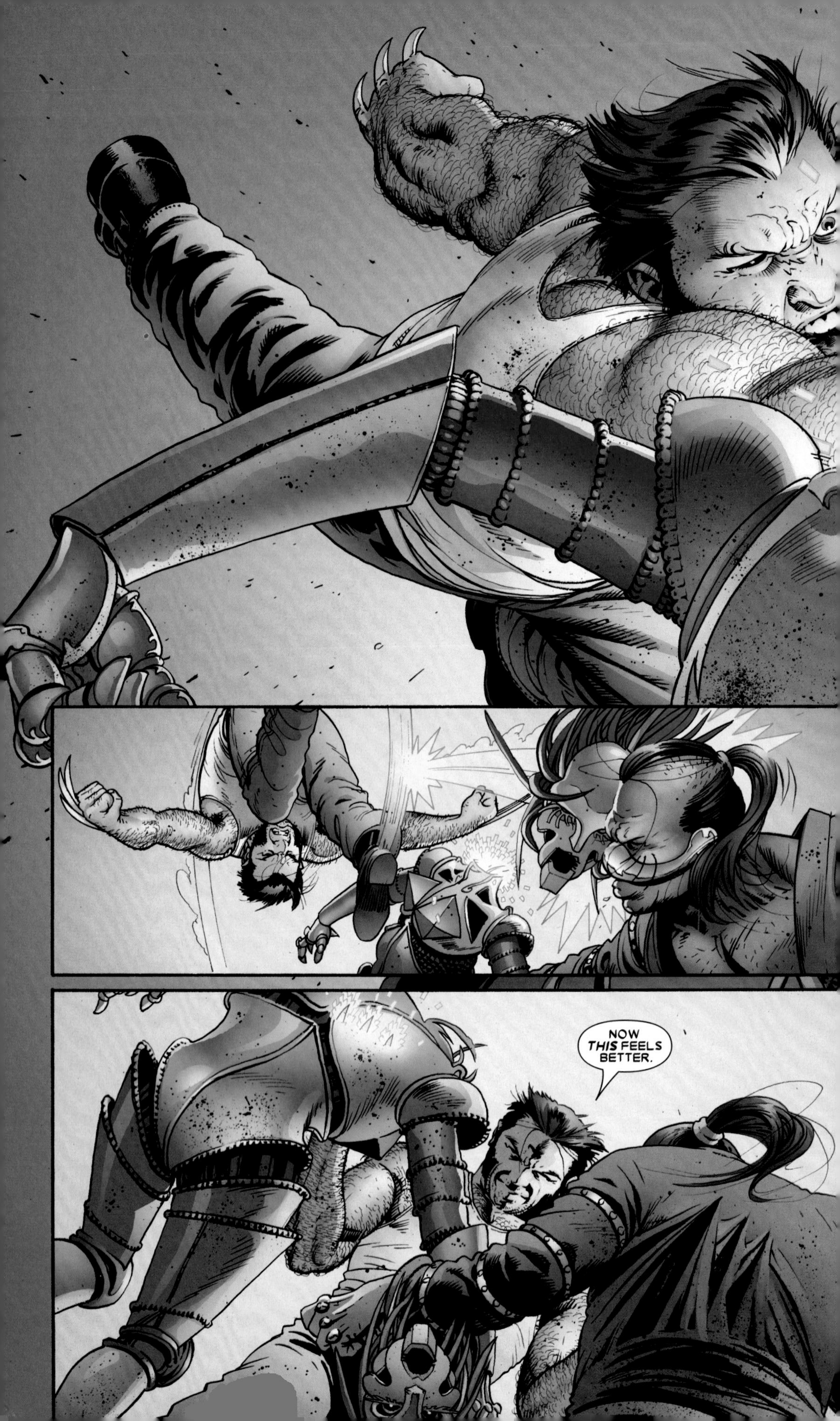
NOW *THIS* FEELS BETTER.

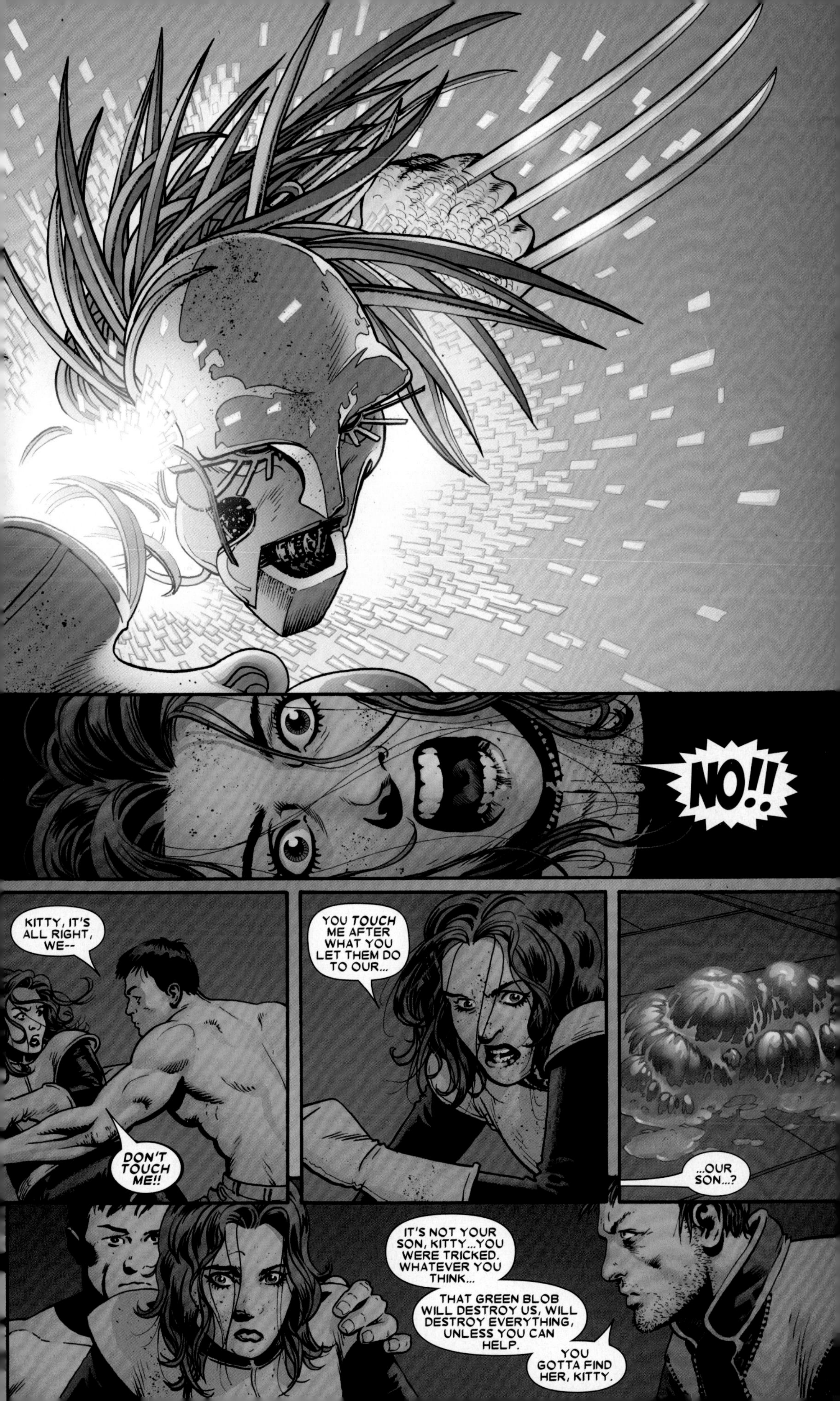
NO!!
KITTY, IT'S ALL RIGHT, WE--
DON'T TOUCH ME!!
YOU TOUCH ME AFTER WHAT YOU LET THEM DO TO OUR...
...OUR SON...?
IT'S NOT YOUR SON, KITTY...YOU WERE TRICKED. WHATEVER YOU THINK...
THAT GREEN BLOB WILL DESTROY US, WILL DESTROY EVERYTHING, UNLESS YOU CAN HELP.
YOU GOTTA FIND HER, KITTY.

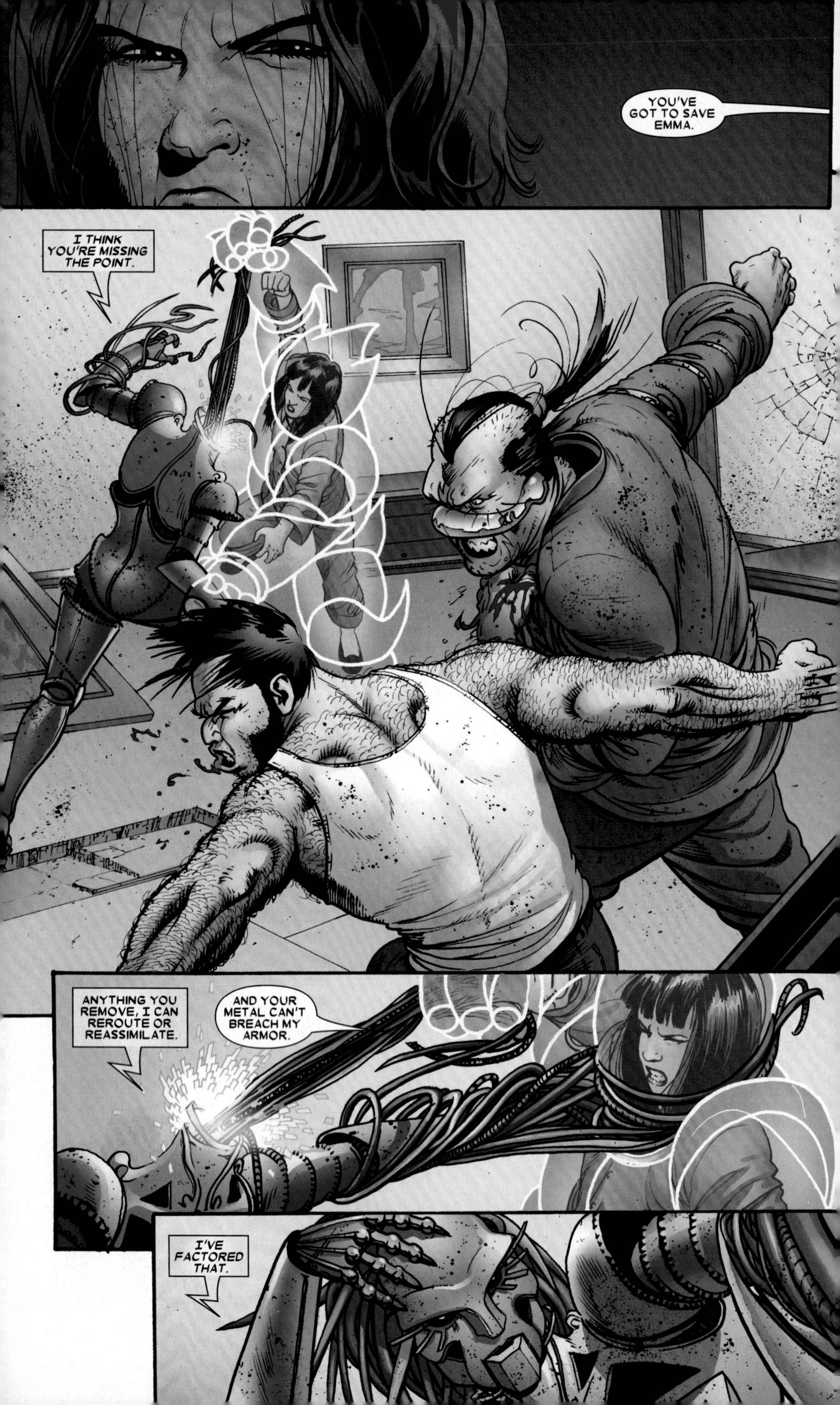
YOU'VE GOT TO SAVE EMMA.
I THINK YOU'RE MISSING THE POINT.
ANYTHING YOU REMOVE, I CAN REROUTE OR REASSIMILATE.
AND YOUR METAL CAN'T BREACH MY ARMOR.
I'VE FACTORED THAT.

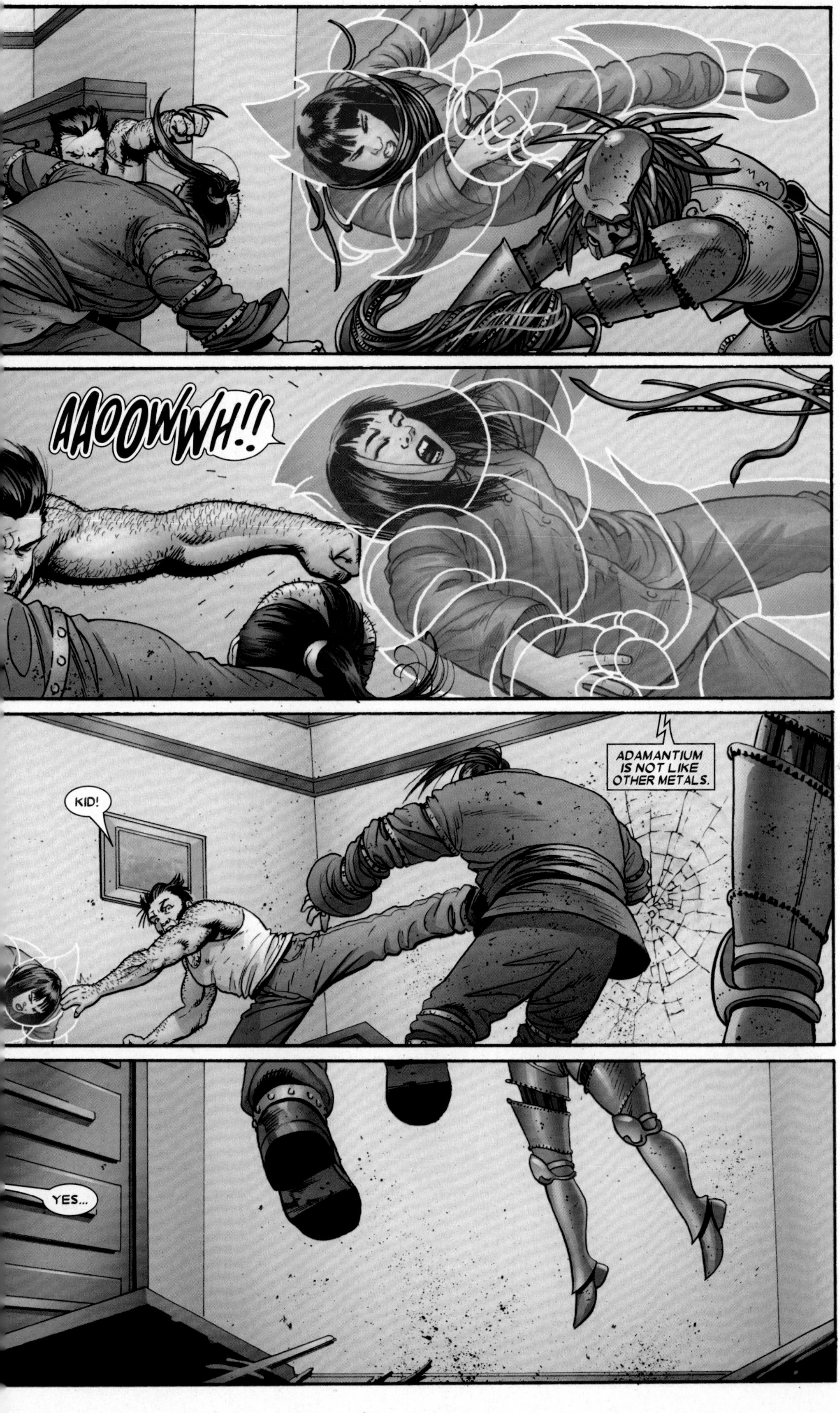
AAOOWWH!!
ADAMANTIUM IS NOT LIKE OTHER METALS.
KID!
YES...

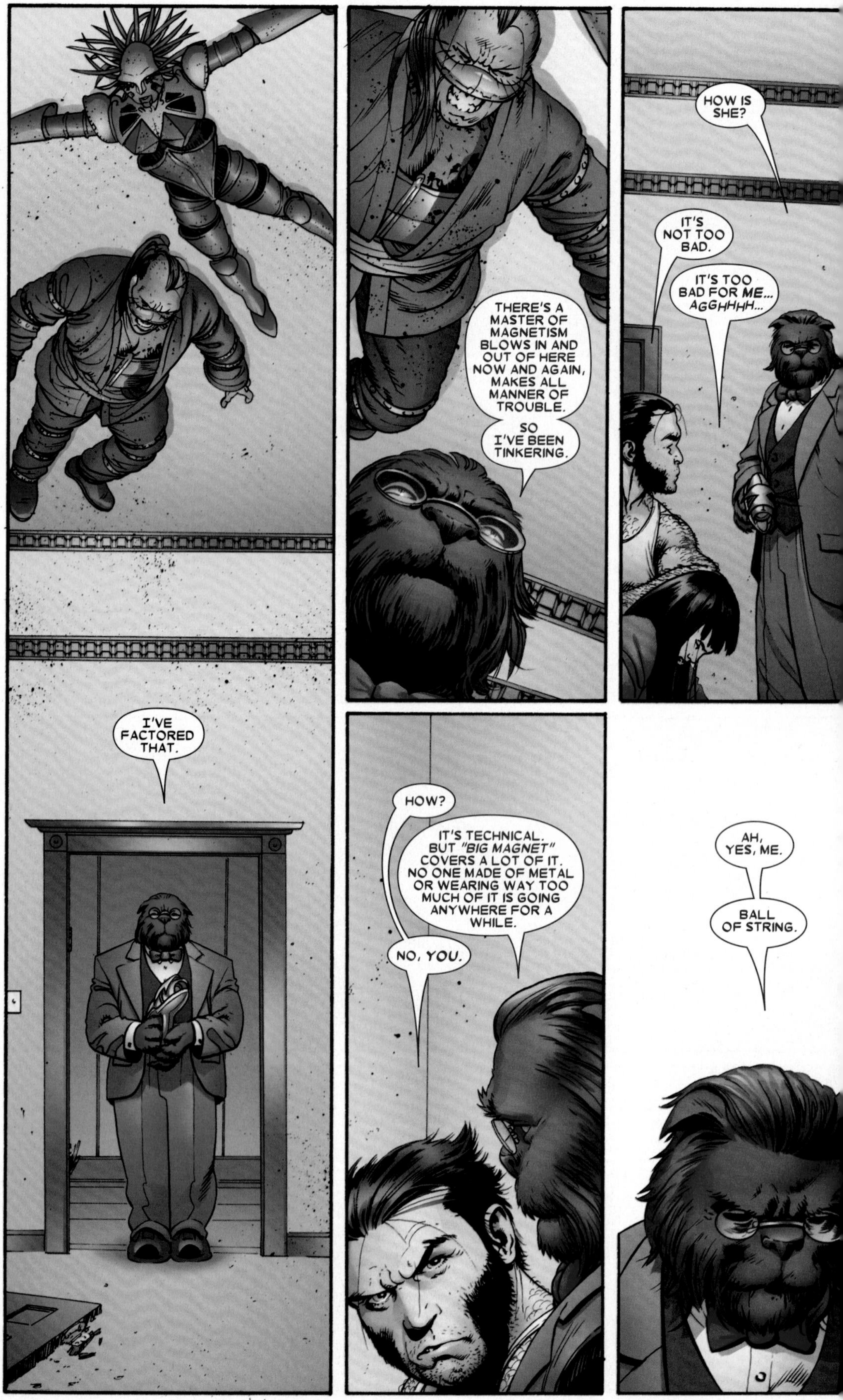
THERE'S A MASTER OF MAGNETISM BLOWS IN AND OUT OF HERE NOW AND AGAIN, MAKES ALL MANNER OF TROUBLE.
SO I'VE BEEN TINKERING.
HOW IS SHE?
IT'S NOT TOO BAD.
IT'S TOO BAD FOR ME... AGGHHHH...
I'VE FACTORED THAT.
HOW?
IT'S TECHNICAL. BUT "BIG MAGNET" COVERS A LOT OF IT. NO ONE MADE OF METAL OR WEARING WAY TOO MUCH OF IT IS GOING ANYWHERE FOR A WHILE.
NO, YOU.
AH, YES, ME.
BALL OF STRING.

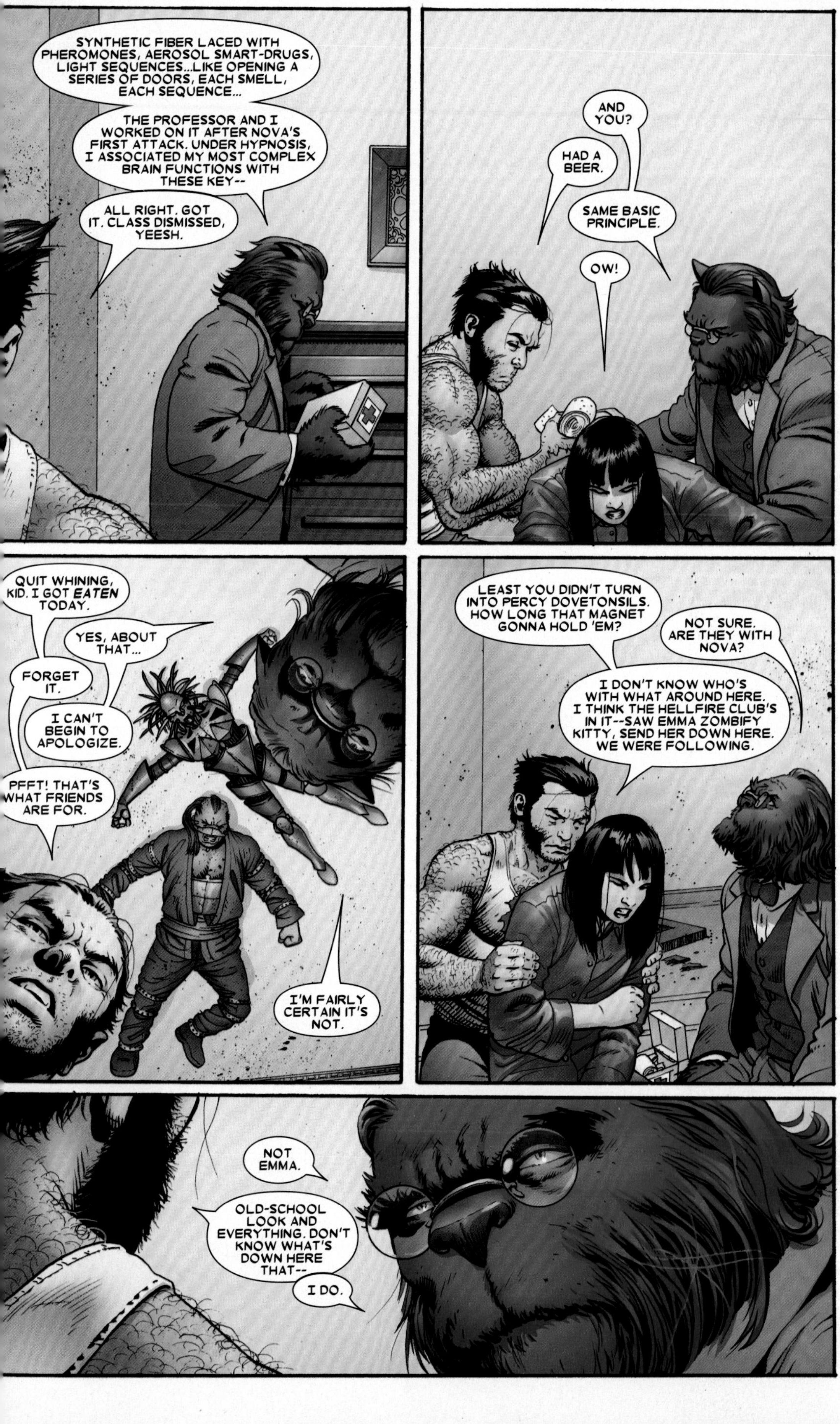
SYNTHETIC FIBER LACED WITH PHEROMONES, AEROSOL SMART-DRUGS, LIGHT SEQUENCES...LIKE OPENING A SERIES OF DOORS, EACH SMELL, EACH SEQUENCE...
THE PROFESSOR AND I WORKED ON IT AFTER NOVA'S FIRST ATTACK. UNDER HYPNOSIS, I ASSOCIATED MY MOST COMPLEX BRAIN FUNCTIONS WITH THESE KEY--
ALL RIGHT. GOT IT. CLASS DISMISSED, YEESH.
AND YOU?
HAD A BEER.
SAME BASIC PRINCIPLE.
OW!
QUIT WHINING, KID. I GOT *EATEN* TODAY.
YES, ABOUT THAT...
FORGET IT.
I CAN'T BEGIN TO APOLOGIZE.
PFFT! THAT'S WHAT FRIENDS ARE FOR.
I'M FAIRLY CERTAIN IT'S NOT.
LEAST YOU DIDN'T TURN INTO PERCY DOVETONSILS. HOW LONG THAT MAGNET GONNA HOLD 'EM?
NOT SURE. ARE THEY WITH NOVA?
I DON'T KNOW WHO'S WITH WHAT AROUND HERE. I THINK THE HELLFIRE CLUB'S IN IT--SAW EMMA ZOMBIFY KITTY, SEND HER DOWN HERE. WE WERE FOLLOWING.
NOT EMMA.
OLD-SCHOOL LOOK AND EVERYTHING. DON'T KNOW WHAT'S DOWN HERE THAT--
I DO.

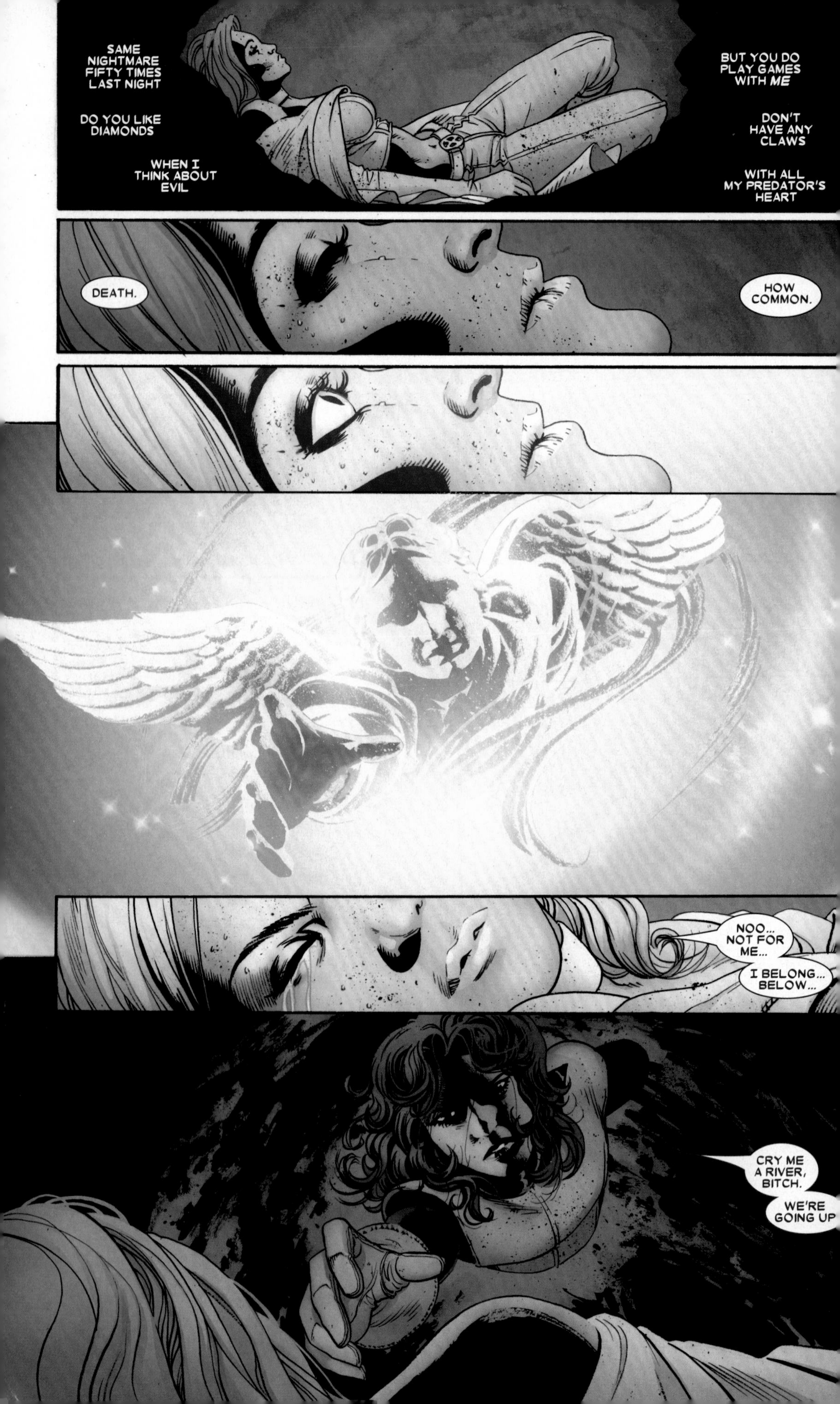
SAME NIGHTMARE FIFTY TIMES LAST NIGHT
DO YOU LIKE DIAMONDS
WHEN I THINK ABOUT EVIL
BUT YOU DO PLAY GAMES WITH *ME*
DON'T HAVE ANY CLAWS
WITH ALL MY PREDATOR'S HEART
DEATH.
HOW COMMON.
NOO... NOT FOR ME...
I BELONG... BELOW...
CRY ME A RIVER, BITCH.
WE'RE GOING UP

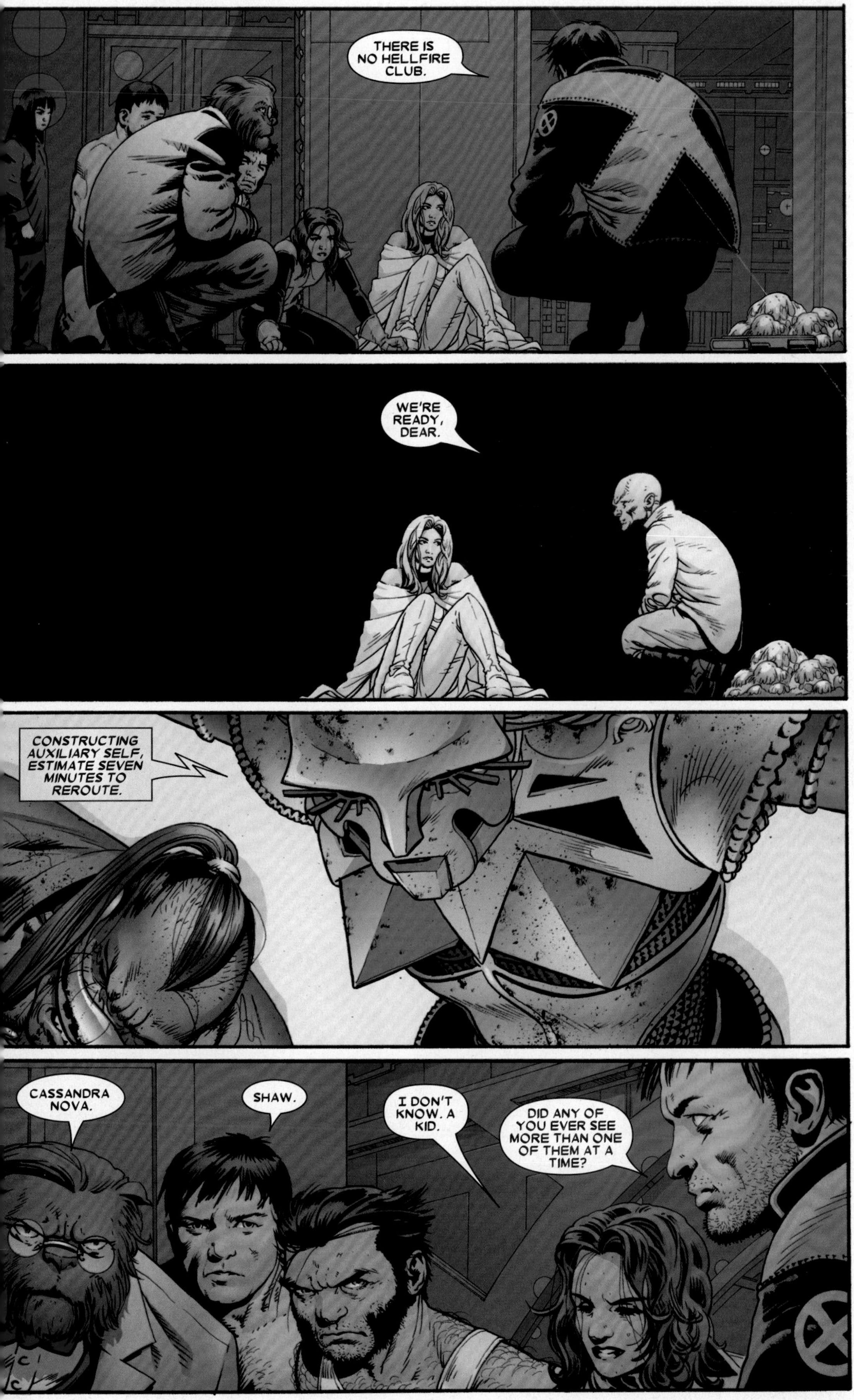
THERE IS NO HELLFIRE CLUB.
WE'RE READY, DEAR.
CONSTRUCTING AUXILIARY SELF, ESTIMATE SEVEN MINUTES TO REROUTE.
CASSANDRA NOVA.
SHAW.
I DON'T KNOW. A KID.
DID ANY OF YOU EVER SEE MORE THAN ONE OF THEM AT A TIME?

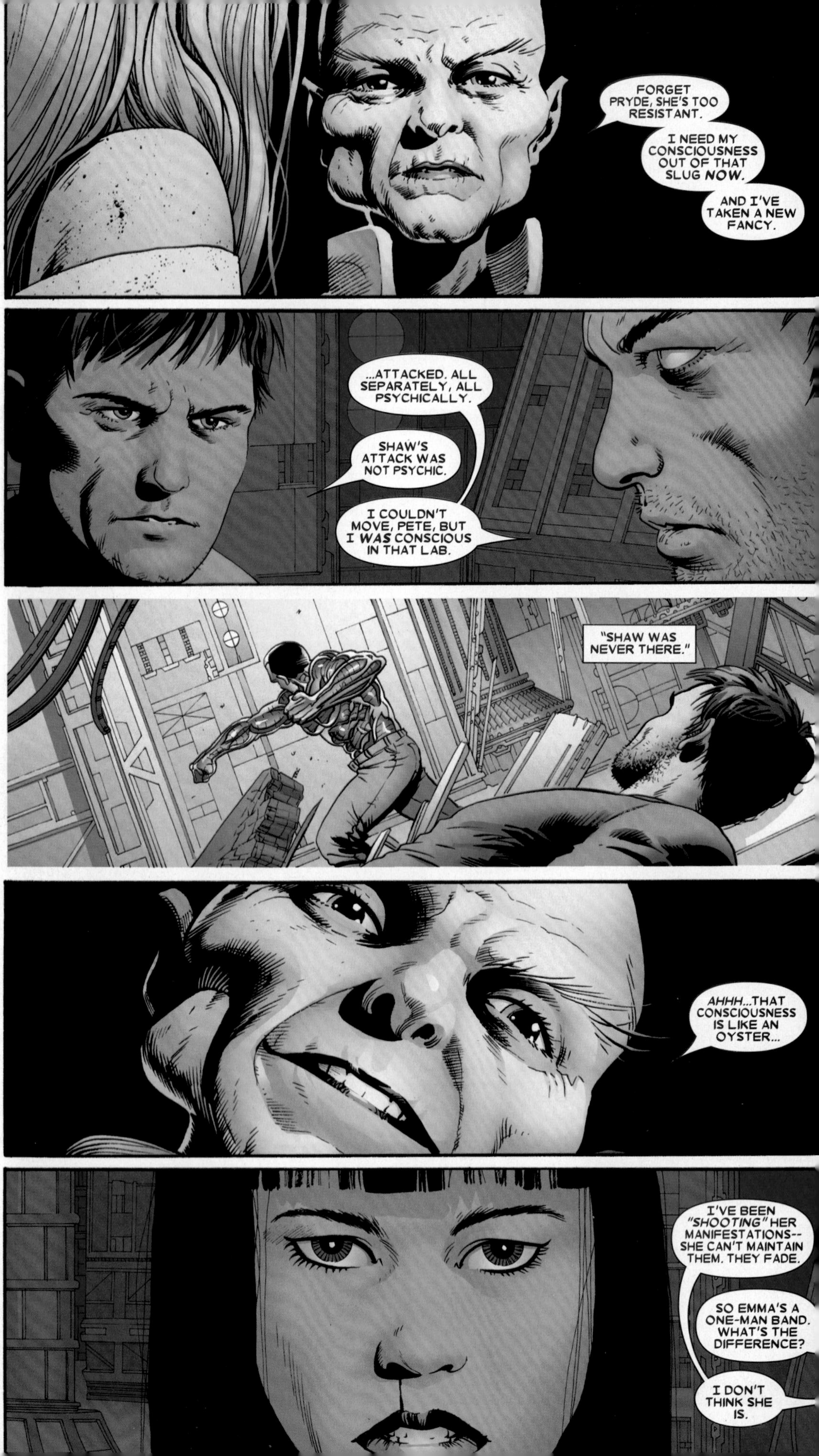
FORGET PRYDE, SHE'S TOO RESISTANT.
I NEED MY CONSCIOUSNESS OUT OF THAT SLUG NOW.
AND I'VE TAKEN A NEW FANCY.
...ATTACKED. ALL SEPARATELY, ALL PSYCHICALLY.
SHAW'S ATTACK WAS NOT PSYCHIC.
I COULDN'T MOVE, PETE, BUT I WAS CONSCIOUS IN THAT LAB.
"SHAW WAS NEVER THERE."
AHHH...THAT CONSCIOUSNESS IS LIKE AN OYSTER...
I'VE BEEN "SHOOTING" HER MANIFESTATIONS--SHE CAN'T MAINTAIN THEM. THEY FADE.
SO EMMA'S A ONE-MAN BAND. WHAT'S THE DIFFERENCE?
I DON'T THINK SHE IS.

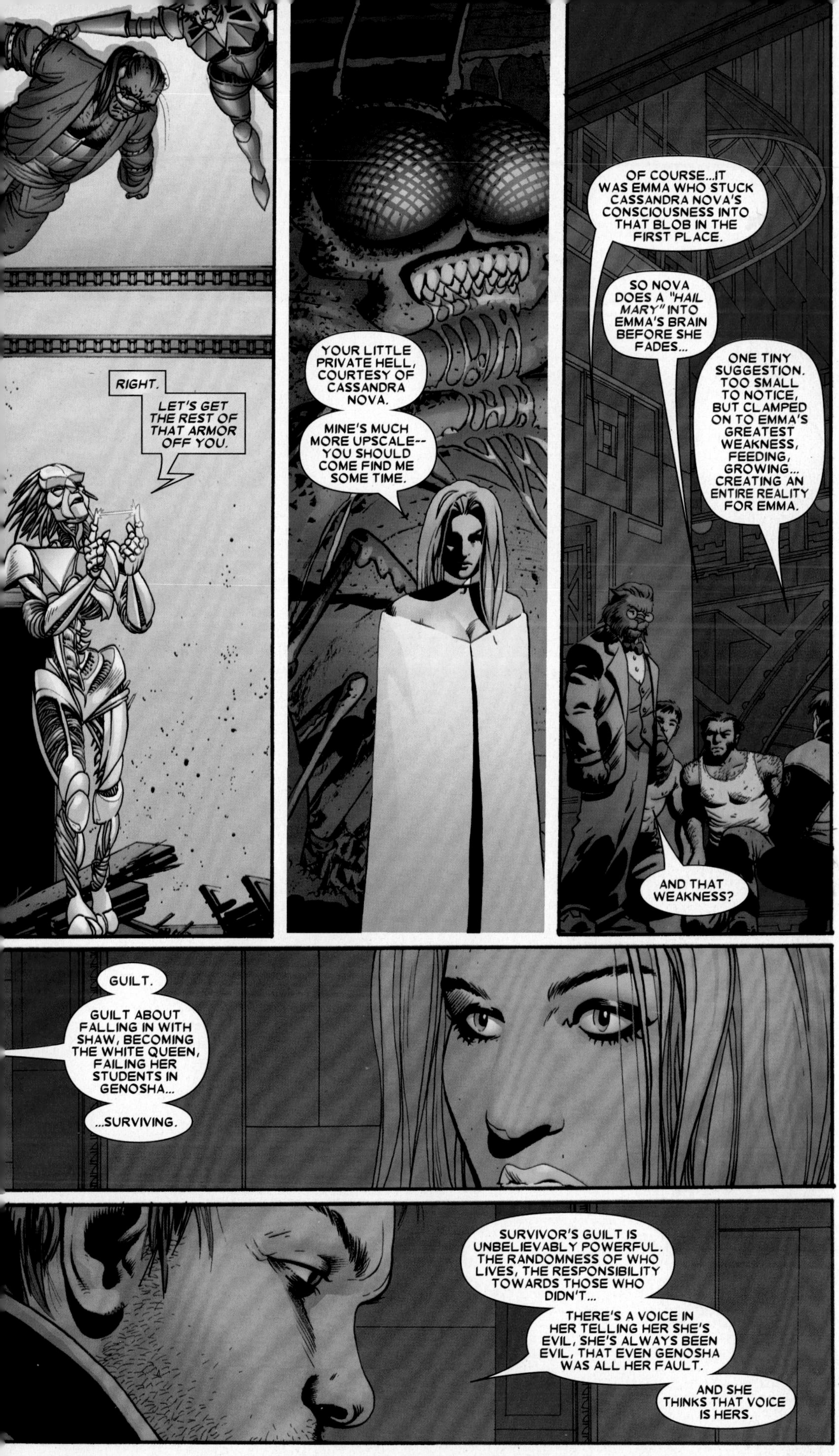
RIGHT.
LET'S GET THE REST OF THAT ARMOR OFF YOU.
YOUR LITTLE PRIVATE HELL, COURTESY OF CASSANDRA NOVA.
MINE'S MUCH MORE UPSCALE-- YOU SHOULD COME FIND ME SOME TIME.
OF COURSE...IT WAS EMMA WHO STUCK CASSANDRA NOVA'S CONSCIOUSNESS INTO THAT BLOB IN THE FIRST PLACE.
SO NOVA DOES A "HAIL MARY" INTO EMMA'S BRAIN BEFORE SHE FADES...
ONE TINY SUGGESTION. TOO SMALL TO NOTICE, BUT CLAMPED ON TO EMMA'S GREATEST WEAKNESS, FEEDING, GROWING... CREATING AN ENTIRE REALITY FOR EMMA.
AND THAT WEAKNESS?
GUILT.
GUILT ABOUT FALLING IN WITH SHAW, BECOMING THE WHITE QUEEN, FAILING HER STUDENTS IN GENOSHA...
...SURVIVING.
SURVIVOR'S GUILT IS UNBELIEVABLY POWERFUL. THE RANDOMNESS OF WHO LIVES, THE RESPONSIBILITY TOWARDS THOSE WHO DIDN'T...
THERE'S A VOICE IN HER TELLING HER SHE'S EVIL, SHE'S ALWAYS BEEN EVIL, THAT EVEN GENOSHA WAS ALL HER FAULT.
AND SHE THINKS THAT VOICE IS HERS.

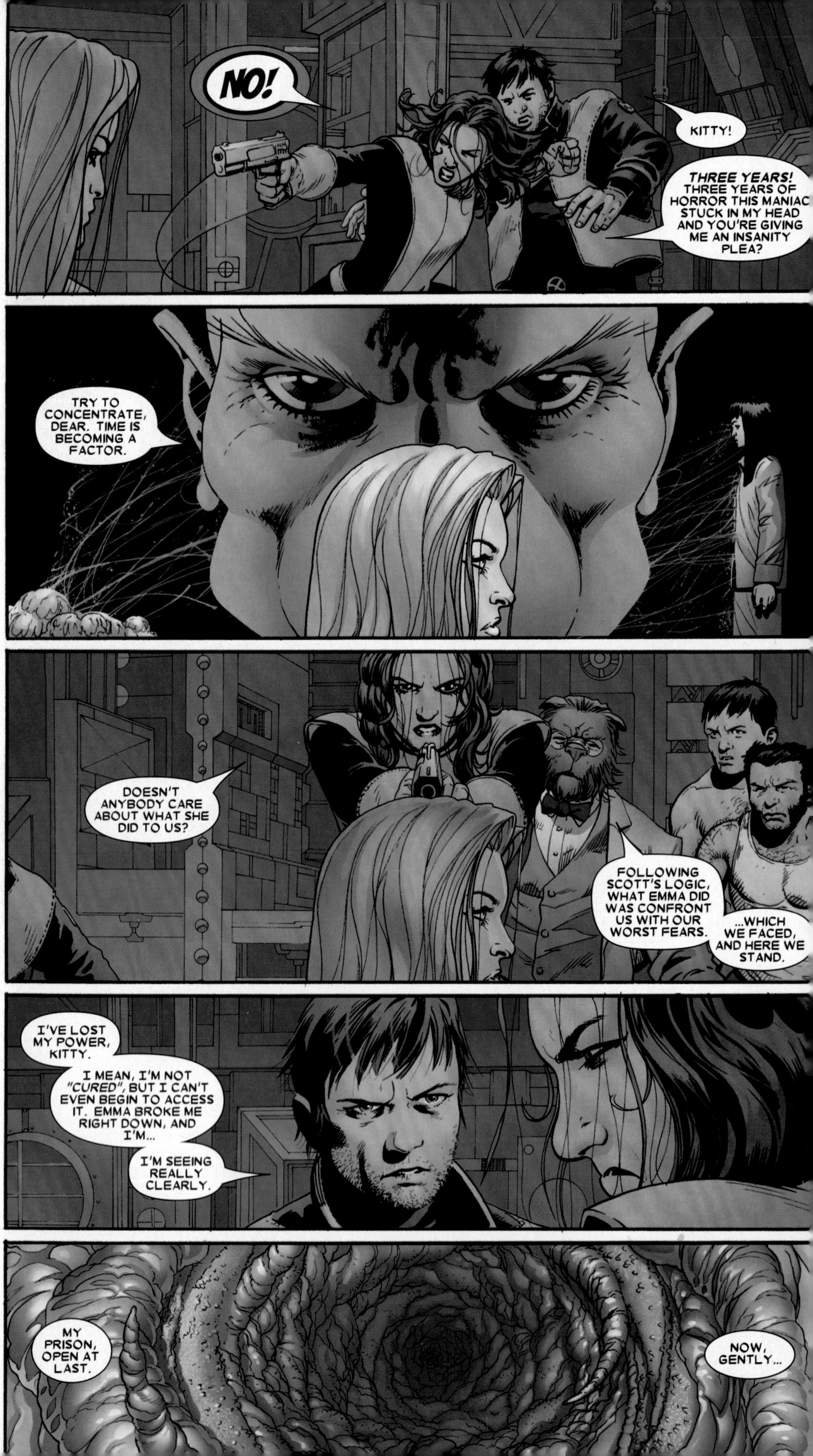
NO!
KITTY!
THREE YEARS! THREE YEARS OF HORROR THIS MANIAC STUCK IN MY HEAD AND YOU'RE GIVING ME AN INSANITY PLEA?
TRY TO CONCENTRATE, DEAR. TIME IS BECOMING A FACTOR.
DOESN'T ANYBODY CARE ABOUT WHAT SHE DID TO US?
FOLLOWING SCOTT'S LOGIC, WHAT EMMA DID WAS CONFRONT US WITH OUR WORST FEARS.
...WHICH WE FACED, AND HERE WE STAND.
I'VE LOST MY POWER, KITTY.
I MEAN, I'M NOT "CURED", BUT I CAN'T EVEN BEGIN TO ACCESS IT. EMMA BROKE ME RIGHT DOWN, AND I'M...
I'M SEEING REALLY CLEARLY.
MY PRISON, OPEN AT LAST.
NOW, GENTLY...

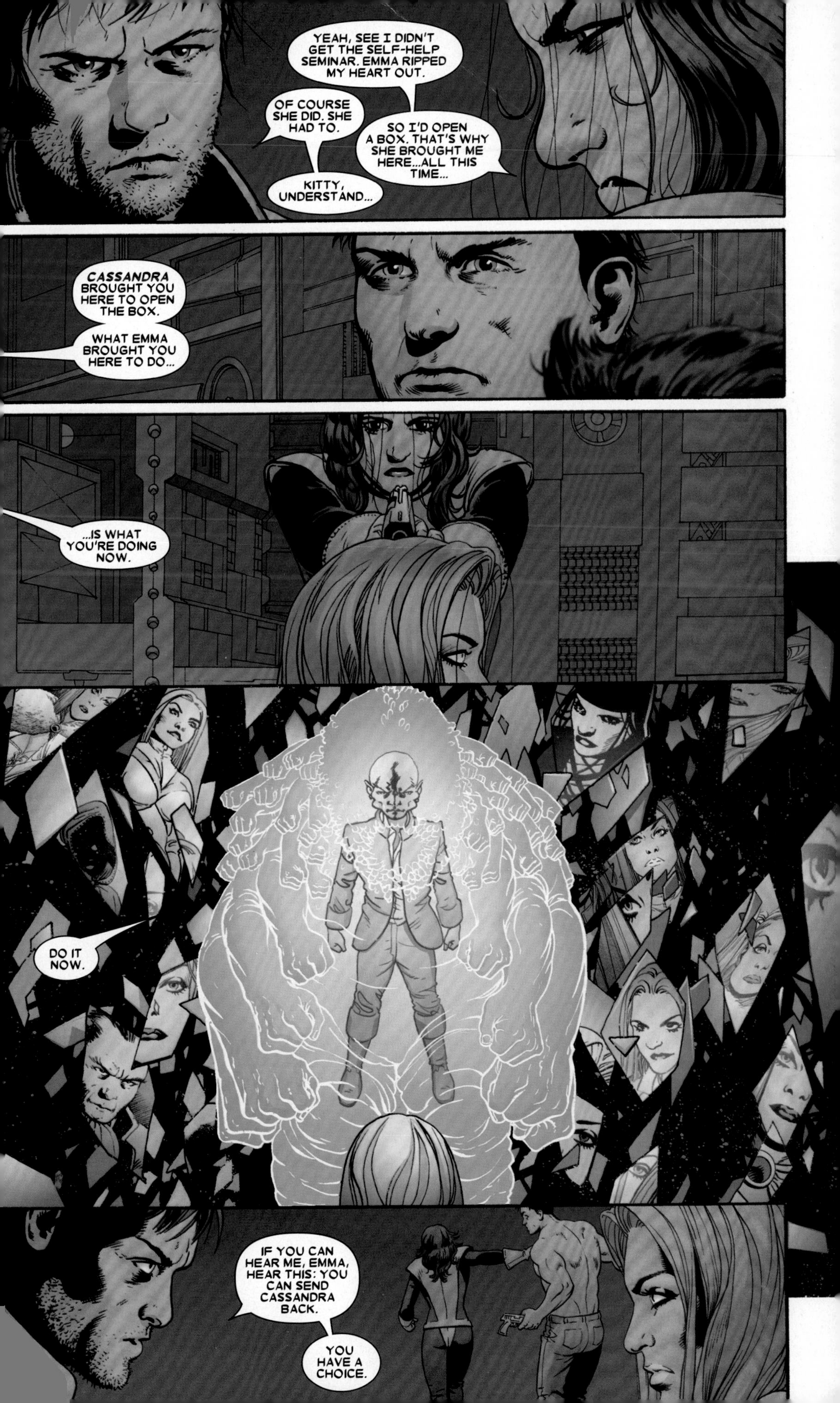
YEAH, SEE I DIDN'T GET THE SELF-HELP SEMINAR. EMMA RIPPED MY HEART OUT.
SO I'D OPEN A BOX. THAT'S WHY SHE BROUGHT ME HERE...ALL THIS TIME...
OF COURSE SHE DID. SHE HAD TO.
KITTY, UNDERSTAND...
CASSANDRA BROUGHT YOU HERE TO OPEN THE BOX.
WHAT EMMA BROUGHT YOU HERE TO DO...
...IS WHAT YOU'RE DOING NOW.
DO IT NOW.
IF YOU CAN HEAR ME, EMMA, HEAR THIS: YOU CAN SEND CASSANDRA BACK.
YOU HAVE A CHOICE.

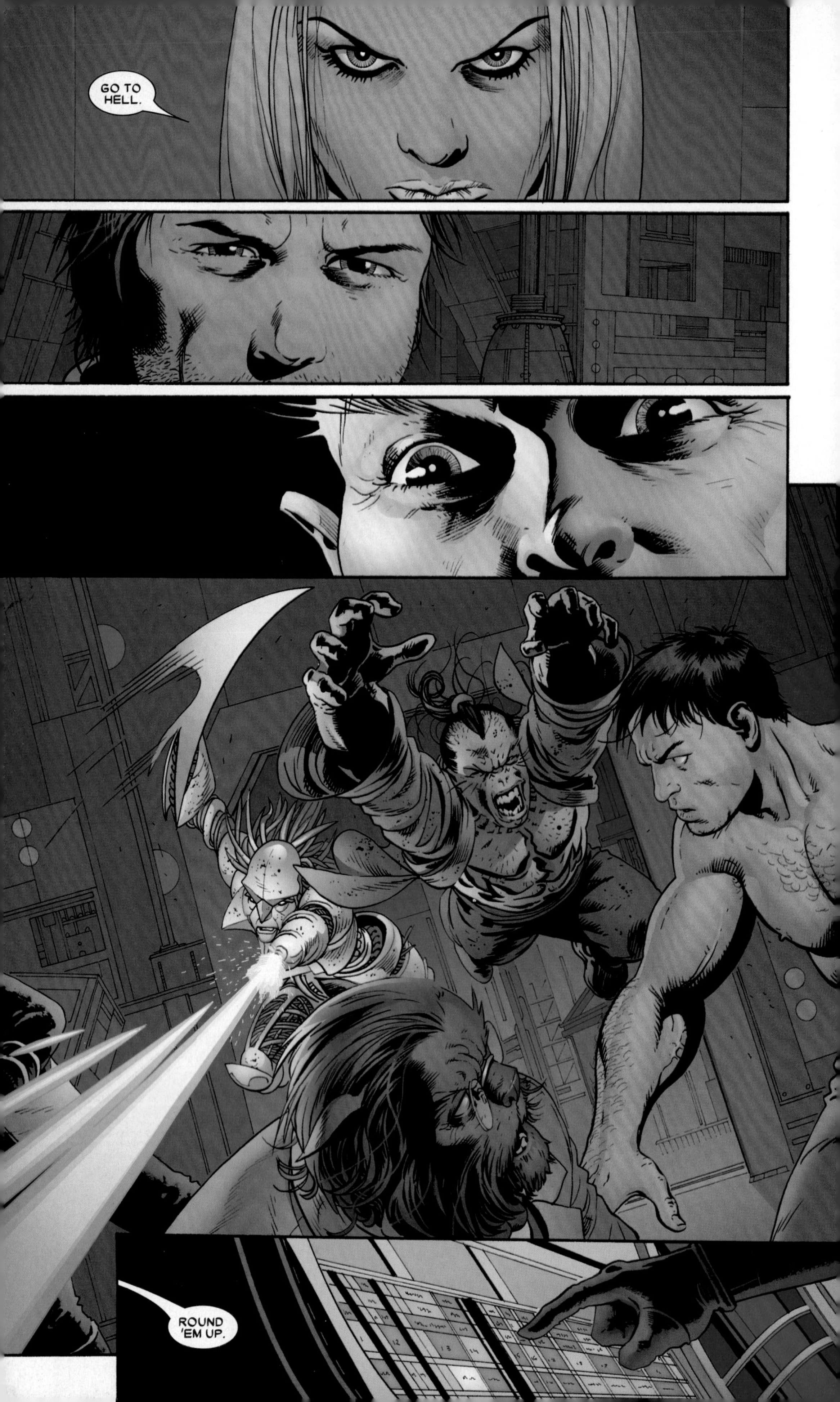
GO TO HELL.
ROUND 'EM UP.

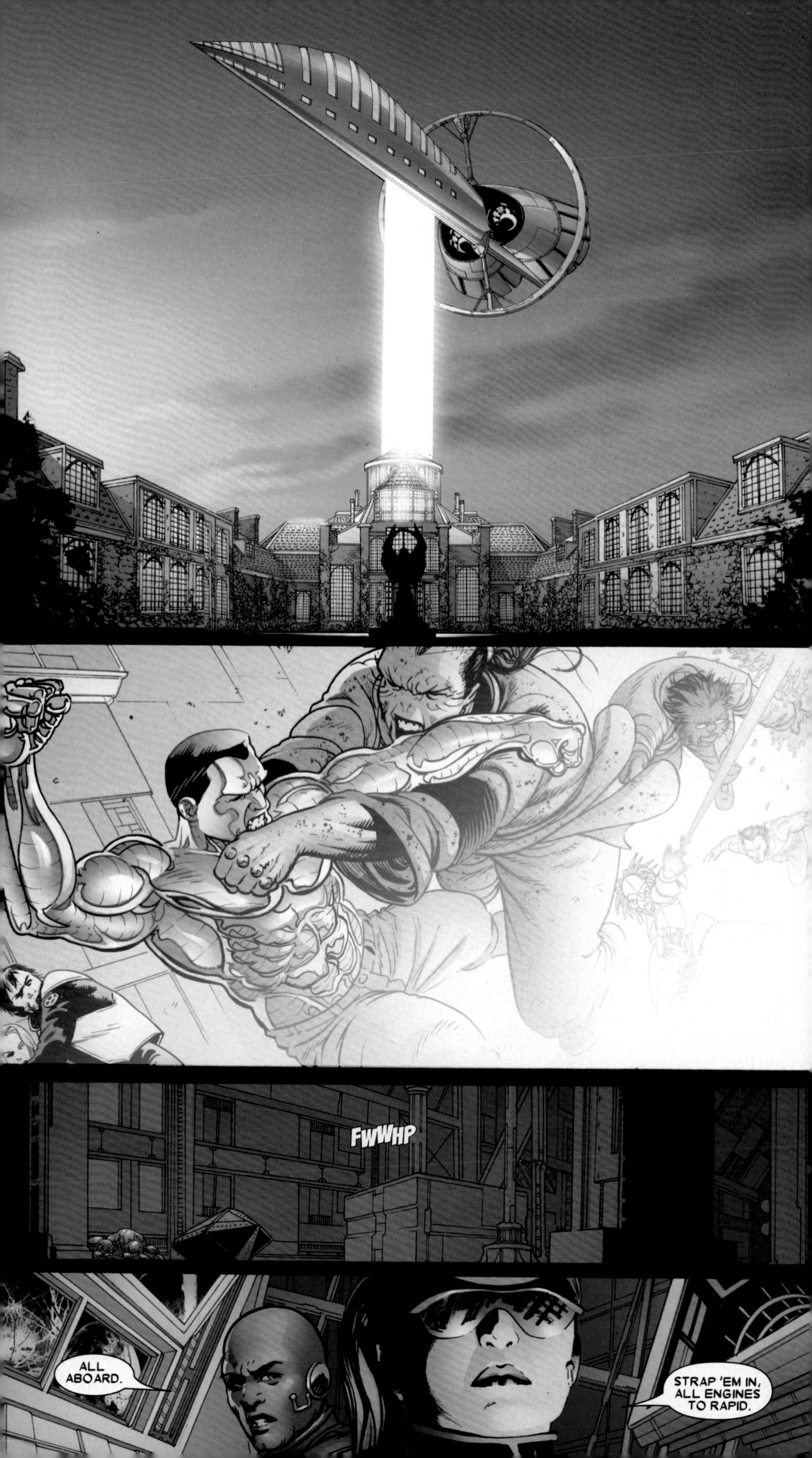
FWWHP
ALL ABOARD.
STRAP 'EM IN, ALL ENGINES TO RAPID.

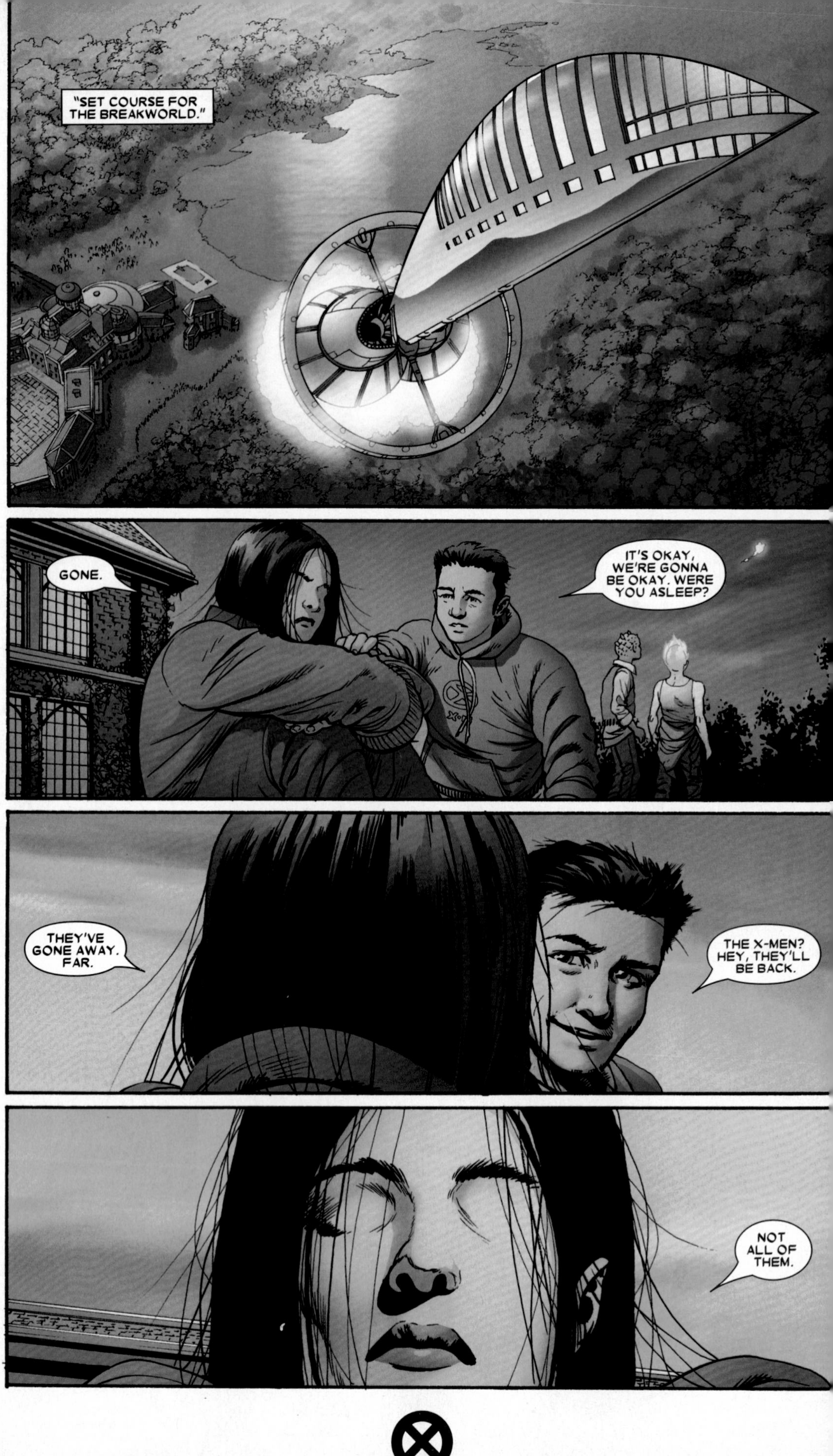
"SET COURSE FOR THE BREAKWORLD."
GONE.
IT'S OKAY, WE'RE GONNA BE OKAY. WERE YOU ASLEEP?
THEY'VE GONE AWAY. FAR.
THE X-MEN? HEY, THEY'LL BE BACK.
NOT ALL OF THEM.

Issue #13 Sketch Variant
by John Cassaday

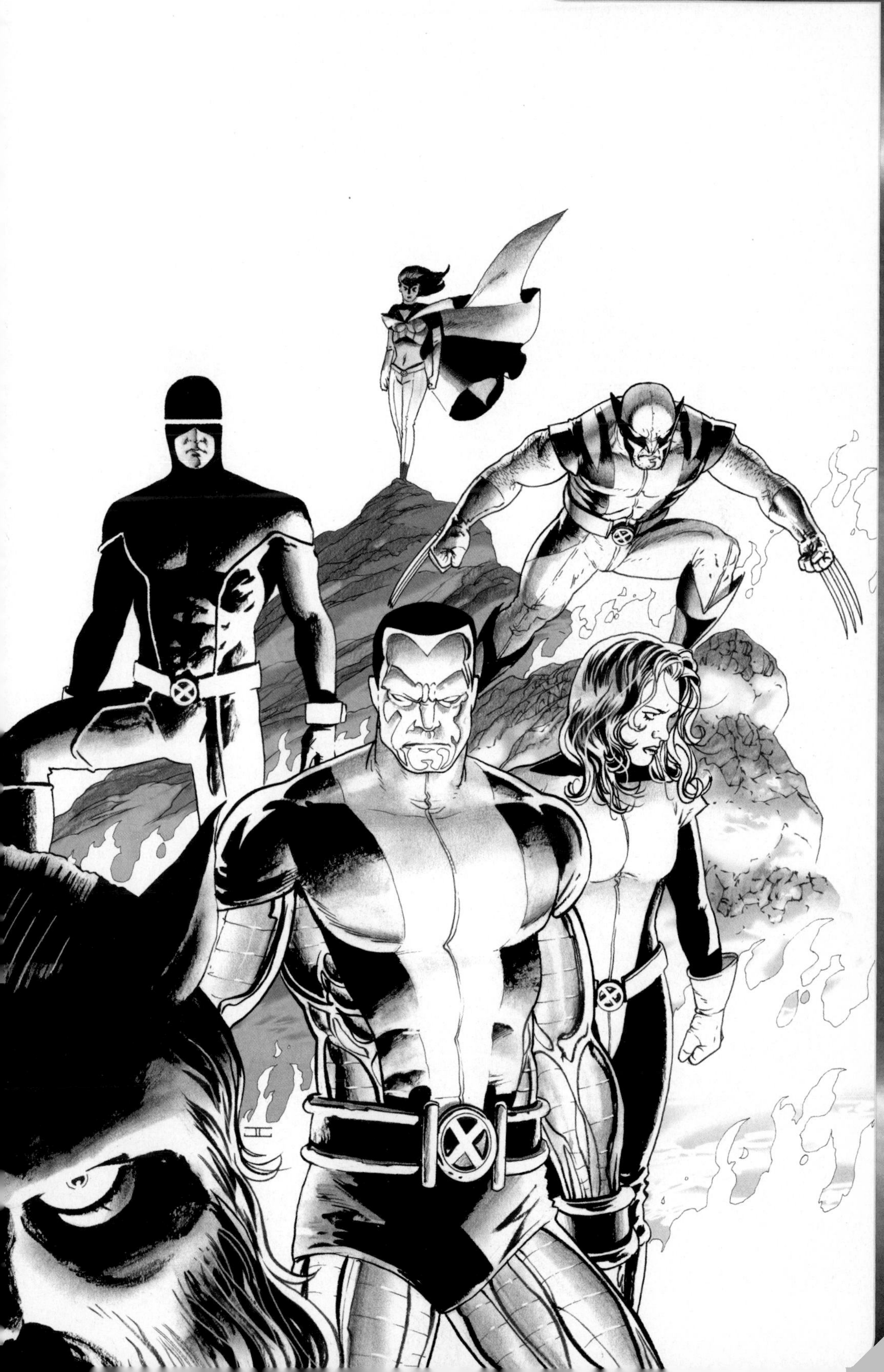

Issue #16 Cover Pencils
by John Cassaday

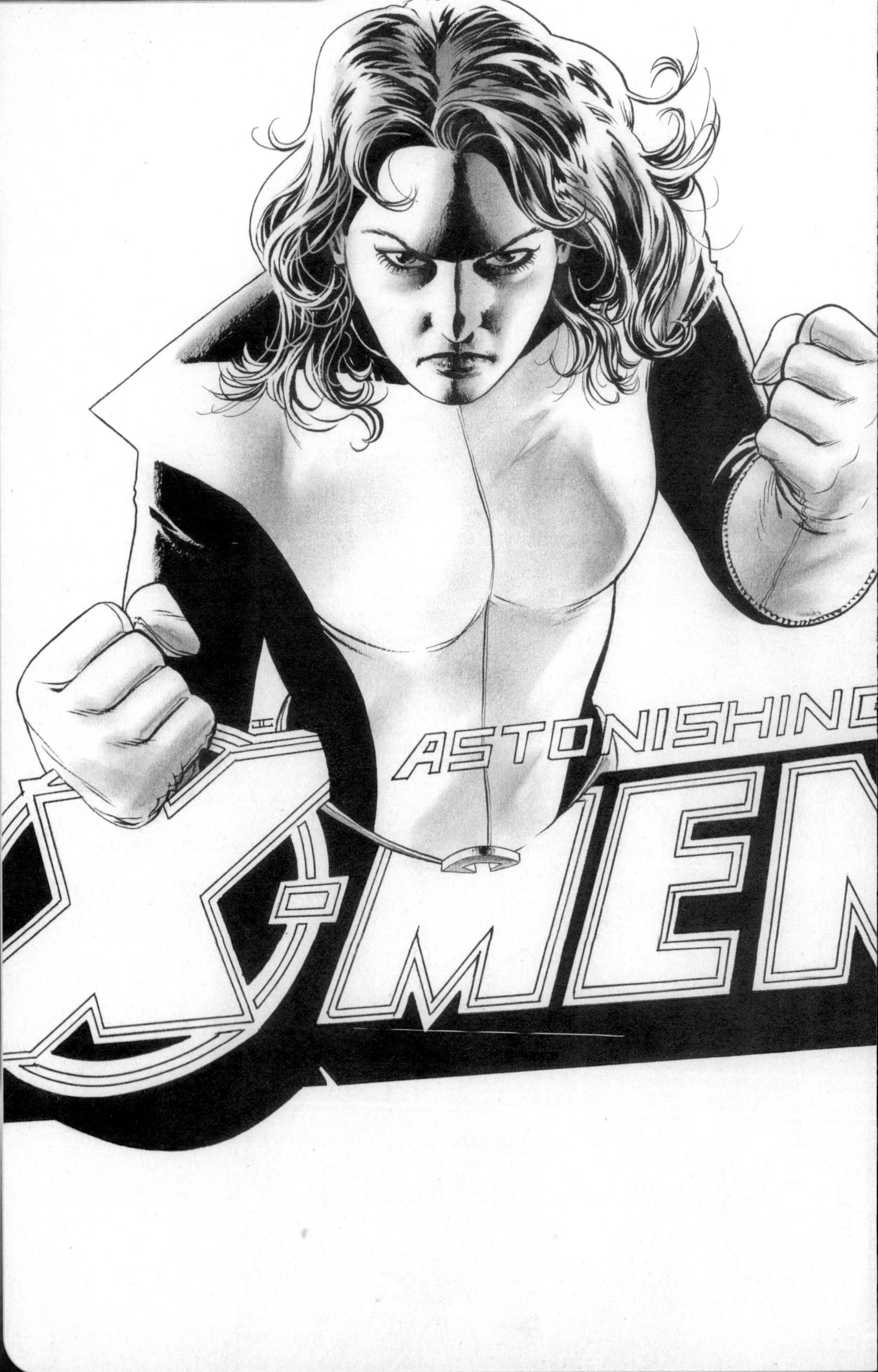
ASTONISHING
X-MEN

Issue #18 Cover Pencils
by John Cassaday

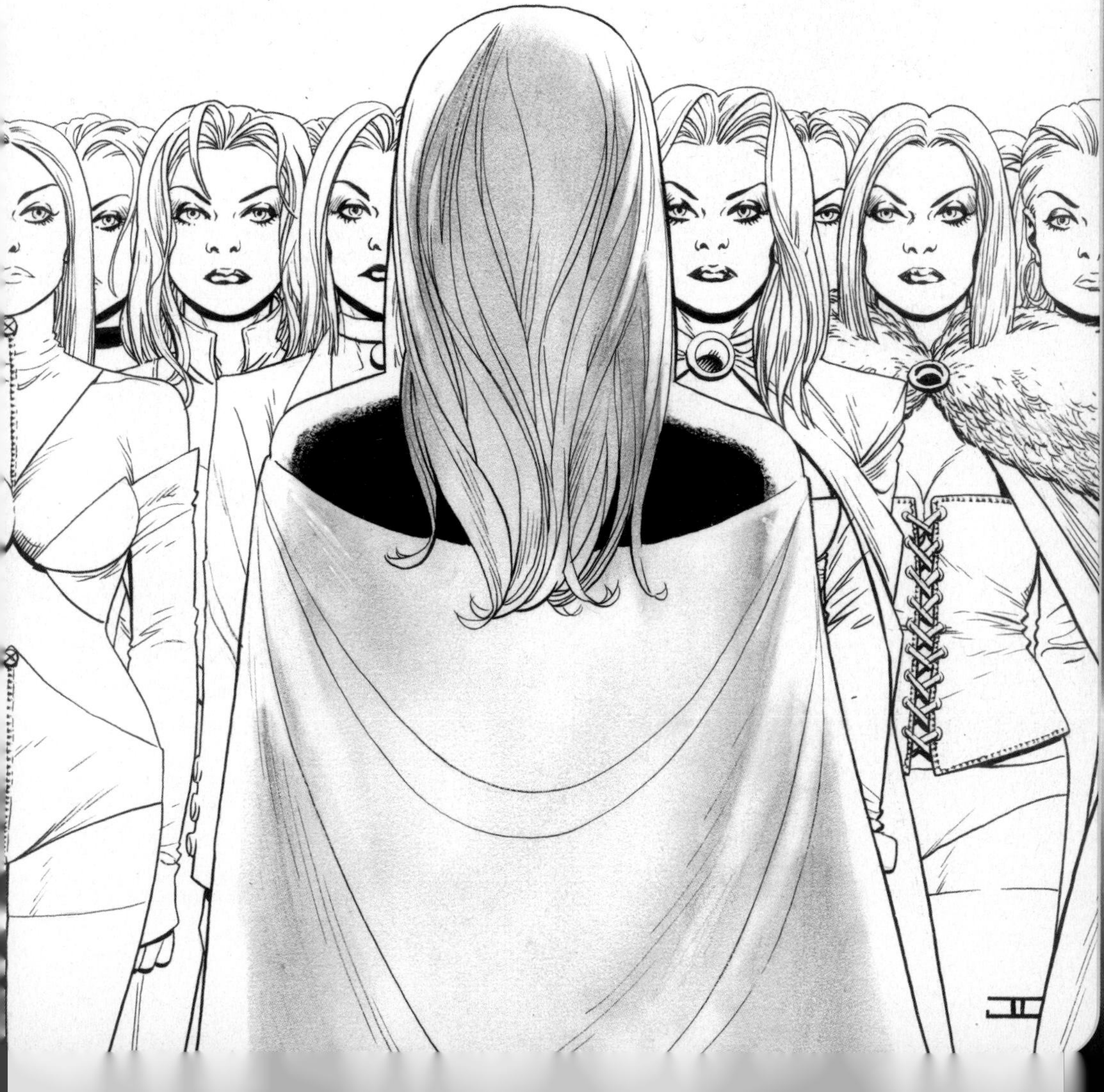

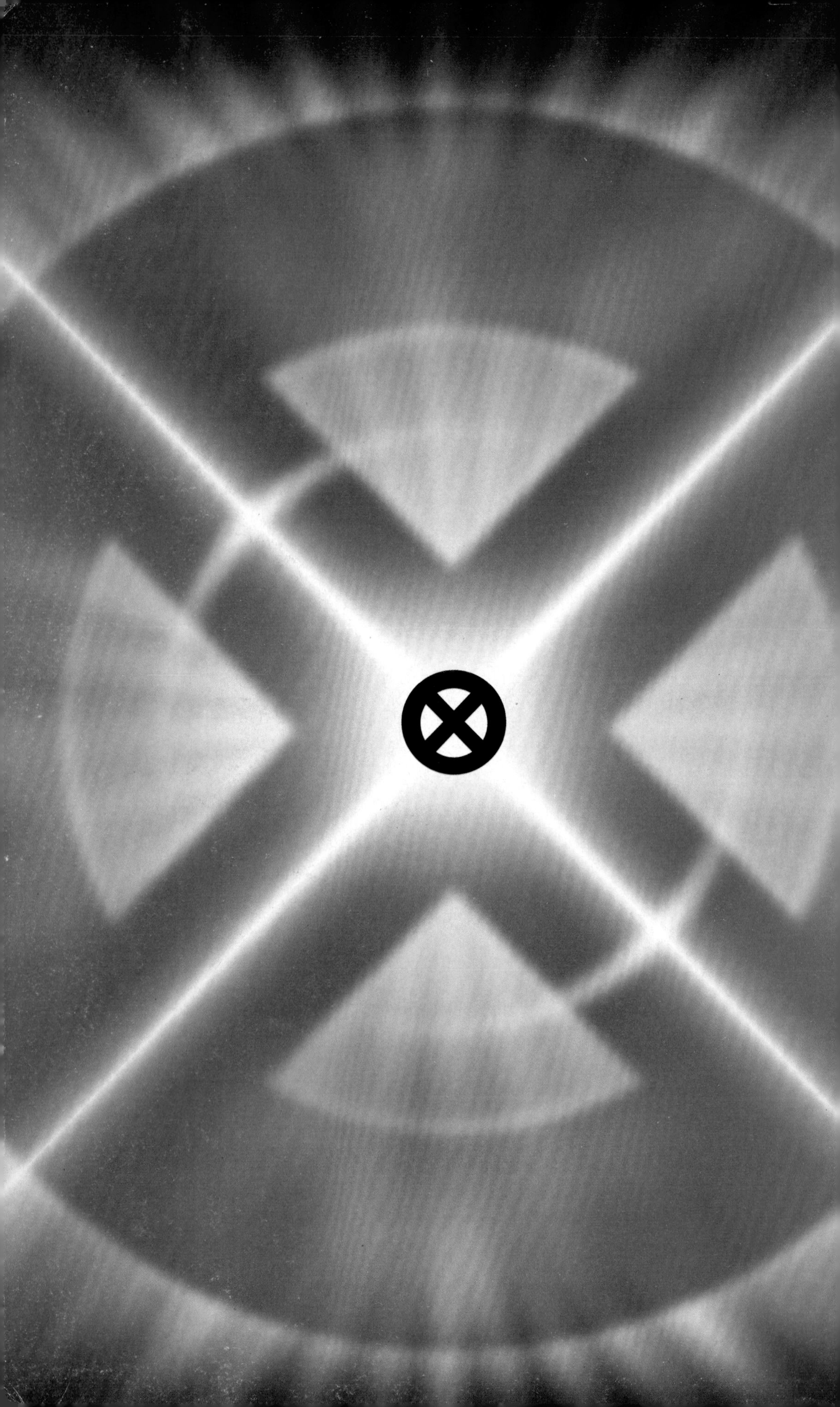